Beauty in Sufism

Beauty in Sufism

The Teachings of Rūzbihān Baqlī

Kazuyo Murata

SUNY PRESS

Published by State University of New York Press, Albany

Printed in the United States of America

For information, contact State University of New York Press, Albany, NY
www.sunypress.edu

Production, Diane Ganeles
Marketing, Anne M. Valentine

Library of Congress Cataloging-in-Publication Data

Names: Murata, Kazuyo (Lecturer in Islamic studies), author.
Title: Beauty in Sufism : the teachings of Ruzbihan Baqli / Kazuyo Murata.
Description: Albany : State University of New York Press, [2016] | Includes bibliographical references and index.
Identifiers: LCCN 2016007681 (print) | LCCN 2016008781 (ebook) | ISBN 978-1-4384-6279-0 (hardcover : alk. paper) | ISBN 978-1-4384-6278-3 (pbk : alk. paper) | ISBN 978-1-4384-6280-6 (e-book)
Subjects: LCSH: Aesthetics--Religious aspects--Islam. | Sufism. | Baqlī, Rūzbihān ibn Abī al-Naṣr, -1209 or 1210.
Classification: LCC BL65.A4 M875 2016 (print) | LCC BL65.A4 (ebook) | DDC 297.4--dc23
LC record available at http://lccn.loc.gov/2016007681

10 9 8 7 6 5 4 3 2 1

ای آفتاب حسن برون آ دمی ز ابر
کان چهرهٔ مشعشع تابانم آرزوست

O Sun of Beauty! Come out for a moment from the clouds,
For that beaming, resplendent countenance is my wish.

—Mawlānā Jalāl al-Dīn Muḥammad Balkhī Rūmī

CONTENTS

ILLUSTRATIONS

ACKNOWLEDGMENTS

My deep gratitude goes to Professor Gerhard Böwering of Yale University for his generous support and insightful advice that sustained the doctoral research that became the basis of this book. He has been my Doktorvater in the truest sense, and I cannot thank him enough for all he has done over the years. My sincere thanks also go to Professor Denys Turner and Professor William Chittick for sharing the scholarly acumen that helped improve my work. Part of the research for this book was conducted in Tehran during my yearlong academic residence at the Institute of Philosophy (*Anjuman-i Ḥikmat wa Falsafa-yi Īrān*) thanks to Yale's McMillan Center International Dissertation Fellowship. I am truly thankful to all the individuals who helped make my research year in Tehran so fruitful, in particular Dr. Gholamreza Aavani, Dr. Pari Riyahi, Ms. Mahin Riyahi, Dr. Fereshteh Kazempour, Dr. Shahram Pazouki, Dr. Saeed Anvari, Dr. Mehdi Mohaghegh, and Dr. Noushafarin Ansari. I am grateful to Prof. Ghasem Kakaei of Shiraz University for giving me a precious opportunity to present my work in Rūzbihān's hometown, Shiraz, and to see Mount Bamū, where Rūzbihān had spent some years. I would also like to express my thanks to Mojtaba Shahsavari for generously sharing his unpublished critical edition of Rūzbihān's *Manṭiq al-asrār*. I am thankful to Dr. Leonard Lewisohn for sharing his vast knowledge of existing literature both modern and premodern. I am also indebted to Matthew Melvin-Koushki for his comments on an earlier version of this book. My deep gratitude goes to Prof. Sachiko Murata for all her academic and moral support over the years.

I remain forever grateful to my family, Seiya Murata, Junko Murata, and Rie Murata, without whose trust and support I could not have completed this work. I am also grateful to the Department of Theology and Religious Studies at King's College London, in particular Prof. Paul Joyce and Dr. Carool Kersten, for their support while I completed this book. Finally, I would like to express my sincere thanks to the late Nancy Ellegate of SUNY Press, who gave me indispensable support and advice throughout the pre-production process but left us before this book saw the light of day.

NOTE ON TRANSLITERATION

For transliterating Arabic and Persian words, the *International Journal of Middle East Studies* system has been employed with the following exception—no distinction is made in transcribing the identical letters appearing in Arabic and Persian texts, i.e.:

ث is transliterated as *th* throughout, not as s̱ in Persian texts

ذ is transliterated as *dh*, not ẕ

ض is transliterated as *ḍ*, not ż

و is transliterated as *w*, not *v* or *u*

ة is transliterated as *a* or *at* (in the *iḍāfa* construction), not *ih*

Introduction

As Rūzbihān entered the ʿAtīq mosque through the bazaar, he overheard the following conversation between a woman and her daughter:

> "My dear! I am giving you some advice. Cover your face and don't show it to everyone from the window of beauty—lest someone should fall into temptation because of your beauty! You hear my words—won't you take my advice?"
>
> When Rūzbihān heard this conversation, he wanted to tell that woman: "Even if you advise her and try to prevent her from showing herself, she won't listen to you or take your advice, because she has beauty, and she won't be at rest with [her] beauty until it is joined by passionate love."[1]

Muhammad famously proclaimed, "God is beautiful and He loves beauty." In a world, however, where politicized, militant Islam dominates the news, it has become almost counterintuitive to associate beauty with Islam. Some may even wonder if there is any room for it in the religion. Edward Farley, a scholar of Christian theology, argues that this is in fact a common postmodern situation:

> Beauty (the aesthetic) is not among the primary values or deep symbols of postmodern societies.... Certain features of postmodern society...tend to diminish beauty both as an important value and

> as an interpretive concept. Contributing to the postmodern effacement of beauty is a hermeneutic legacy, a tradition of interpretation, governed by dichotomies between the ethical and the aesthetic, religion (faith) and the aesthetic, and religion (faith) and pleasure. Accordingly, a contemporary aesthetic (or theological aesthetic) that seeks to restore beauty as important to human experience of religious faith faces the deconstructive task of exposing and breaking down these dichotomies. The displacement of the aesthetic by aesthetics (philosophy of the arts) in recent times has contributed to the suppression of beauty in hermeneutics, philosophy and criticism. A contemporary theological aesthetic also works in the setting of a centuries-long marginalization—in some cases suppression—of the aesthetic by Hebraic and Christian iconoclasm, asceticism and legalism.[2]

It is not only theologians who bemoan the banishing of beauty from modern human life. For instance, the British poet and writer Kathleen Raine expresses this sentiment by way of quoting the poignant words of the Irish poet George William Russell (d. 1935): "One of the very first symptoms of the loss of the soul is the loss of the sense of beauty."[3] A contemporary scholar of aesthetics, Elaine Scarry, published *On Beauty and Being Just* (Princeton: Princeton University Press, 1999) as a manifesto for protecting beauty from various postmodern attacks and reviving it in contemporary discourse. A more recent attempt at "recovering beauty" can be found in Corinne Saunders et al., *The Recovery of Beauty: Arts, Culture, and Medicine* (Basingstoke: Palgrave Macmillan, 2015).[4]

It is not the purpose of the present study to reinstate "beauty" at the forefront of Islam, as Farley tries to do for Christianity. It aims, rather, to draw people's attention to a neglected dimension of Islamic thought, a dimension that was current especially among premodern Muslim intellectuals and literary figures. In their way of seeing things, beauty had a central place in the universe and human life. They saw God as beautiful in Himself and as creator of an inherently beautiful world, and they regarded the pursuit of beauty at all levels (e.g., material, ethical, spiritual, and divine) as part and parcel of the life of a good Muslim. My aim is to investigate the significance of beauty in Muslim conception of God, the world, and the human being taking as a case study the works of one prominent and prolific Sufi thinker, Rūzbihān Baqlī (1128–1209), who presented some of the most fully developed discussions on the idea of beauty to be found in Muslim literature.

The questions to be addressed in this study include the following: Why did Rūzbihān talk so much about beauty? What is the significance of beauty for his understanding of God, the world, and the human being? How can God's beauty be contrasted with beauty in His creation—including that of humans, angels, and animals? What role does beauty have in the process of God's creation of the world and human beings? Does beauty have any soteriological significance? What determines the degree of beauty found in a thing or perceived by an individual? Does beauty have any role in the ideal way of life? Does the pursuit of beauty have any practical implications for the daily lives of Muslims? What exactly is the connection between love and beauty? Is there any Qurʾānic foundation for Rūzbihān's discussions of beauty (*jamāl, ḥusn, iḥsān,* etc.)? What key symbols and imagery does he employ in speaking about beauty? Overall, what is the place of beauty in the intelligible structure of Rūzbihān's thought specifically and in the underlying worldview of traditional Muslim thinking generally?

Despite the refined nature of Rūzbihān's theory of beauty, his view on beauty—or for that matter, his thought in general—remains largely unexplored and unknown mostly because of his famously convoluted style. Moreover, even among scholarly publications on love and beauty in Sufism, there is nothing that focuses on the concept of beauty, as most discuss love and treat beauty in passing. This is the first book that is devoted to a systematic analysis of the concept of beauty as such in Sufism and that attempts a reconstruction of the worldview in which Rūzbihān and many other Sufis situate the idea of beauty.[5]

In order to analyze the exact role and significance of beauty in Rūzbihān's thought, the following two steps must be taken: first to decipher his technical terminology and often cryptic and flowery language, and second to undertake a systematic analysis of his numerous works so as to reconstruct his overall worldview, which is nowhere explicitly stated in his works nor presented in the secondary literature.

I should say at the outset that the focus of the present study is not aesthetics, a term coined by the German philosopher Alexander Gottlieb Baumgarten (1714–1762), who wrote a two-volume treatise in Latin called *Aesthetica* (1750–58)[6] and derived the term from the Greek, *aisthētika,* meaning "perceptible things."[7] The proper subject of aesthetics is perceptible things, such as artifacts and nature. A modern dictionary defines it as the "study of the feelings, concepts, and judgments arising from our appreciation of the arts or of the wider class of objects considered moving, or beautiful, or sublime."[8] Although aesthetics can be a theoretical investigation into the nature of beauty and the engagement with objects in the world that are pleasing to the senses, Rūzbihān's concern (and that of most premodern Muslim intellectuals) was to understand beauty for the sake of coming to know God. Knowing the created world itself was a secondary concern, even if the nature of the world has close connections with theological principles. For Rūzbihān, inquiry into beauty is inquiry into the origin, end, and purpose of human existence. The story of beauty is the story of the unfolding of divine beauty through its two mirrors, the universe (the macrocosm) and the human being (the microcosm).

A number of scholars have noticed the significance of beauty in Rūzbihān's writings. Nazif Hoca writes, for example, "At the center of his thought is divine self-manifestation (*tajallī*) and the worship of God through human beauty."[9] Some scholars have even categorized Rūzbihān's thought as *jamāl-parastī* or *zībāʾī-parastī* ("beauty-adoration"), a term used to characterize a number of Sufis and philosophers,[10] including Aḥmad Ghazālī (d. 1126; the younger brother of Abū Ḥāmid al-Ghazālī), ʿAyn al-Quḍāt Hamadānī (d. 1131; a disciple of Aḥmad Ghazālī), ʿAṭṭār (d. 1221; a Persian Sufi poet), Awḥad al-Dīn Kirmānī (d. 1238; a Persian poet and friend of Ibn al-ʿArabī), Rūmī (d. 1273), Fakhr al-Dīn ʿIrāqī (d. 1289; a follower of Ibn al-ʿArabī), and ʿAbd al-Raḥmān Jāmī (d. 1492; a Persian litterateur and major scholar in the school of Ibn al-ʿArabī).[11] As can be seen from the list, "beauty-adoration" does not refer to a unified historical movement, but functions rather as an ahistorical label for characterizing various authors from different times and places who happen to share a common tendency in thinking, though many of them may well have had historical connections.

Among the authors who frequently spoke about their love for beauty, Rūzbihān is especially worthy of attention. His works contain a substantial amount of discussion of beauty of all sorts, divine, human, and cosmic. Although key passages on the subject are scattered throughout his works, they are held together by an overall worldview and common themes. His discussions of beauty are multidimensional, encompassing the fields of theology, cosmology, cosmogony, anthropology, psychology, and prophetology. His firm training in the religious sciences—such as the Qurʾān, Ḥadīth, Arabic grammar, jurisprudence, and dogmatic theology (particularly Ashʿarism)—adds depth to his discussions while allowing him to approach the notion of beauty from multiple angles.

Rūzbihān's Life

Rūzbihān's life has been the subject of extensive discussion by several scholars, so I will only present the essentials here. The standard story is that he was born in 1128 in the town of Pasā (also transcribed as Fasā or Basā in Arabic) in the Fārs province in southwestern Persia, near the ancient capitals of Pasargadae and Persepolis. He lived during the Seljuk period under the local Salghurid dynasty, whose capital was Shiraz, where Rūzbihān spent most of his adult life.[12] Hence, he is called "Shīrāzī," though originally he was "Fasāʾī," that is, from Pasā.

Rūzbihān started having visions as early as at age three, and a vision at age fifteen left him in an ecstatic state for a year and a half, leading him to join up with Sufis.[13] Paul Ballanfat argues that Rūzbihān was twenty-three years old when he first moved to Shiraz, where he commenced his formal studies in a Sufi convent established by Sirāj al-Dīn Maḥmūd b. Khalīfa b. ʿAbd al-Salām b. Aḥmad b. Sālba (d. 1165), from whom he is said to have received a *khirqa,* or a tattered cloak of initiation.[14]

Thereafter, Rūzbihān led an ascetic life at Mount Bamū in the outskirts of Shiraz, where he remained for seven years.[15] Not all the details of his life are clear, but at some point he undertook travels to various regions, such as Iraq, Ḥijāz (including Mecca), Syria, and possibly Alexandria.[16] When he settled again in Shiraz, he established his own convent at the age of thirty-eight, in 1165.[17] After spending some time in Pasā around 1174,[18] he went back to Shiraz and became established as a scholar-preacher in the grand mosque, known as Masjid-i ʿAtīq.[19] He continued to instruct the public and his disciples until his passing in 1209.

Rūzbihān's Works

Rūzbihān is known to have composed at least forty-five works in Arabic and Persian in diverse fields, such as Arabic grammar, Qurʾānic exegesis, Ḥadīth commentaries, jurisprudence, principles of jurisprudence, dogmatic theology (*kalām*), and Sufism. The last category has the greatest number of works, thirty-one, some of which are extant in print or in manuscript form, and some of which are lost.[20] The present study draws on works from four of these categories, though the perspective in all of these works is Sufi: Qurʾānic exegesis (*ʿArāʾis al-bayān fī ḥaqāʾiq al-qurʾān*), Ḥadīth commentary (*al-Maknūn fī ḥaqāʾiq al-kalim al-nabawiyya*), dogmatic theology (*Masālik al-tawḥīd*), and Sufism (*ʿAbhar al-ʿāshiqīn, Mashrab al-arwāḥ, Ghalaṭāt al-sālikīn, Kitāb al-ighāna, Kashf al-asrār, Lawāmiʿ al-tawḥīd, Manṭiq al-asrār, Risālat al-quds, Sayr al-arwāḥ, Sharḥ-i shaṭḥiyyāt*). I pay particular attention to works that have not received much scholarly attention, either because they are relatively new publications, were written in Persian rather than Arabic, or were simply too obscure to read. These include *ʿArāʾis al-bayān*, which had been available in an Indian lithograph edition but was newly printed by Dār al-Kutub al-ʿIlmiyya in Beirut in 2008; *al-Maknūn fī ḥaqāʾiq al-kalim al-nabawiyya* (published in Iran in 2002); *Masālik al-tawḥīd* (edited by Ballanfat in 1998; unstudied except for a brief discussion by the editor), *ʿAbhar al-ʿāshiqīn* (two editions by Muʿīn and Corbin and by Nūrbakhsh have been available for decades but have received little scholarly attention in the West, perhaps because of the high-flown Persian style), and *Mashrab al-arwāḥ* (published in 1973 but little studied until now).[21]

Among these works, perhaps the most systematic in presentation is *Mashrab al-arwāḥ*, in which Rūzbihān explains the journey of human spirits from God to the world and back to God through a series of 1,001 stations. Systematic in a different way is his *Masālik al-tawḥīd*, which is his sole extant work in dogmatic theology. He presents key theological terms in a rigid structure following the standard language in *kalām*. This is in good contrast to the language he uses in his other works, which is rather cryptic, allusive, ambiguous, and literary. His Qur᾽ān commentary follows a standard structure of *tafsīr* works, which is to say that he cites clusters of verses and comments on them from the first chapter to the last, though it is a thoroughly Sufi work.

Previous Scholarship on Rūzbihān

Much of the modern scholarship on Rūzbihān in the early twentieth century reflects the secondary interest of scholars working on figures preceding Rūzbihān. The most prominent example is the work of Louis Massignon, the first Western scholar to pay attention to Rūzbihān's writings. He tried to reconstruct the lost corpus of the famous Sufi martyr al-Ḥallāj (d. 920) by salvaging snippets of his sayings quoted by Rūzbihān.[22] A few scholars then took an interest in reconstructing Rūzihān's life—Vladimir Ivanow (1928),[23] followed by Muḥammad Taqī Dānishpazhūh (1969)[24] and Paul Nwyia (1970).[25]

The first scholar to focus on the content of Rūzbihān's thought was Henry Corbin, who edited two of Rūzbihān's Persian works, *ʿAbhar al-ʿāshiqīn* (1958)[26] and *Sharḥ-i shaṭḥiyyāt* (1966).[27] He also devoted half of his major work, *En Islam iranien: Aspects spirituels et philosophiques, vol. III, Les fidèles d'amour: Shîʿisme et soufisme* (1972), to a textual analysis of three of Rūzbihān's works, namely *Kitāb al-ighāna, Kashf al-asrār*, and *ʿAbhar al-ʿāshiqīn*. As suggested by the title of this volume, *Les fidèles d'amour*, which is Corbin's translation of *ʿAbhar al-ʿāshiqīn* (literally, "The Jasmine of Passionate Lovers"), Corbin devoted most of his study to this treatise by Rūzbihān. Forty years after the publication of his book, it remains the most in-depth analysis of Rūzbihān's overall thought.

Also active around the same time as Corbin was the Turkish scholar Nazif Hoca, who edited two of Rūzbihān's Arabic works, *Kashf al-asrār* (1971)[28] and *Mashrab al-arwāḥ* (1974).[29] In Iran, Jawād Nūrbakhsh published an improved edition of *ʿAbhar al-ʿāshiqīn* based on a newly discovered manuscript.[30] He also published two short Persian treatises by Rūzbihān[31] and the hagiography written by his great-grandson, Sharaf al-Dīn Rūzbihān Thānī, which had also been published by Dānishpazhūh.[32]

Annemarie Schimmel was perhaps the first to draw English readers' attention to Rūzbihān's writings through her works on Persian poetry, even though she never wrote a separate article or book on Rūzbihān himself.[33] Her interest in Rūzbihān was carried on by her former student, Carl Ernst, who became the first major scholar to publish on Rūzbihān in English. His *Rūzbihān Baqlī: Mysticism and the Rhetoric of Sainthood in Persian Sufism* (Richmond: Curzon, 1996) is still the only monograph on him. In it, Ernst focuses on the history of the Rūzbihāniyya order from its formation to its gradual institutionalization, the history of Rūzbihān's family, and an analysis of the "inner structure of sainthood," in which he mainly treats Rūzbihān's visionary experiences. Ernst's earlier work, *Words of Ecstasy in Sufism* (Albany: SUNY Press, 1985), devoted a section to the ecstatic aspect of Rūzbihān's writings. He also translated *Kashf al-asrār* in 1997. Firoozeh Papan-Matin recently published a critical edition of *Kashf al-asrār* (Leiden: Brill 2006).

The scholar who has been most prolific in writing about Rūzbihān in recent years is Paul Ballanfat, who has edited a number of Rūzbihān's Arabic works[34] and translated his visionary diary, *Kashf al-asrār*, into French.[35] In his long French introduction to the *Quatre traités inédits de Rûzbehân Baqlî Shîrâzî*, Ballanfat pays close attention to two things: the historical reconstruction of Rūzbihān's biography and an analysis of what he considers to be the key features of Rūzbihān's thought. Ballanfat's attempt at reconstructing Rūzbihān's life is probably the most extensive among all existing biographical work on him. Ballanfat's analysis of Rūzbihān's thought seems to feature aspects that might be unexpected, such as the "problem of evil" and Iblīs, which have more to do with Rūzbihān's influential predecessor, al-Ḥallāj. Ballanfat also pays significant attention to Rūzbihān's "equivocal" language.[36] One of his contentions is that love, contra Corbin, is not central to Rūzbihān's thought, so he focuses on other sides to it that he finds more central or important.

1

Discourse on Beauty

The concept of beauty has inspired generations of Muslim intellectuals—philosophers, Sufis, dogmatic theologians, jurists, and litterateurs—to engage in discourse from various angles, ranging from poetry to metaphysics. Some took a practical interest in the subject, discussing how to create beautiful and persuasive writings (as in poetics) or whether it is permissible to display external beauty (as in jurisprudence); others took a more theoretical approach, analyzing the concept of beauty as such. Among all these Muslim intellectuals, two groups have made notable contributions on both the practical and the theoretical levels: Sufis and philosophers. Sufis saw God as their beautiful beloved and sought intimacy with Him by beautifying their inner qualities. Philosophers, not least because of the influence of the *Theology of Aristotle*, a compilation of paraphrases from Plotinus's *Enneads*, equated beauty with being, their fundamental subject of analysis.

Close examination of key discussions in three major schools of thought—philosophy (*falsafa*), Sufism (*taṣawwuf*, *ʿirfān*), and dogmatic theology (*kalām*)—reveals Muslim thinkers' wide-ranging yet interconnected reflections on the notion of beauty (*jamāl*, *ḥusn*). It is these reflections that provide the intellectual milieu in which Rūzbihān's theory of beauty may be situated. It must be noted that the lines separating these three schools of thought are not clear-cut, because many scholars, like al-Ghazālī, combine the various perspectives.

The foundation of much Muslim discourse on beauty (*jamāl*) is the saying of Muhammad, "Indeed, God is beautiful and He loves beauty" (*Inna Allāh jamīl yuḥibb al-jamāl*).[1] This ḥadīth has had practical and theoretical implications for generations of Muslims, who took it as an encouragement to pursue beauty on various levels—from personal grooming to the improvement of one's moral qualities to the quest for an encounter with God. There are many other ḥadīths and Qurʾānic verses of import for the Muslim understanding of beauty, most often using the other Arabic word root denoting beauty: *ḥ-s-n*. These include such Qurʾānic verses as *Blessed is God, the most beautiful* (*aḥsan*) *of creators* (Q 23:14) and *We have created the human being in the most beautiful stature* (Q 95:4).

Among ḥadīths, one that plays an especially important role is the so-called ḥadīth of Gabriel, according to which the angel Gabriel appeared to Muhammad in front of a number of companions to ask him about the religion that he was teaching them. Muhammad explained that it has three basic dimensions—*islām* (submission), *īmān* (faith), and *iḥsān* (doing what is beautiful; a fourth-form derivation from *ḥasuna,* i.e., to be beautiful). Doing what is beautiful means to "worship God as if you see Him, for even if you do not see Him, He sees you."[14] On the basis of this statement, Muslims have understood the complementarity of the acts of submission, faith, and beautiful intention, with the last holding the key to the perfection or "beautification" of Muslim faith and worship.

If we turn to Muslim cultural production, we find poets, litterateurs, Qurʾān reciters, and calligraphers searching for the best sensory means of expressing beauty—whether literary, auditory, or visual. In contrast, philosophers, dogmatic theologians, and Sufis tended to ponder the nature of beauty primarily on the intelligible level, so as to understand the principles behind beautiful phenomena in the world, while striving for an experience of beauty beyond the sensible world.

In terms of the sheer diversity of the angles through which beauty was analyzed as a concept and as a sensible phenomenon, no group surpasses the philosophers (*falāsifa*). Their investigation ranges over fields such as rhetoric, poetics, optics, and music.[2] Along with the Sufis and, to a lesser degree, the dogmatic theologians, the philosophers also paid close attention to beauty in the areas of metaphysics, cosmology, psychology, and ethics. In fact, it is these last four fields of inquiry that lie at the center of the shared discourse on beauty among Muslim intellectuals.

Recent Western scholarship has pointed out that despite the abundance of philosophical discussion of the idea and phenomena of beauty, aesthetics—i.e., investigation of the principles of beauty and human taste on the sensible level—was never a major topic of discussion in Muslim philosophy. As Deborah Black writes,

> On the whole, Islamic philosophers did not view artistic and literary creativity as ends in themselves. Rather, their interest was in explaining the relations of these activities to purely intellectual ends. In the case of poetics and rhetoric in particular, the emphasis in Islamic philosophy was pragmatic and political: poetics and rhetoric were viewed as instruments for communicating the demonstrated truths of philosophy to the populace, whose intellectual abilities were presumed to be limited.[3]

For the philosophers, the pursuit of the principles of beauty in the sensible order of things (art, literature, speech, etc.) was a means to an end—i.e., to maximize the effect of their words on the masses in their effort to convey philosophical truths to them for educational purposes. This is in contrast to the *udabāʾ* ("litterateurs"), whose goals did not usually go beyond the very act of producing beautiful literature that appeals to human sensibility. Aaron Hughes argues that the philosophers focused primarily on the process of intellection in the human aesthetic experience, that is, the soul's encounter with a beautiful object:

> Although Muslim and Jewish philosophers approached aesthetics from what we would today call a number of different disciplinary perspectives, common to all is the role and function of beauty in the noetic development of the individual. This involves…a process whereby an individual

> encounters a beautiful object, resulting in a subsequent correspondence between the soul of the knower and the object known. This correspondence in turn allows the individual to recognize the beauty of the intelligible world.[4]

Common to the philosophers, dogmatic theologians, and Sufis is the notion that the highest degree of beauty belongs to the most perfect being, which the philosophers call the "Necessary Being" or "First Cause," and which the dogmatic theologians and Sufis call "God." Although the language and approach used by each group differs, the general content of their discussion can be categorized into the following main themes: ontology (i.e., beauty as perfection of being), theology (beauty as an attribute of God), cosmogony and cosmology (the role of beauty in the origination and structure of the world), ethics (how to beautify one's soul by acquiring virtues), and psychology (the effect of beauty on the human soul).

Ontology

The most fundamental aspect of the philosophical discourse on beauty is ontology. Al-Fārābī (d. 950), for instance, argues that beauty (*jamāl*) is found in that which "is in its most excellent state of existence and…has attained its ultimate perfection."[5] Al-Fārābī maintains that the intensity of beauty is proportionate to the degree of a thing's ontological perfection. Hence, he concludes, "[S]ince the First is in the most excellent state of existence, its beauty surpasses the beauty of every other beautiful existent."[6]

Ibn Sīnā (Avicenna; d. 1037) writes: "There cannot exist beauty (*jamāl*) or splendor beyond that [being whose] quiddity is purely intelligible, purely good, free from any deficiency, and unique in all respects. The Necessary Being has pure beauty and splendor."[7] Here Ibn Sīnā is speaking about the same being that al-Fārābī has referred to as "the First," but he adds another point: since ultimate beauty can be found only in the perfect being that is purely intelligible and good, it cannot be found in the sensible world, which is a realm of deficiency and imperfect being.

Al-Ghazālī (d. 1111), who inherited elements from various intellectual schools including philosophy (while publicly presenting himself as a critic of philosophy), offers a similar ontological analysis of beauty though with a subtle difference. He argues that every single thing has a unique perfection proper to itself, and its particular beauty depends on the degree to which it has actualized the perfection that is meant for it.

> Each thing's beauty (*jamāl* and *ḥusn*) is for the perfection that is fitting and possible for it to be present with it. When all its possible perfections are present, it will be in the utmost limit of beauty. If only some of them are present, it will have beauty in the measure of what is present. Thus a beautiful horse is that which combines all that is fitting for a horse, such as appearance, shape, color, beautiful running, and ease in attack and retreat. A beautiful script is that which combines all that is fitting for a script, such as the proportion of the letters, their alignment, their being in the right sequence, and the beauty of their order.
>
> Each thing has a perfection that is fitting for it, and its opposite may be fitting for something else. So the beauty of each thing lies in its fitting perfection. Thus the human being is not beautiful through what makes a horse beautiful, nor is a script beautiful through what makes a voice beautiful, nor are vessels beautiful through what makes clothing beautiful, and so on with other things.[8]

What is noteworthy here is that instead of regarding sensible things as imperfect beings in contrast to its ultimate source—God—al-Ghazālī recognizes a relative perfection of each thing, that is to say, a perfection that is specific and uniquely proper to each object. The degree of each thing's relative perfection accounts for its beauty. By acknowledging that each thing has a relative perfection, al-Ghazālī is able to analyze the beauty of sensible objects on their own terms without constant recourse to God as the highest principle of beauty—thus venturing into the area of aesthetics proper. Underlying all these discussions by al-Fārābī, Ibn Sīnā, and al-Ghazālī is the fundamental notion of beauty as the perfection of being.

Theology

The dogmatic theologians addressed the issue of beauty on the basis of the Qurʾān's ascription of the most beautiful names (*al-asmāʾ al-ḥusnā*) to God (7:180; 17:110; 20:8; 59:24). Many concluded that the names should be numbered ninety-nine and extracted from the language of the Qurʾān itself. They were able to establish a more or less standard list of God's most beautiful names, with a good deal of variation.[9] On the basis of the lists of the divine names, they divided a major cluster into two types: the names of gentleness (*luṭf*) and the names of severity (*qahr*), corresponding to the two opposing aspects of God seen in relation to His creation.[10] They also called these two types the names of bounty (*faḍl*) and justice (*ʿadl*), or mercy (*raḥma*) and wrath (*ghaḍab*). For example, the name "life-giver" (*muḥyī*) indicates God's gentle or merciful side, and "death-giver" (*mumīt*) shows His severe or wrathful side. According to this schematization of the divine names, the names of gentleness are seen to attract human beings to God and create intimacy between them, whereas the names of severity inspire fear in human beings and put them at distance from God. These two opposing categories of divine names came to be also referred to as the names of beauty (*jamāl*) and names of majesty (*jalāl*).[11]

That God has these two dimensions—the beautiful and the majestic, the gentle and the severe—is a widespread theme in Sufi texts, be they commentaries on the divine names, such as those of al-Qushayrī, al-Ghazālī, Samʿānī, and Ibn al-ʿArabī, or other works that deal with theological issues. The general question of the divine attributes interested philosophers as well. Their main concern was the exact ontological relationship between the divine attributes (*ṣifāt*) and the divine essence (*dhāt*)—in other words, whether the attributes were identical with the essence, and if not how it would then be possible to maintain God's oneness. For instance, in Book Eight of *al-Shifā*, "On Knowing the First Principle of All Existence and On Knowing His Attributes," Ibn Sīnā has a chapter entitled, "On the relation of the intelligibles to Him; on making it clear that His positive and negative attributes do not necessitate multiplicity in His essence; that to Him belong the most tremendous splendor, the loftiest majesty, and infinite glory; on explaining in detail the state of intellective pleasure."[12]

If the dogmatic theologians sought to systematize their understanding of God's beauty by setting up schemes to categorize the Qur'ānic names of God, the philosophers engaged mainly in the analysis of God's beauty in terms of ontology, leading them to the conviction that beauty and being are identical. As for the Sufis, for the most part they agreed with the views of both philosophers and theologians, but they also stressed the implications of God's beautiful names for human life, as people should study and know the divine names with the aim of beautifying the soul by embodying God's most beautiful qualities. They took a variety of approaches to this task, as we will see with Rūzbihān.

Cosmology

In addressing the cosmological significance of beauty, we might begin by recalling the original sense of the Greek word *cosmos*—"order." It is this that constituted beauty for the ancient Greeks. The Muslim philosophers show a strong Greek influence in their analysis of beauty; especially prominent are elements of Pythagoreanism and Neoplatonism, both of which had been transmitted to the Muslim world through Syriac and Arabic translations before the tenth century. A perfect example of the combination of the Pythagorean and Plotinian understanding of beauty is found in the Ikhwān al-Ṣafā' ("the Brethren of Purity"), a group of anonymous tenth-century philosophers who composed an encyclopedic work, *al-Rasā'il* ("The Epistles"), covering a vast range of philosophical topics. In their discussion of music, for example, the Ikhwān speak of the music of the spheres, which appears in accordance with the Pythagorean principle of proportion, as well as the moral benefit of music in taming the animal soul.[13]

As for the Neoplatonic side of the discussion, the Ikhwān explain that a human aesthetic experience depends on the mutual relationship between the universal and the particular souls. Perceiving beauty in a sensible object is an occasion for the particular soul to be reminded of its higher origin, the universal soul that lies in the intelligible realm, which is the realm of true beauty. Such an experience calls the soul to return to its origin by making it turn away from corporeal existence. The Ikhwān write,

> When the traces of beautiful (*ḥisān*) sensory things take form in particular souls, these [souls] come to resemble and correspond to the universal soul, yearn for it, and wish to join with it. When they become separate from the bodily frame, they will ascend to the kingdom of heaven and join with the highest plenum.[14]

By "the highest plenum" (*al-mala᾽ al-a῾lā*), the Ikhwān explain, they mean "the residents of the heavens and the celestial spheres."[15]

The above passage echoes Plotinus's discussion in the *Ennead* I.6.2: "the soul, since it is by nature what it is and is related to the higher kind of reality in the realm of being, when it sees something akin to it or a trace of its kindred reality, is delighted and thrilled and returns to itself and remembers itself and its own possessions."[16] For both Plotinus and the Ikhwān al-Ṣafā᾽, the true experience of beauty pertains to the intelligible world, not to the sensible. At the same time they also recognize that sensible beauty prompts the individual soul to conform or attune[17] itself to its original state of beauty through the process of recollection.

The notion that the individual soul mirrors the beauty of higher order resonates with much of Sufi thinking as well. Though it is almost impossible to pinpoint where Muslim writings come under direct Greek influence outside the philosophical tradition, especially in the later centuries, the general Muslim discourse on beauty—especially among the

Sufis—has certain striking similarities to the Plotinian understanding whether there be direct or indirect influence or not.

Cosmogony

As for the function of beauty in cosmogony, beauty plays a significant role especially in the general Sufi understanding of creation (*khalq*). There is a crucial "creation myth" found in many Sufi texts. This is the so-called ḥadīth of the Hidden Treasure, in which God says, "I was a Hidden Treasure, and I loved to be recognized. So I created the creatures so that I may be recognized."[18] In general, Sufis interpret this saying in the following manner. The clause "I was a Hidden Treasure" corresponds to the state of God in His solitude without the presence of anything else. While God knew and loved Himself in His solitude, He wanted something else to appreciate and come to know His Treasure. Hence, God created the world so that His Hidden Treasure would no longer be hidden. Thus, God's love for Himself and His desire to be known are the driving force for the creation of the world.

In conjunction with another key ḥadīth, "God is beautiful and He loves beauty," the ḥadīth of the Hidden Treasure has contributed to the idea that creation was driven by God's desire to manifest His *beauty* so that it might be witnessed and known by others. Creation is then the self-disclosure (*tajallī*) of God's beauty as a result of His overflowing love for His own beauty. This process also brings about the duality of subject and object, knower and known, lover and beloved. Without creation, God's beauty could not have been known or loved by *anything else*.

Ethics and Chivalry

Ethics (*ʿilm al-akhlāq*) and etiquette (*ādāb*) are subjects discussed by practically all groups of Muslim intellectuals, though it was the philosophers who established ethics as a discipline. They often regarded it as "medicine for the soul," just as there is medicine for the body. The philosopher-physician

Abū Bakr al-Rāzī (Rhazes), for example, wrote an ethical treatise entitled *Spiritual Medicine* (*al-Ṭibb al-rūḥānī*), full of advice on how to control one's lower self or soul (*nafs*) and to treat its various illnesses, such as envy, anger, and lust, all of which are generally considered ugly qualities of the human soul. The goal of philosophical ethics can be taken as the beautification of the soul, which involves the removal of the vices of the lower soul that hinder the higher functions of the rational soul.

The emphasis on disciplining and beautifying the soul is even more evident in Sufism, where the soul is described as being in need of ascending a stairway back to God in the footsteps of the Prophet in his *miʿrāj*. Each step in the path is understood as an increase in proximity to the divine beauty, and the steps are typically understood as refinements and beautifications of the soul. Rūzbihān's *Mashrab al-arwāḥ* is an example of the genre.

Sufi literature addresses ethics in a variety of ways. One of the most distinctive instances is a current of thought and practice known as *futuwwa*, or "chivalry," which is characterized by the training of the soul in ethics, that is, the beautiful traits of the soul, such as generosity, self-sacrifice, humbleness, camaraderie, and mutual respect. *Futuwwa* literally means "young-manliness," representing the "young man" (*fatā*) ideal characterized by the above-listed virtues. Sufis often discuss Abraham and Joseph as representatives of the young man ideal as the Qurʾān calls each a *fatā*, along with the Companions of the Cave, who in Maybudī's view encapsulate the young man ideal.[19]

Among prominent Sufi authors who wrote on *futuwwa* were al-Sulamī (d. 1021), Shihāb al-Din ʿUmar al-Suhrawardī (d. 1234), and Ibn al-ʿArabī (d. 1240). Though essentially a practical discipline, underlying the ideals of *futuwwa* is a radical commitment to *tawḥīd*, or the assertion of God's oneness, in everyday human conduct by giving no significance to anything other than God, above all one's own ego. By sacrificing self-concern in interhuman transactions, Sufi "chevaliers" strive to live up to the beautiful young man ideal modeled on Abraham, who was ready to sacrifice his own beloved son for the sake of God.

On a more general level, Sufi ethics also revolves around the idea of "becoming characterized by the character traits of God" (*takhalluq bi-akhlāq Allāh*)—which comes from a statement ascribed to Muhammad and which Sufis took to mean the cultivation or internalization of the most beautiful names of God. In support of this ideal, al-Ghazālī quotes another ḥadīth connected with God's most beautiful names: "God has ninety-nine character traits: whosoever becomes characterized by one of them will surely enter the Garden."[20]

Psychology of Beauty and Love

Psychology, or the study of the soul (*ʿilm al-nafs*) is a well-established subfield of philosophy, so it is no surprise to find philosophers analyzing beauty in psychological terms. Ibn Sīnā explores the psychology of beauty in a treatise called *Risāla fī al-ʿishq* ("Treatise on Love"), which contains a detailed analysis of various kinds of love. In keeping with the Aristotelian psychology adopted by most Muslim thinkers, Ibn Sīnā divides the "soul" into several kinds, each of which embraces the qualities of the lower kind—the vegetative, animal, human, and angelic—and argues that each kind possesses a kind of "love" according to its own nature.[21]

When Ibn Sīnā analyzes the animal and rational souls, he points out that *sensible* beauty causes love in the *animal* soul, while *intelligible* beauty causes love in the *rational* soul. He explains that loving sensible beauty brings human beings down to the level of beasts, and loving *intelligible* beauty raises the soul to its most noble level. Such a view comes from his basic understanding that intelligible beauty serves as a ladder for the human being to come closer to the Absolute Good (which he calls elsewhere the Necessary Being or God). This Good is the rational soul's ultimate object of contemplation. It is the cause and origin of all sensible and intelligible beauty, the possessor of the highest beauty, and the ultimate object of love.[22] Ibn Sīnā thus discovers a necessary connection between beauty and love on all levels of existence and considers the Absolute Good as the most proper object of love for the rational soul. In explaining such hierarchical scheme of love and beauty, Ibn Sīnā places a definite emphasis on the significance of intelligibility even in the human experience of love.

Love also plays an extremely important role in Sufi psychology. Generations of Sufis have written works explaining the distinctions to be drawn among the soul (*nafs*), the spirit (*rūḥ*), the heart (*qalb*), and the secret core (*sirr*). They investigated various states (*aḥwāl*) of the human soul, such as hope, fear, joy, sorrow, bewilderment, and love. They also wrote many works revolving around the theme of love and beauty. The Persian poet Jalāl al-Dīn Rūmī (d. 1273) is one of the most famous Sufis who spoke about the necessity of love in human life and the path to God. Other Sufis known for their talk of love and beauty include Aḥmad Ghazālī (d. ca. 1126), Aḥmad Samʿānī (d. 1140), ʿAyn al-Quḍāt Hamadānī (d. 1131), Shihāb al-Dīn Yaḥyā Suhrawardī al-Maqtūl (d. 1191), Rūzbihān Baqlī (d. 1209), and Ibn al-ʿArabī (d. 1240).

Most Sufis were aware that love and beauty are inseparable, for the source of all love in the universe is the fact that God loves beauty. As a result, human love necessarily takes beauty as its object. Aḥmad Ghazālī points out that beauty always needs a lover: "The eye of beauty is shut to its own beauty, for it cannot perceive the perfection of its own beauty except in the mirror of the lover's love. Hence, in this respect, beauty must have a lover so that the beloved may feed on its own beauty in the mirror of the lover's love and seeking."[23] Here emerges a basic Sufi picture of beauty as the perennial beloved (*maḥbūb, maʿshūq*). Just as the philosophers regard the First Cause or the Necessary Being as the ultimate object of contemplation and love for the rational soul, the Sufis also see God as their eternal beloved, with whom they strive forever, in this world and the next, to achieve union.

Psychology of Beauty and Pleasure

In psychological analyses of beauty, philosophers often associate beauty with the pleasure (*ladhdha*) that accompanies the perception of beauty. They point out that the more beautiful a thing is, the greater the pleasure is in perceiving it. Hence, given that the First is the most perfect and the most beautiful being, the pleasure It causes is also the greatest—to the point that it is beyond human comprehension. Al-Fārābī writes, "Pleasure and delight and enjoyment result and increase only when the most accurate apprehension concerns itself with the most beautiful…objects."[24] Moreover, "since the First is absolutely the most beautiful…the pleasure which the First enjoys is a pleasure whose character we do not understand and whose intensity we fail to apprehend, except by analogy."[25]

In contrast to al-Fārābī, Ibn Sīnā focuses on the intense pleasure that people experience in the cognition of intelligible beauty. He argues that since intelligible beauty is superior to sensible beauty and causes more intense pleasure, human beings must separate themselves from their bodily dimension in order to experience it. He writes, "If we become isolated from our body by examining our essence—when it has become an intellective world corresponding to the true existents, the true beauties, and the true pleasures and become conjoined with them as the intelligible is conjoined with the intelligible—then we will find infinite pleasure and splendor."[26] Ibn Sīnā's emphasis on the necessity of separating the intellect from the body to experience the true pleasure of perceiving beauty may echo the Plotinian disdain for the body and the search for beauty in the intelligible realm, but the emphasis on the intelligible over the sensible is common across all currents of philosophical (and Sufi) thinking in Islam.

Psychology of Beauty and Sorrow

If the perception of beauty causes love and pleasure, the failure to perceive beauty, that is, the object of one's love, will result in sorrow (*ḥuzn*), as some Muslim thinkers point out. The connection between beauty and sorrow is a theme that appears in the Qurʾān itself and is a well-developed literary theme in post-Qurʾānic literature. The Qurʾān's twelfth chapter consists mainly of a narrative on the life of Joseph, and the Qurʾān calls it *the most beautiful of tales* (Q 12:3). Joseph's beauty was the reason that Jacob had a particular attachment to him among all his sons, and due to the loss of Joseph Jacob fell into despair and sorrow.

This Qurʾānic narrative inspired the Illuminationist (*ishrāqī*) philosopher Suhrawardī to compose the allegorical tale, "On the Reality of Love" (*Risāla fī ḥaqīqat al-ʿishq*), to depict the interrelationship among beauty, love, and sorrow, by presenting them as three brothers with distinct personalities.[27] In this allegory, Beauty is the eldest brother to whom the second brother Love clings, but when Love is separated from Beauty, Sorrow becomes Love's constant companion. Sorrow also befriends both Jacob upon the loss of his son and Zulaykhā, the unnamed wife of the vizier of Egypt (biblical Potiphar) in the Qurʾān, who suffers unfulfilled love for Joseph.

If we combine our earlier discussion of the divine names with the present analysis of human psychology, the following picture emerges: when human beings encounter God's mercy, gentleness, and beauty (*jamāl*), their natural reaction to it will be attraction and love. When faced with God's wrath, severity, and majesty (*jalāl*), they will likely experience alienation and sorrow. This theological fact is reflected in the art of Qurʾānic recitation, according to Michael Sells: in the recitation of verses that highlight human beings' encounter with God's majesty or their alienation from Him, the dominating tone is that of sorrow.[28]

Summary

The general picture that emerges from this analysis of the Muslim discourse on beauty is as follows. It begins with the understanding that the first principle, the perfect being, is beautiful. God is the possessor of the most beautiful names, but in relation to the world, He can be beautiful or majestic, merciful or wrathful. He knew His own beauty for eternity, and He created the world because of His desire to make His beauty known in the temporal realm.

God's beauty is reflected in the cosmic order. Higher levels of beauty correspond with higher levels of intelligibility, and lower levels appear in the sensible realm. The harmony produced by this cosmic order reminds the human soul, which is engrossed in corporeality, of its higher origin and invites it to turn away from the sensible world toward the intelligible world. The human aesthetic experience—that is, finding beauty through the senses—has the proper function of directing attention to that which is beyond the sensible world. Beauty is a powerful force that attracts human beings and redirects them toward the intelligible realm because all beauty derives from the ultimate principle of beauty, perfection, and intelligibility.

Human beings are naturally drawn to beauty and find it lovable by nature. In their search for beauty, they may find pleasure in attaining the object of their love, but they will experience sorrow if they lose access to their beloved—be it divine, human, animal, vegetative, or even mineral—because it is the very nature of human beings to love beauty. Sorrow is then the longing for a lost or unattainable beauty, and pleasure and joy result from attaining beauty.

When human beings realize that the ultimate source of all beauty is God, they become lovers of God and strive to see more of His beauty. They realize that this requires the refinement of their inner qualities, for the beautiful God cannot be seen by someone whose heart is rusty and full of ugly character traits. In this process, they try to turn away from the lower animal soul and its egoistic desires so as to seek ultimate beauty alone. As a result of perseverance in this quest, they become purified of the lower realm. It is in such state of purity that the heart can reflect a beautiful image of the divine in itself, and they themselves become beautiful.

For many of the thinkers examined above, to search for beauty was to seek God. For both the philosophers and Sufis, an aesthetic experience is a reminder or sign of God, because they know that every beautiful object derives from its beautiful Creator. Perhaps the role of the dogmatic theologians in shaping this view was less discernible than the philosophers and Sufis, but they still had the important function of providing a terminological framework for speaking about God as "beautiful," for example, in their discussion of the divine names. However, the dogmatic theologians' strictly rationalist interpretation of Qurʾānic language and their rejection of the cognitive value of images and symbols seem to have restricted their discussion on the nature of beauty to a limited and rigid framework.

In contrast, philosophers did not limit themselves to language drawn from the Qurʾān and the Ḥadīth. They felt free to use terminology based on Arabic translations of Greek sources or the Persian intellectual tradition. They approached beauty in terms of things' intelligibility, for they saw the sensible world per se as a realm of imperfection, deficiency, and ugliness, unless one saw through its phenomena to their intelligible sources, that is, the realities of things in the divine. Ultimate beauty per se is to be found only in the intelligible world, in the most perfect being, which transcends human cognitive capacity. By exercising the intellect fully, they strove to come ever closer to a pure cognition of the most perfect being as far as humanly possible. In contrast to the dogmatic theologians' focus on the abstractions of reason, the philosophers also turned their attention to the sensible world to illustrate how the principles of beauty left their traces in the sensible order of things, and this attention to the world resulted in the development of aesthetic theories in optics, rhetoric, and poetics.

For their part Sufis sought to attain the highest beauty by a process of inner transformation—i.e., purification and beautification—driven by their love for God. Given that it is God's love and beauty that brought the world into existence, it is that same love and beauty that bring human beings back to the divine presence. While this is a picture that emerges from those of the Muslim thinkers who have specifically written about beauty, we can say that most Muslim thinkers have traditionally understood that the search for beauty in various areas of human life is part of their religious path—the path to human perfection—for all beauty is a pointer to its origin, God.

2

The Language of Beauty

Over the centuries, various intellectuals—from medieval Sufis to modern Western scholars—have remarked that Rūzbihān's language is dense and recondite, particularly difficult to understand, let alone translate. A well-known scholar of Sufism and Persian literature, the late Annemarie Schimmel noted,

> What so profoundly impresses the reader in Rūzbihān's writing, both in his commentary on the *Shaṭḥiyāt* and his *ʿAbhar al-ʿāshiqīn*...is his style, which is at times as hard to translate as that of Aḥmad Ghazzālī and possesses a stronger and deeper instrumentation. It is no longer the scholastic language of the early exponents of Sufism, who tried to classify stages and stations, though Baqlī surely knew these theories and the technical terms. It is the language refined by the poets of Iran during the eleventh and twelfth centuries, filled with roses and nightingales, pliable and colorful.[1]

Carl Ernst—a scholar on Rūzbihān and former student of Schimmel—calls his style "at times...admittedly convoluted and obscure" and even lists the names of highly educated premodern Muslims—including Jāmī (d. 1492), a prolific writer in later theoretical Sufism and Persian literature, and Dārā

Shukūh (d. 1659), a Mughal scholarly prince—who regarded Rūzbihān as a difficult writer to understand centuries ago.[2] Ernst quotes Jāmī as saying, "He has sayings that have poured forth from him in the state of overpowering ecstasy that not everyone can understand."[3]

Though these statements point to the difficulty of Rūzbihān's language, the reason suggested for it in each case is different—from his flowery style in Persian (Schimmel) to the ecstatic nature of his utterances (Jāmī). In fact there are numerous possible reasons for the difficulty of his language, including his multidimensional learning, the shifting target audiences, his sensitive theologico-political concerns, the varying tones of his voice from the personal to expository, ecstatic to reserved—all the while being as poetic as the context permits—and last but not least, his highly developed technical terminology.

It is the purpose of the present chapter to decipher this last aspect—Rūzbihān's technical terminology—with a focus on several terms that are essential to his discussions of beauty—namely, *ḥusn, jamāl, mustaḥsan, mustaqbaḥ,* and *qubḥ*. While these are all Arabic terms—as most of his technical terms are (even in his Persian works)—Persian equivalents will be introduced whenever applicable. The first section introduces the two most important terms—*ḥusn* and *jamāl*—and traces their usage in the Qurʾān and Ḥadīth, the two key sources for Rūzbihān's technical terminology. The second and main section of this chapter investigates his usage of these terms in his works, while examining how the specific senses in which he employs these terms relate to precedents in the Qurʾān, Ḥadīth, and other Muslim literature that was available to him.

As *ḥusn* and *jamāl* are two concepts central to Rūzbihān's discussion of beauty, which is the topic of this book, I will limit the treatment of these terms in this chapter to the basic terminological distinction between them, while also paying attention to two other terms that are characteristic of his discussions of beauty: *mustaḥsan* and *mustaqbaḥ*. In addition to exposing the basic linguistic framework of Rūzbihān's discourse on beauty, the present chapter aims at bringing out a provisional picture of his *ontology* of beauty. In the subsequent chapters, we shall see how the bare skeleton of his ontological scheme (as shown in a chart at the end of this chapter) grows into a complex theology of beauty (chapter 3), a cosmology and anthropology of beauty (chapter 4), and a prophetology of beauty (chapter 5).

"Beauty" in the Language of the Qur'ān and Ḥadīth

Two key Arabic terms are normally translated as "beauty" in English: *ḥusn* and *jamāl*. Any Muslim discourse touching upon the subject of beauty utilizes either or both of these terms. The present section examines their contextual basis in the Qur'ān and Ḥadīth in order to prepare the ground for Rūzbihān's usage.

Ḥusn

We will begin with *ḥusn* and its derivatives, as they have a more prominent role to play in the Qur'ān than *jamāl*. Medieval lexicographers—such as Ibn Fāris (d. 1004), al-Jawharī (d. ca. 1006), and Ibn Manẓūr (d. 1311), who lived relatively close to Rūzbihān's time—present *ḥusn* first of all as an antonym of *qubḥ* ("ugliness"), implying the meaning of "beauty" for *ḥusn*.[4] The sense of beauty inherent in the Arabic root *ḥ-s-n* is further confirmed by the fact that al-Jawharī compares *tazyīn* ("to ornament/decorate") to *taḥsīn* (a transitive verbal noun from the same root *ḥ-s-n*), which he apparently understands in the sense of "to make something beautiful."[5] However, "ugliness" (*qubḥ*) is *not* the only antonym that Arabic lexicographers list for *ḥusn*. Another antonym that they commonly mention is *sū'*,[6] which is usually translated as "evil" or "badness."[7] This second antonym suggests *ḥusn*'s additional connotation of "goodness." Hence, *ḥusn* denotes both beauty and goodness at the same time.

As *ḥusn* encompasses both goodness and beauty without an internal distinction, the term may remind some readers of the Greek *kallos,* which also signifies goodness and beauty without an internal distinction. This word is present as a prefix in English, for example, *calli*graphy, meaning "*beautiful* writing." Due to the double sense of *ḥusn,* scholars have often wavered between translating it as "goodness" or "beauty." For instance, the lexicographer Edward William Lane lists the following words as possible English equivalents of *ḥusn*: "goodness, or goodliness, [generally the latter,] beauty, comeliness, or pleasingness"; "symmetry; or just proportion of the several parts of the person, one to another"; "anything, moving the mind, that is desired, or wished for."[8]

To complicate the matter further, when scholars wanted to translate *ḥusn* in the sense of "beauty" in a text where the term *jamāl* also appears, they often resorted to translating *jamāl* as "beauty" while choosing one of its synonyms in English to translate *ḥusn*, such as "loveliness," "prettiness," and "comeliness." Thereby they attempted to maintain a distinction between the two terms in the English translation, even though the original author is likely to have employed them in the same meaning, using both together for emphasis or harmony of language, a literary technique especially common in Persian writings.

It must be noted, however, that the challenge of translating *ḥusn* into English has more to do with the linguistic framework of the English language than anything else. This is also clear from the fact that Persian speakers, when they want to translate *ḥusn*, have an apt Persian equivalent: *nīkūʾī*, which denotes both goodness and beauty.[9] For instance, both Aḥmad Ghazālī and the Illuminationist thinker Yaḥyā Suhrawardī (d. 1191) use *nīkūʾī* as a Persian equivalent of *ḥusn*.[10] Moreover, Aḥmad's elder and famous brother, Abū Ḥāmid al-Ghazālī (d. 1111) employs *nīkūʾī* in his discussion of beauty in *Kīmiyā-yi saʿādat* ("The Alchemy of Happiness").[11] In the present book, both *jamāl* and *ḥusn* will be translated as "beauty" rather than using the cumbersome double translation of "goodness-and-beauty" for *ḥusn*. However, the Arabic will be noted in parentheses in many cases where the distinction between the two terms is important.

In the Qurʾān, words derived from the root *ḥ-s-n* appear 193 times in various forms, including (but not limited to): verbs (*ḥasuna, aḥsana*); nouns (*ḥusn, ḥasana*); an adjective (*ḥasan*); an active participle (*muḥsin*); and a verbal noun (*iḥsān*). Seventy-seven of these are related to the forth-form verb, *aḥsana* ("to do what is good and beautiful"), occupying a prominent place in the Qurʾān. Toshihiko Izutsu explains,

"The verb *aḥsana* (inf. *iḥsān*) is one of the key ethical terms in the Qurʾan. Most generally it means 'to do good,' but in the actual Qurʾanic usage this word is applied mainly to two particular classes of 'goodness': profound piety towards God and all human deeds that originate in it, and acts motivated by the spirit of *ḥilm* ['forbearance']."[12] In fact, it was the moral overtone of being "good" inherent in the root *ḥ-s-n* that prompted the late Izutsu, an eminent scholar of Islamic thought, to undertake a detailed analysis of this word root in his *Ethico-Religious Concepts in the Qurʾān*,[13] though it must be noted that his analysis of *ḥusn* is limited by the very nature of his book: "ethico-religious." What falls outside the scope of his book is an ontological analysis of *ḥusn*, which is essential for a full grasp of the term.

Key Qurʾānic verses that contain *ḥ-s-n* derivatives include: *Blessed is God, the most beautiful (aḥsan) of creators* (Q 23:14), *To God belong the most beautiful* (*ḥusnā*) *names* (Q 7:180), *To Him belong the most beautiful* (*ḥusnā*) *names* (Q 17:110, 20:8, 59:24), *Surely you have a beautiful (ḥasana) example in God's messenger—for those who hope for God and the Last Day, and who remember God much* (Q 33:21), *Indeed We created the human being in the most beautiful (aḥsan) stature* (Q 95:4), *He formed you then made your forms beautiful (aḥsana)* (Q 40:64, 64:3), *Verily God loves those who do what is beautiful (muḥsinīn)* (Q 2:195), and *who made beautiful (aḥsana) everything He has created* (Q 32:7). Though the above is only a small sample of the verses containing *ḥ-s-n* derivatives, it is already clear that in the Qurʾān *ḥ-s-n* is used to designate beauty in a whole range of beings—from God Himself (Q 23:14, 37:125, 7:180, 17:110, 20:8, 59:24) to the prophet Muhammad (Q 33:21), human beings (Q 40:64, 64:3, 95:4, 2:195), and all of God's creation (Q 32:7).

As for the Ḥadīth literature, whose corpus is much vaster than the Qurʾān, there are countless instances where *ḥ-s-n* derivatives appear. One of the most famous ḥadīths that feature these is known as the aforementioned ḥadīth of Gabriel, in which the archangel Gabriel appears to Muhammad in front of a few of his companions to ask him the meaning of *islām* ("submission"), *īmān* ("faith"), and *iḥsān* ("doing what is beautiful"). With regard to the third, the Prophet replies, "*Iḥsān* is that you worship God as if you see Him, for even if you do not see Him, He sees you." While this is one of the most famous ḥadīths among Sunnis, it does not have a key role in Rūzbihān's discussion of *ḥusn* (though he does refer to it in his writings).

Much more prominent in Rūzbihān's discussion of beauty is the ḥadīth, "I saw my Lord in the most beautiful form" (*Raʾaytu rabbī fī aḥsan ṣūra*).[15] Here, the word *aḥsan*—the superlative of *ḥasan*, "beautiful"—describes the "form" in which God appeared to the Prophet. This ḥadīth plays an important role in Rūzbihān's discussion of the vision (*ruʾya*) of God, which took place for him often in indescribably beautiful forms. In fact the vision of the beautiful God is a major theme in Rūzbihān's writings, particularly in his diary of visions, *Kashf al-asrār* ("The Unveiling of Secrets"),[16] which will be examined in subsequent chapters.

In short, *ḥ-s-n* derivatives abound in the Qurʾān and Ḥadīth, which gives them an official status as scriptural terms to describe the beauty of both God and creatures. The above and other passages in the Qurʾān and Ḥadīth containing *ḥ-s-n* derivatives form the fundamental textual basis for later Muslim discourse—including Rūzbihān's own—on the beauty (*ḥusn*) of God and His creation.

Jamāl

The other key term that denotes "beauty," *jamāl,* is a noun derived from the root *j-m-l*, which has the basic root meanings of "to be beautiful," "to gather," and "that which pertains to the camel" (*jamal*).[17] Even though it is not impossible to see relationships among these three senses, they appear quite distinct from one another, and here we are concerned only with the first. *Jamāl* is almost without exception translated into English as "beauty." In modern Arabic, it is the standard word for beauty, much more commonly used than *ḥusn,*[18] whereas in the Qurʾān, it has only a marginal presence.

In fact, the word *jamāl* appears in the Qurʾān only once: *And the cattle—He created them for you; in them is warmth, and uses various, and of them you eat. There is beauty in them for you when you bring them home to rest and when you drive them forth abroad to pasture* (Q 16:5–6). In this single Qurʾānic usage, *jamāl* is a quality of beauty ascribed to an animal—in this case, the cattle.

The adjectival form, *jamīl* ("beautiful"), appears in the Qurʾān seven times. In three of these it is used in conjunction with the word *patience* as in "*Beautiful patience!*" (*ṣabr*^{un} *jamīl*^{un}). This phrase appears twice as the words of Jacob in his despair over the loss of his beloved son, Joseph (Q 12:18, 12:83), and it is understood more generally to encourage patience in times of affliction. The third instance is found as part of God's admonishment: *So be thou patient with a beautiful patience* (Q 70:5).

In the Qurʾān, *jamīl* occurs twice as a description of the manner in which women should be set free if divorce is agreed upon: *Set them free in a beautiful manner* (*sarāḥ*^{an} *jamīl*^{an}) (Q 33:49); *I will set you free in a beautiful manner* (Q 33:28). It also appears once to describe the act of "pardoning" (*ṣafḥ*): *So pardon thou, with a beautiful pardoning* (Q 15:85). It also appears once to designate the proper manner of "leaving" or "abandoning" some people: *And bear thou patiently what they say and leave them beautifully* (*hajr*^{an} *jamīl*^{an}) (Q 73:10). Thus, in only eight verses does the Qurʾān talk about beauty using the Arabic root *j-m-l*, in contrast to *ḥ-s-n*, which it mentions nearly two hundred times.

In these eight verses the term *jamāl/jamīl* is always applied to *creatures*—first to *animals* and then to the ideal manner of *human* conduct—from how to set women free to manners of pardoning or abandoning people. What this implies is that the Qurʾān itself does not ascribe the quality of *jamāl* to God. One of the visible consequences of this fact is the absence of *al-jamīl* (the Beautiful) in many early lists of the ninety-nine names of God.

Daniel Gimaret in *Les noms divins en Islam* points out that while *jamīl* does not appear as a divine name in the Qurʾān, it has come to be considered as such by some Muslims on the basis of the aforementioned ḥadīth, "Indeed God is beautiful and He loves beauty." He further explains that the notion of divine beauty became a popular subject among certain groups of Muslims, such as naive anthropomorphists and Sufis, but cautiously treated by most dogmatic theologians, including both Muʿtazilites and Ashʿarites. Among the Muslim thinkers who have compiled lists of divine names and included *al-jamīl* ("the Beautiful") as a divine name, Gimaret mentions al-Qushayrī (d. ca. 1072) and Abū Ḥāmid al-Ghazālī (d. 1111).[19]

The origin of attributing *jamāl* to God is without doubt the well-known saying of Muhammad, "Indeed God is beautiful and He loves beauty" (*Inna Allāh jamīl yuḥibb al-jamāl*). It is found in both the *Ṣaḥīḥ* of Muslim and the *Musnad* of Ibn Ḥanbal. In both cases, it is situated in a dialogue between Muhammad and a certain man. Muhammad first says, "No one who has a dust mote's weight of arrogance in his heart will enter paradise." In Ibn Ḥanbal's versions, the man notes that he loves to adorn himself with beautiful (*ḥasan*) outer garments and asks the Prophet directly: "Is that arrogance?" The Prophet replies by saying in one version "No, that is not arrogance," and in another, "No, that is beauty (*jamāl*)." Then he proceeds to remark, "Indeed God is beautiful and He loves beauty."[20] In Muslim's version, after the same initial statement by the Prophet it reads: "Then a man said, 'A man likes his garment and sandals to be beautiful (*ḥasan*).' He replied, 'Indeed God is beautiful and He loves beauty. Arrogance is to be insolent toward God and to despise people.'"[21]

The most apparent meaning of this ḥadīth is that adorning oneself properly is not an act of arrogance, but rather one done out of love for beauty. Hence, it means that there is no blame in loving beauty and adorning oneself with it, because this is to follow the divine custom of loving beauty. Another point to be noticed here is that the Prophet takes *jamāl* to be a synonym of *ḥusn,* which is clear from the fact that he responds to the man who likes his clothes to be *ḥasan* by confirming that it is fine because God loves *jamāl,* using the other Arabic word for beauty.

A more striking point made in this ḥadīth is this: not only does God love beauty but He Himself is *jamīl*. Hence, the first half of this ḥadīth—"God is beautiful"—introduces a significant leap from the seemingly mundane discussion of the quality of one's clothing to that of the beauty of God. This establishes a prophetic precedence for ascribing *jamāl* to God, not just to creatures, as was done in the Qur᾽ān. Being a sound ḥadīth, it has hence given *jamāl/jamīl* an official status as an appropriate term to describe God, sowing the seed for the flowering of the medieval theological, philosophical, and mystical discourse on *jamāl* as an attribute of God.

Another noteworthy point about this ḥadīth is that the seeming "leap" from the mundane beauty of an outer garment to the divine beauty is not presented as a leap in the statement, but rather as the result of an evident interconnection between the beauty of God and that of creatures. In other words, in keeping with much of Muslim discourse, God and His creation are not cut off from each other as if they constitute the two separate domains of the sacred and the profane. Rather, the world always *reflects* God's characteristics or attributes—including beauty—as if it is God's *mirror*. This is a standard interpretation of the word *āya,* "sign," frequently used in the Qurʾān to designate natural phenomena, prophetic miracles, and the Qurʾān's own verses.

Thus, we can see that even if the Qurʾān never ascribed *jamāl* to God, the word gains a wide significance in Muslim theological discourse because of its prophetic endorsement. It is no overstatement to say that this ḥadīth, "Indeed God is beautiful and He loves beauty," is the foundation of all Muslim discourse on God as *jamīl*.

Rūzbihān's Definitions

Among Rūzbihān's works, the Arabic treatise, *Mashrab al-arwāḥ* ("The Drinking Place of Spirits")[22]—also called by the Persian title *Hazār wa yak maqām* ("One Thousand and One Stations")—is arguably the best source for studying his terminology. As the Persian title indicates, this work consists of an exposition of 1,001 stations (*maqāmāt,* sing. *maqām*) through which human spirits travel—from their creation by God and their pre-earthly life in the presence of God to their embodied existence on earth and their eventual return to God. In each section of this book, Rūzbihān provides an exposition of a single station. Each of these designates a state of human beings as they progress on the Sufi path—e.g., repentance, hope, fear, joy, love, bewilderment, certitude, and annihilation. Such a structure allows the work to be used almost as an annotated lexicon of Rūzbihān's terminology. What interests us here is the fact that both *ḥusn* and *jamāl* appear among the "1,001" stations.

It must be noted that while there is a general sense of a hierarchical order in the progression of the twenty chapters in *Mashrab al-arwāḥ*, the ordering of individual stations inside a chapter does not always appear strictly hierarchical. In other words, just because the station of *ḥusn* appears before that of *jamāl,* it does not necessarily mean that *ḥusn* is a lower station than that of *jamāl*. Another point to be made about the *Mashrab* is that while 1,001 is the "official" total number of the stations that it presents, in reality there are 1,004 stations presented in the work, as there are three chapters that contain one extra station each (i.e., chapters 1, 5, and 8). However, since in each of these chapters, the additional station holds a special, high place in relation to all the previous stations, perhaps they are not meant to be counted like the rest.

Ḥusn and *Jamāl*

In the section on the station of *ḥusn,* Rūzbihān writes: "Understand that *ḥusn* is one of the attributes of God and is eternal because His essence is eternal.…God's *ḥusn* is one of His most specific descriptions. God said, *Blessed is God, the most beautiful* (*aḥsan*) *of creators* [Q 23:14]."[23] Rūzbihān cites this Qurʾānic usage of the word *aḥsan*—"the most beautiful"—to corroborate his view that *ḥusn* is an attribute of God. The idea that God possesses *ḥusn* is confirmed among others by Muhammad's saying, "I saw my Lord in the most beautiful form," which Rūzbihān takes to be a testimony to the Prophet's "vision of God the Exalted in the clothing of *ḥusn*."[24] Thus, the Prophet saw the *most beautiful creator* in "the most beautiful form."

We saw that the Prophet had used *ḥusn* and *jamāl* as synonyms in the conversation leading to his famous saying, "Indeed God is beautiful and He loves beauty." In *al-Maknūn fī ḥaqāʾiq al-kalim al-nabawiyya* ("The Hidden in the Realities of the Prophetic Speech"), also known as *Arāʾis al-ḥadīth* ("The Brides of Ḥadīth"), Rūzbihān explains the ḥadīth in this manner: "He loves inner beauty (*jamāl al-bāṭin*), such as love, recognition, and certitude, and external beauty, such as humility and submissiveness."[25] He thus explains that the *jamāl* that God loves consists of certain states invisible to outside observers (i.e., "inner beauty") and attitudes that are perceivable through one's conduct (i.e., "outer beauty") befitting the God-human relationship.

It is worth asking if Rūzbihān discerns any difference between *ḥusn* and *jamāl*. In one place he rejects any differentiation between the two concepts: "The difference between *ḥusn* and *jamāl* is [only] in words, and there is no difference in the realities of the meanings of the[se] attributes."[26] However, after saying this he admits two distinct perspectives in comparing the two: one that treats them as synonyms and the other that distinguishes them as having slightly different connotations. From the first perspective, both *ḥusn* and *jamāl* would generically indicate "beauty." Rūzbihān does not provide any further explanation of this view, treating it as self-explanatory. From the second perspective, however, he points out a subtle difference: *ḥusn* is a more gentle and inviting kind of beauty than *jamāl*. *Ḥusn* inspires hope and joy in its perceiver, while *jamāl* is more intimidating due to its association with "fear and recognizing majesty."[27] Furthermore, he argues that because of the awe-inspiring connotations of *jamāl*, it can only cause *maḥabba*, a love less intense than *ʿishq* ("passionate love"), which is caused by *ḥusn*.[28]

This subtle distinction between *ḥusn* and *jamāl* made by Rūzbihān, as we shall see, lies at the heart of his highly sophisticated theory of beauty. For the purposes of the present chapter, let us simply note that in this little passage on the contrast between *jamāl* and *ḥusn*, we can already glimpse how Rūzbihān gives *ḥusn* a higher status than *jamāl* in his grand metaphysical scheme, which is perfectly in keeping with the Qurʾānic primacy of the term *ḥusn* over *jamāl*.

Mustaḥsan: "What Is Deemed Beautiful"

Mustaḥsan is a term that has a notable presence in Rūzbihān's writings on beauty, playing an important role in his discussion of the relationship between divine beauty and beautiful things in the world. The word is a passive participle from the verb *istaḥsana*, a tenth-form derivative of *ḥ-s-n*. As a tenth-form verb it has the sense of "to consider" or "to deem" something to be something. In modern Arabic usage, *istaḥsana* is commonly taken to mean "to deem something right or good" or "to approve."[29] The verbal noun *istiḥsān* has a specific usage in the technical terminology of Islamic jurisprudence (*fiqh*), often translated as juristic "preference."[30] In Rūzbihān's usage of the word *istiḥsān,* he preserves its root meaning and Qurʾānic connection to *ḥusn*. In other words, he takes it to mean "to deem something *ḥasan,*" that is, (good and) beautiful. Hence, he uses the verb's passive participle, *mustaḥsan,* "what is deemed beautiful," applying it to objects that people *perceive* as beautiful.

Rūzbihān's use of *mustaḥsan/istiḥsān* finds little parallel in other Muslim texts. The term does not appear in the Qurʾān nor does it seem to originate in the Ḥadīth. The most probable source for Rūzbihān's usage of the term is a work by Abū al-Ḥasan ʿAlī b. Muḥammad al-Daylamī (fl. ca. 950), *Kitāb ʿaṭf al-alif al-maʾlūf ʿalā al-lām al-maʿṭūf* ("The Book of the Inclination of the Familiar *Alif* toward the Inclined *Lām*"), one of the earliest Arabic compendia on passionate love or "eros" (*ʿishq*), a book with which Rūzbihān was thoroughly familiar.[31]

There is no doubt that al-Daylamī's *ʿAṭf al-alif* has strong presence in Rūzbihān's discussions of love and beauty, most notably in his celebrated Persian treatise, *ʿAbhar al-ʿāshiqīn* ("The Jasmine of Passionate Lovers"). Al-Daylamī's *ʿAṭf* revolves around the question of the permissibility of ascribing passionate love to the God-human relationship—a question also posed by a female interlocutor at the beginning of Rūzbihān's *ʿAbhar al-ʿāshiqīn*. The latter book contains a chapter entitled "On the excellence of *ḥusn, ḥasan,* and *mustaḥsan,*"[32] and this finds a clear parallel in chapter 3 of al-Daylamī's *ʿAṭf,* which is called "Mention of some of the features belonging to love and passionate love." It has four subsections: (1) On the excellence of beauty (*ḥusn*); (2) On the excellence of the beautiful (*ḥasan*); (3) On the excellence of what is deemed beautiful (*mustaḥsan*); and (4) On the excellence of love and passionate love. In the third subsection al-Daylamī writes,

> Know that things deemed beautiful derive [their] beauty (*ḥusn*)[33] from the universal beauty that is in the proximity of the Real. Then the strength of beauty partly remains upon them in proportion to

> their proximity to the universal [beauty] after being issued forth, while it becomes weak and diminished in proportion to their distance from it, even to the extent that almost no beauty may be noticed in them due to its hiddenness in them. And no one will become aware of it except the folk of recognition.[34]

Though "the folk of recognition" (*ahl al-maʿrifa*) is most likely a reference to the Sufis, the explanation of beauty (*ḥusn*) that al-Daylamī provides here is strikingly Neoplatonic—from the idea of being "issued forth" (*inṣidār*), which is evocative of "emanation" (*ṣudūr* or *fayḍ*) to the idea of the universal beauty (*al-ḥusn al-kullī*). These terms are part of the language that was imported from the Greek philosophical tradition and naturalized in the Arabic language through the writings of philosophers such as al-Kindī, al-Fārābī, and Ibn Sīnā,[35] though this is not to say that the content of such Muslim philosophical discussions is also foreign.

One passage in Rūzbihān's work is reminiscent of the above quotation from al-Daylamī: "Every one and every thing is given a ray of that light [of God]. In this world, passionate lovers have sweet basil from the garden of the beauty (*jamāl*) and majesty (*jalāl*) of the One. In proximity to that light, the shade of beauty (*ḥusn*) increases. In distance from the quarry, beauty (*ḥusn*) decreases."[36] Here Rūzbihān presents God, the One, as the source of beauty. The closer one comes to the source, the more beauty one is able to perceive; the farther one is from God, the less beauty one is able to perceive.

In a similar way, Rūzbihān says, "That which is deemed beautiful is deemed beautiful because of the manifestation of God's beauty (*ḥusn*) within it."[37] Thus, things deemed beautiful derive their beauty from God's *ḥusn*. God as the Beautiful is the source of all beauty found in the world, or more specifically, in things deemed beautiful. Rūzbihān's language is not as noticeably philosophical as that of al-Daylamī, but his understanding of the relationship between *mustaḥsan* and *ḥusn* fits squarely in al-Daylamī's metaphysics. For both scholars, *mustaḥsan* represents individual or partial beauty, that is, each object in the world having a share of that universal beauty by way of what may be called the process of derivation, participation, emanation, or creation (depending on one's perspective).

Concerning the Qur'ānic verse, *Blessed is God, the most beautiful of creators* (Q 23:14), Rūzbihān says, "He described Himself as bringing into being what is deemed beautiful in His kingdom [i.e., this world] by manifesting His beauty (*ḥusn*) within it."[38] Hence, the most beautiful creator is He who creates things deemed beautiful to manifest His own beauty. Rūzbihān then gives as an example of divine manifestation through something deemed beautiful Moses's encounter with God through the intermediary of the mountain (Q 7:143). In this verse, Moses says to God, *"My Lord, show me so that I may look upon Thee."* The verse goes on: *He said, "Thou shalt not see Me but look at the mountain. If it stays firmly in its place, then thou shalt see Me." When his Lord disclosed Himself (tajallā) to the mountain, He made it crumble to dust, and Moses fell down in a swoon*. Rūzbihān writes, "That which is deemed beautiful is deemed beautiful because of the manifestation of God's beauty within it, and this is the beauty (*ḥusn*) of His self-disclosure (*tajallīhi*) within it, just as He disclosed Himself in the mountain to Moses."[39] Hence, the idea of God as the most beautiful creator has two significations: not only is God beautiful in Himself, but also what He creates is beautiful and should be deemed beautiful by humans.

Mustaqbaḥ: "What Is Deemed Ugly"

If everything God creates is beautiful in reality and we should deem it beautiful, why do we still perceive some things to be ugly? *Mustaqbaḥ,* the antonym of *mustaḥsan,* is Rūzbihān's answer to this question. The word is a tenth-form passive participle from *qubḥ* ("ugliness") denoting "what is deemed ugly." It is important to remember the strong connotation of "deeming" or "regarding" inherent in tenth-form words, for there is a difference between things in themselves and human perception of them, a point Rūzbihān explains in the context of things' beauty.

We have seen that according to Rūzbihān God possesses beauty and is the source of all beauty found in the world. Where then does ugliness (*qubḥ*) stand in his ontological scheme? Does it *exist* to begin with, and is that why we perceive it in the world? On this question, Rūzbihān explicitly states that "God is the creator of things deemed beautiful and things deemed ugly."[40] This is to say that while God is beautiful Himself, His creation is either deemed beautiful or deemed ugly by humans. It is also important to note that "what is deemed beautiful" and "what is deemed ugly" refer to the realm of creation only, not to the Creator, who is beautiful by definition, not merely *deemed* beautiful, and never ugly nor deemed ugly because ugliness implies imperfection, while God is perfect being.

Rūzbihān argues that it is a grave mistake to identify things that are deemed either beautiful or ugly with God Himself. This would constitute unbelief (*kufr*), because it blurs the fundamental distinction between the Creator and the created.[41] However beautiful a thing in the world may be, it cannot be God because its beauty derives from God. It is ontologically dependent on Him and its beauty is inferior to His in every respect. The same principle applies to identifying an ugly thing with God. It also constitutes unbelief because it involves mixing up the created and the Creator. Moreover, it would entail the additional theological error of equating a deficient/ugly being with God, who is a perfect/beautiful being. Even though Rūzbihān does not provide such a full explanation, such an understanding seems to underlie his argument that neither things deemed beautiful nor things deemed ugly can be identified with God without the charge of unbelief.

To come back to the initial question, why do some created things appear beautiful and some ugly? Put differently, where is the line that divides things that appear beautiful from those that appear ugly? On this matter Rūzbihān writes,

> If God disclosed Himself through a thing to a thing, that thing would be beautiful (*ḥasuna*) through His self-disclosure in the eyes of all the recognizers and the witnessers. If He curtained Himself from a thing, that thing would be ugly in the eyes of the viewers, and that would be in the station of intimacy. Aḥmad b. ʿAṭāʾ said concerning the meaning of recognition: "Things deemed ugly are ugly through

> being curtained, while things deemed beautiful are beautiful through His self-disclosure." The recognizer said—may God be pleased with him—"Deeming things beautiful does not occur to anyone except the one who sees the Existence-giver of things in things."[42]

In short, Rūzbihān argues that a thing appears ugly when it hides God and beautiful when it reveals God. At the end of the passage, he encapsulates this station in the voice of his alter ego, "the recognizer": perception of beauty in things depends on one's ability to see God in things. Thus, he introduces an element of individual human perception into his discussion of beauty.

Rūzbihān calls this ability to find God's *ḥusn* in created objects "the eye of contentment" (*ʿayn al-riḍā*), which is a well-established Sufi technical term that he uses in the new context of *beauty*. The basic sense of *riḍā* as most Sufis understand it is contentment, satisfaction, or approval in the face of both ease and adversity, or divine mercy and wrath.[43] While contentment appears as one of the 1,001 stations in the *Mashrab,* Rūzbihān does not provide a concentrated discussion of the eye of contentment as such in this work. However, we find a useful discussion in *ʿArāʾis al-bayān,* in which he writes, "The eye of contentment sees the ugly as beautiful (*ḥasan*) among all, just as it was said: The eye of contentment is dim toward every shortcoming / but the eye of evil makes appear evil traits. It was said: The eye of enmity is responsible for evil traits / while the eye of contentment is dim toward shortcomings."[44] This is Rūzbihān's basic explanation of the term.

However, when he employs the term in his discussion of beauty, a new horizon opens: "When the eye of contentment is opened…one will see the quiddity of being and the beauty (*ḥusn*) of God's artisanry (*iṣṭināʿ*) that becomes manifest from [that quiddity] in every atom."[45] Then one will "deem all things decreed by the Unseen as beautiful."[46] "Then," he says,

> the vision of beauty (*ḥusn*) and ugliness will become equal, because in the vision of [divine] tremendousness, no trace of temporally originated things[47]

> remains and the acts of [divine] severity and gentleness will be equal. All things will come out from the source of all with a single description. That is why God praised Himself for giving existence to the realm of being and what is within it and explained that nothing emerges from Him except the perfection of beauty with His words, *Who made beautiful everything He has created*. (Q 32:7)[48]

Thus, Rūzbihān argues that in reality everything in the world is beautiful (*ḥasan*) because it is God's handiwork, endowed with a perfection of beauty. It is important to note that here only *ḥasan* would be appropriate in this discussion, not *jamīl;* put another way, it would be right to say that everything is *ḥasan* but wrong to say everything is *jamīl*—for reasons that will become clear in the next chapter. With the eye of contentment a person will be able to see everything in creation as *mustaḥsan* rather than *mustaqbaḥ,* because however far removed a thing is from God, or however defective a thing may be, insofar as it exists, it is God's creation and therefore beautiful and to be appreciated.

The question of *mustaqbaḥ* versus *mustaḥsan* thus turns out to be an issue of human perception in accordance with one's level of knowledge. Rūzbihān's choice of the tenth-form words aptly captures the human judgmental factor of "deeming" in this process of perceiving beauty and ugliness in created things. To put it in a philosophical language, in the realm of creation there are only things *deemed* beautiful or *deemed* ugly, not beauty or ugliness itself. Depending on people's perspectives, the same things may appear beautiful or ugly. What then is beautiful or ugly in itself, not relative to human perception? One may say that "beauty" (*ḥusn*) itself belongs to God alone (as a divine attribute), whereas "ugliness" (*qubḥ*) itself is nonexistence, that is, sheer deficiency (of beauty), which by definition does not exist, therefore, is a mere theoretical construct. Rūzbihān does not speak in this exact manner, but such a philosophical explanation does not contradict with his understanding of beauty either. However, he maintains that with the eye of contentment it is possible to see everything as beautiful (*ḥasan*).

If we construct a scheme representing the interrelationship among *ḥusn, mustaḥsan, mustaqbaḥ,* and *qubḥ,* we may get the following picture:

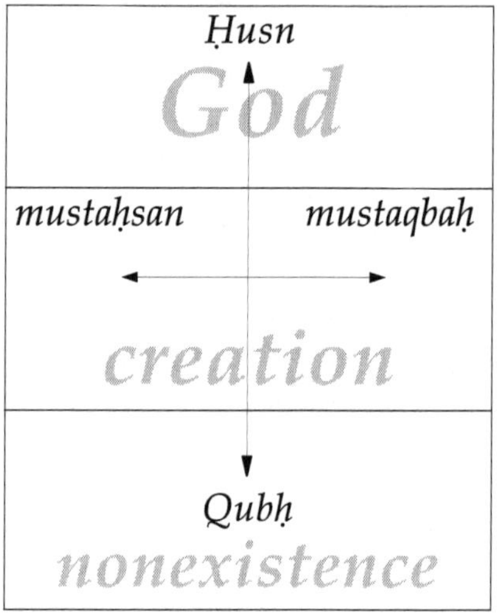

Figure 2.1 An ontological scheme of beauty and ugliness

God stands alone as the sole possessor of *ḥusn* as such, while His creation, or the world, is the domain in which *ḥusn* is either manifest or veiled—depending on individual human perception. Hence, creation is the domain of *mustaḥsan* and *mustaqbaḥ* rather than of *ḥusn* or *qubḥ* itself.

Alternatively, to use a philosophical language once again, at the top of this ontological hierarchy lies universal or absolute (*kullī* or *muṭlaq*) beauty, which is the realm of the necessary being (*wājib al-wujūd*). Here no ugliness can be found, for ugliness is by definition a lack of beauty or being. At the bottom of this ontological hierarchy is the conceptual opposite of absolute beauty, that is, absolute ugliness, which equals absolute nonexistence or impossible being (*mumtaniʿ al-wujūd*). In between absolute beauty and absolute ugliness lies partial or relative (*juzʾī* or *nisbī*) beauty, which is the realm of possible being (*mumkin al-wujūd*) or the domain of creation (or "generation and corruption"), consisting of things that come to be and cease to be. While both beauty and ugliness may be perceived in this middle domain, they are relative, not absolute, which is to say that things in this domain can only be *mustaḥsan* or *mustaqbaḥ*, that is, *deemed* beautiful or ugly, but never beauty or ugliness itself. Since Rūzbihān mostly avoids philosophical language and prefers a more literary style, he does not draw such direct parallels between his own language and the more commonly used language of Muslim intellectuals. However, once one gets past the linguistic barrier of his peculiar phraseology and terminology, it is possible to discern such a structured ontology of beauty in his writings.

Summary

Upon analysis, Rūzbihān's essential terms of beauty reveal a worldview that revolves around the notion of beauty, which can be understood ontologically as the fullness or perfection of being. God is called *jamīl* ("beautiful") and is the possessor of *ḥusn* ("beauty"). He is "the most beautiful (*aḥsan*) creator" of a world through which He manifests His own beauty (both *jamāl* and *ḥusn*). In Rūzbihān's ontology, there is nothing that truly exists but God's *ḥusn*; everything else (i.e., creation) is a reflection or shadow of His *ḥusn*. If human beings focus on the manner in which something reveals God's beauty, it will appear beautiful (*mustaḥsan*) to them. If they fix their eyes on the manner in which it veils God's beauty, it will appear ugly (*mustaqbaḥ*) to them.

Put another way, perception of beauty and ugliness is perception of God's presence and absence, respectively. God's presence in the world is mind-independent reality; God exists whether or not human beings sense His presence. The same goes for beauty. Those who sense God's presence more strongly than His absence will find the object of their perception beautiful; those who sense God's absence more than His presence will find it ugly. That is the reason why the same objects can appear beautiful to some people and ugly to others. In Rūzbihān's view, it is up to individual human beings to attain the right perception of reality, which is possible by cultivating "the eye of contentment."

In this light, one may say that according to Rūzbihān it is *ugliness* that lies in the eye of the beholder. This is to say, beauty is reality and all there is to be perceived; its reality neither depends on nor is relative to individual human perception. Perception of ugliness in the world simply indicates *defective* individual perception or ignorance on the part of its perceiver, for what exists is *ḥusn* and what we call ugliness is nonexistence.

By extension, one can draw an analogy between the above view and a contemporary discussion in psychology: Rūzbihān's contrast between *mustaḥsan* and *mustaqbaḥ* is like the difference between perceiving a glass of water to be "half full" and regarding it as "half empty," respectively. In the first perspective—that is, deeming something *beautiful* or the glass to be half *full*—one's attention is fixed on the *presence* of something. In contrast, the second perspective—finding something *ugly* or the glass to be half *empty*—highlights what is *absent*, indicating the perceiver's incapacity to recognize what is present. In an everyday situation, people who always see things from the second perspective are likely to be constant complainers, who fail to be grateful for what they have. This certainly would be considered a vice in Islam, constituting *kufr*, for the term means not only "unbelief" but also "ingratitude," being the antonym of both "faith" (*īmān*) and "gratitude" (*shukr*).[49]

Moreover, the first perspective in the above instance goes well with the notion of "contentment" (as in "the eye of contentment"), because whoever takes this perspective appreciates and is content with what is present, as this person's attention is not drawn to any lack. This is a mode of perceiving each thing in the world as equal in beauty to everything else insofar as it exists. For example, one would perceive a tree in full bloom as beautiful as when it is withered, for both are God's creation and how He intends them to be. A person with the eye of contentment is able to see God and His beauty in the tree in both situations.

Implicit in Rūzbihān's presentation of the eye of contentment is his understanding of creation. The eye of contentment emphasizes the sameness of things because of the presence of being in each and every one of them—as he had said, "When the eye of contentment is opened…one will see the quiddity of being and the beauty (*ḥusn*) of God's artisanry that becomes manifest from [that quiddity] in every atom."[50] In other words, beauty (*ḥusn*) lies in being; ugliness lies in nonbeing (*ʿadam*).

Thus, Rūzbihān's analysis of beauty (*ḥusn*) in contrast to ugliness (*qubḥ*) is quite ontological in nature. Having understood his basic terminology and ontology of beauty, we are now ready to explore his understanding of beauty in God, the world, and the human being, which are the subjects of the subsequent chapters. The next chapter will examine God's beauty, more specifically the notion of God as *jamīl* as well as the possessor of *ḥusn* and of the most beautiful names (*al-asmāʾ al-ḥusnā*) with a view to uncovering the difference between *ḥusn* and *jamāl* in Rūzbihān's theology.

3

The Theology of Beauty

> There is nothing like Him.
>
> —Qurʾān 42:11

> To God belong the most beautiful names.
>
> —Qurʾān 7:180

> Were there no unveiling of His beauty
> how could there be love in people's spirits?
> He made Himself recognized in the signs
> Then He gave out the descriptions of the attributes.
>
> —Rūzbihān Baqlī

The story of beauty[1] for Rūzbihān—and for that matter, all Muslims who talk of it—begins with God Himself, God in His aloneness. In mythic language, the story goes like this: Once upon a time—or, "before" there was time or any temporal existence—God was, and nothing was with Him. To this state alludes a famous monologue attributed to God and frequently mentioned in Sufi literature: "I was a Hidden Treasure, so I loved to be recognized. So I created the creatures so that I may be recognized."[2] Like many others, Rūzbihān understands the unfolding of the Hidden Treasure as the process of God's self-disclosure, first within Himself, then in creation. In the course of this process the divine beauty becomes manifest.

In order to understand the place of beauty in Rūzbihān's theology, several key questions need to be addressed at the outset. First, what is the difference between God's *jamāl* and *ḥusn*? Where are the two situated in Rūzbihān's theological framework? And, what exactly is his theological framework? One of the biggest challenges in answering these questions is Rūzbihān's abstruse language. Rūzbihān, like Sufis in general, likes to use figurative and imagistic language often drawn from the Qurʾān and the Ḥadīth, the same sort of language that is preferred by Persian poets in particular. He likes to employ concrete imagery where dogmatic theologians and philosophers would use abstract, technical language. Upon close intertextual analysis of his works, it becomes clear that many of his figurative expressions form part of his systematic terminology, some of which consistently correspond to well-known technical terms in dogmatic theology. Hence, one of the objectives here is to decode and recast Rūzbihān's allusive language into the clearer, more common vocabulary of general Muslim theological discourse. A key text in this endeavor is Rūzbihān's sole extant work in dogmatic theology, *Masālik al-tawḥīd* ("The Paths to Asserting Oneness"), a little-studied work whose content will be examined in conjunction with related discussions in his other works.

The Technical Languages of Dogmatic Theology, Philosophy, and Sufism

To begin discussing the question, "What is God's beauty?" we must first address a more fundamental question, "How can we speak about God?" "Speaking about God"—which is the most basic sense of the word *theology*—was never a simple matter for Muslims. Throughout Muslim intellectual history, the dogmatic theologians (*mutakallimūn*) have tried to co-opt for themselves the function of setting the basic linguistic-conceptual framework for appropriate manners of speaking about God. Although Rūzbihān is primarily known as a Sufi, he was also well versed in the discipline of dogmatic theology (*kalām*) as well as other Muslim religious sciences, like any well-trained scholar.

In order to understand the precise nature of Rūzbihān's language, it might be useful to begin with a brief characterization of "Sufi," "theological," and "philosophical" writings. There are at least two fundamental differences between these three categories of writings: the first is *lexical,* that is, they utilize different sets of technical terms; the second is *epistemological,* that is, their immediate sources of knowledge are different.

First of all, Muslim philosophers (*falāsifa*) redefined standard Arabic words (including those used in the Qur᾽ān) in the light of concepts drawn from Greek philosophy. Moreover, many of them preferred using a language that is devoid of Qur᾽ānic expressions. Thus, instead of "God" (*Allāh*), they liked to use terms like "the necessary being" (*wājib al-wujūd*), "the first cause" (*al-ʿilla al-ūlā*), "the sheer good" (*al-khayr al-maḥḍ*), and so on. With the use of an unambiguous, strictly definition-bound language, Muslim philosophers aimed at gaining indubitable knowledge of the principles behind all things through demonstration (*burhān*), which avoids contradiction.

Dogmatic theologians are similar to the philosophers in their rational argumentative method and their use of a strictly definition-bound language. Thus, each term ideally has a fixed meaning in all contexts, thereby avoiding ambiguity and contradiction in arguments—in contrast to Sufi literature, where intentional ambiguity and contradiction are common features. Dogmatic theologians differ from the philosophers in their preferred technical terms, and they make a point of anchoring their terminology in Qur᾽ānic expressions. Thus, the Qur᾽ān not only provides linguistic tools for them to speak about God but also serves as the fundamental source of their knowledge about God. For dogmatic theologians, the truth of the Qur᾽ān is a given; their task is to interpret its verses with the assistance of rational speculation (*naẓar*) so as to construct a noncontradictory, systematic understanding of God and His creation. For this reason, some translate *mutakallimūn* as "speculative theologians," and *kalām* as "speculative theology." Other common translations are "dogmatic," "dialectic," and "rational" theologians/theology. However, in contrast to the philosophers, who consider observing the world and using the intellect sufficient for obtaining all knowledge, dogmatic theologians take the words of the Qur'ān as the very basis and starting point for all their inquiry. Thus, while both dogmatic theologians and philosophers engage in rational speculation, the former's reliance on the power of the intellect is much more limited than the latter's.

While competing schools of dogmatic theology existed for many centuries, by the time of Rūzbihān in the twelfth century, the dominant school was that of the Ashʿarites, whom he apparently follows and defends in the *Masālik*—often against the claims of the Muʿtazilites. One key difference between these two schools of dogmatic theology lies in their degrees of rationalism: while the Muʿtazilites were outright rationalist theologians, the Ashʿarites—who appeared out of the Muʿtazilite circle to establish the middle ground between rationalist theology and literalist Ḥadīth scholarship—took a more nuanced approach to interpreting the Qur'ān. The general Ashʿarite stance on speaking about God was to employ the words of the Qur'ān as far as possible, as they believed that each Qur'ānic word corresponds to a reality either in a way that humans can understand or beyond human comprehension. Where their rational interpretation of the Qur'ān failed, the Ashʿarites embraced Aḥmad b. Ḥanbal's hermeneutic principle of accepting the apparent meaning of verses "without [asking] how" (*bi-lā kayfa*).

All this suggests that the Ashʿarites were acutely aware of the limits of human rational speculation for understanding God as well as of the inadequacy of human language in describing God as He really is. In other words, they knew that there is a limit to positive (cataphatic) manners of speaking about God. Hence, Ashʿarites also made use of negative (apophatic) descriptions of God.

However, it was the Sufis who took apophatic theological discourse to another level. This is largely because of the very nature of their immediate source of knowledge, namely direct encounters with God, expressed in various ways—vision (*ru'ya*), witnessing (*mushāhada*), audition (*samāʿ*), and so on. Through such direct encounters with God, Sufis attain *maʿrifa*, that is, "recognition" or "experiential knowledge" of God, which is contrasted with *ʿilm,* a bookish type of knowledge that results from memorization of the views of others and rational speculation rather than direct experience. For this reason, Sufis often associate *maʿrifa* with what they call "tasting" (*dhawq*), indicating its personal, direct, and experiential nature. It must be noted, however, that the superiority of *maʿrifa* over *ʿilm* in Sufi understanding holds true only on the human level, for the distinction between these two types of knowledge does not apply to God's knowledge, which is always expressed as *ʿilm* on the basis of the Qurʾānic terminology. The process of attaining *maʿrifa*—which includes Sufis' visionary or auditory encounters with God—is ineffable by nature, as it does not take place on the ordinary plane of consciousness, which is dependent on the five external senses.

Knowing full well that finite human language cannot properly capture such encounters with the infinite God, Sufis tried to cope with—or even play with—the inadequacy of human language in their effort to describe what they "saw" (or "heard," which might be easier to express in words). In their effort to describe the infinite with finite human language, Sufis devised at least three linguistic strategies: the use of (1) poetry, which involves metaphors, symbols, and images to point out how something is *like* something else by analogy; (2) paradoxes and contradictions, in which Sufis simultaneously affirm and deny a quality to God (*coincidentia oppositorum*); and (3) negation (*apophasis*), that is, to describe God by pointing out what He is *not,* highlighting God's transcendence or incomparability (*tanzīh*). These three methods go beyond the limits of human language by intentionally exposing its *collapse,* be it through ultimately inadequate metaphors, contradictions, or negations. This is what Michael Sells calls "the language of unsaying."[3] The Sufi "play" with language—by laying open its vulnerability cum richness through contradictions, negations, and ambiguity—is exactly what distinguishes their language from those of the philosophers and theologians, who try to avoid precisely this: ambiguity and contradiction in their use of language. At the same time, this is precisely what makes Sufi language particularly difficult to understand for those used to philosophical and theological languages.

As for the *lexical* characteristics of general Sufi language, it can contain any mixture of terms from the Qurʾān and Ḥadīth, poetic expressions, and technical terminology of *kalām* and *falsafa*. The Sufis pay special attention to Qurʾānic language, in many cases transforming the words into technical terms of their discipline, for example, "divine self-disclosure" (*tajallī*), "annihilation" (*fanāʾ*), "witnessing" (*mushāhada*), and "unveiling" (*kashf, mukāshafa*). While these terms often characterize Sufi writings, it is important to note that there is no single "Sufi language." Some Sufis are poetic in their expressions, avoiding theological and philosophical terms; others incorporate philosophical and / or theological terms to the exclusion of poetic language. What is actually found in the texts depends on the learning and preference of each Sufi writer. Hence, "Sufi language" is the most multifarious and complicated among the three groups.[4]

Rūzbihān's Language

Rūzbihān's language is no exception. He makes heavy use of metaphors, paradoxes, and negations, and he also utilizes the languages of the Qurʾān and Ḥadīth, Sufism, and dogmatic theology. He shows less interest in adopting the technical terms of philosophy. This is especially evident in the manner in which he makes use of Abū al-Ḥasan al-Daylamī's compendium on the topic of passionate love (*ʿishq*), *ʿAṭf al-alif al-maʾlūf ʿalā al-lām al-maʿṭūf*, which includes many philosophical discussions. As Takeshita has shown in his comparison of al-Daylamī's *ʿAṭf* and Rūzbihān's *ʿAbhar al-ʿāshiqīn*, there is no doubt that Rūzbihān had a thorough familiarity with al-Daylamī's work.[5] Indeed, paraphrases of the *ʿAṭf* can be found in Rūzbihān's various works, not limited to the *ʿAbhar*; however, he rarely mentions any of the philosophical discussions that are plentiful in the *ʿAṭf*.

In contrast to his reticence on philosophy, he does not hide the theological side of his learning, more specifically, his subscription to Ashʿarism. In fact, he even seems to show off his allegiance to Ashʿarism by attacking Muʿtazilism in *Masālik al-tawḥīd*. This is noteworthy given the critical tone of voice in this work, a tone rarely encountered in his other writings, where his Ashʿarite inclination is detectable but rarely emphasized. On reading the *Masālik*, Toby Mayer notes, "The great visionary and mystical exegete, Rūzbehān Baqlī (d. 1209), was strongly Ashʿarite in his theology....In other texts, it is fascinating to see Ashʿarite terms and ideas transposed by Baqlī into a purely mystical context. For instance, the difficult *kalām* issue of the *visio beata* is explored anew, no longer as an episode of the eschaton, or of the Prophet's ascension, but insofar as Baqlī himself claims to have encountered God 'in the most beautiful of forms' in the privacy of his own home."[6] Also, Rūzbihān occasionally uses the Ashʿarite expression "without (asking) how" (*bi-lā kayfa*) in describing his visions of God in his diary of daily visions, *Kashf al-asrār* ("The Unveiling of Secrets"). On this Ernst comments, "Rūzbihān occasionally resorts to conventional theological language, particular [*sic*] the formula 'without (asking) how' (*bi-lā kayf*); pietist groups such as the Ḥanbalīs and Ashʿarīs used this phrase to insist on the literal truth of seemingly anthropomorphic scriptural passages without engaging in intellectual speculation about their modality."[7]

In short, Rūzbihān's language is a mix of (1) terms from the Qurʾān and Ḥadīth, (2) technical terms of Sufism, (3) technical terms of dogmatic theology, (4) a limited number of technical terms from other disciplines such as philosophy, and (5) terms of his own invention, which will be discussed shortly.

Rūzbihān on Ashʿarite Theology: *Kitāb masālik al-tawḥīd*

Among the forty-five works attributed to Rūzbihān, at least three are known to have been written in the field of dogmatic theology: *al-Intiqād fī al-iʿtiqād* ("The Critique in Belief"), *al-Ḥaqāʾiq fī al-ʿaqāʾid* ("The Realities in the Dogmas"), and *Masālik al-tawḥīd*. However, the last one is the sole surviving work in full; the first is lost and the second is preserved only as excerpts.[8] Since Paul Ballanfat published the text of *Masālik al-tawḥīd* in 1998,[9] the work has not attracted much scholarly attention, most likely due to its unoriginal theological content as a précis of the basic Ashʿarite creed. However, for the purpose of the present study, a close textual analysis of the *Masālik* yields a unique benefit: being virtually the only place where Rūzbihān presents the theological system in which his mind operates and defines key terms in dogmatic theology as he understands them, it helps us decipher his Sufi works by revealing the underlying terminological and conceptual framework of his thought that turns out to be deeply rooted in Ashʿarism. Moreover, a comparison of his use of terms in the *Masālik* and in his Sufi works reveals that some of his seemingly poetic expressions found in the latter are in fact his own translations of otherwise well-known technical terms in dogmatic theology.

In *Masālik al-tawḥīd,* which is an Arabic treatise of twenty-two pages in a modern edition, Rūzbihān deals with several well-known points of contention between Ashʿarites and Muʿtazilites, such as the questions of the existence of divine attributes and the possibility of the vision of God. His reasons for choosing to discuss these particular issues in the *Masālik* are not self-evident in the work. The editor of the text, Paul Ballanfat, thinks that the virulent opposition that Rūzbihān expresses toward Muʿtazilism in this treatise indicates the extent to which it still held sway in Fārs, and particularly in Shiraz during his time.[10]

Masālik al-tawḥīd consists of four short chapters, respectively entitled: "The First Pole: On the Recognition of the Essence of God"; "The Second Pole: On the Recognition of the Attributes of God"; "The Third Pole: On the Recognition of the Acts of God"; and "The Fourth Pole: On the Recognition of What Is Heard (*samʿiyyāt*)." Thus, in the first three chapters, he engages in the standard theological discussion of examining the notion of God in terms of essence, attributes, and acts. The final chapter presents various sayings from the Ḥadīth literature, that is, the reports that have been transmitted and heard concerning God. Among the main points Rūzbihān makes in the *Masālik* are: (1) the unknowability of God's essence; (2) affirmation of the seven eternal attributes of God (i.e., knowledge, power, hearing, seeing, speech, desire, and life); and (3) affirmation of everything in this world as divine acts.[11] "Human acts" are in fact divine acts that are, as the Ashʿarites say, "acquired" (*muktasaba*) by human beings.[12]

The three basic theological terms—essence, attribute, and act—are important linguistic tools that Rūzbihān uses to analyze the notion of God's beauty. Dogmatic theologians' tripartite analysis of God implies that when people say "God" (*Allāh*), they could be implicitly referring to God on any of these three distinct levels: (1) His essence (which is unknowable); (2) His attributes (which are knowable); or (3) His acts (which are knowable). Thus, there may be ambiguity inherent in any Muslim discussion of "God" that does not make use of these three technical terms.

Essence (*dhāt*): the Unknowable and Hidden God

One of the first points that Rūzbihān makes in *Masālik al-tawḥīd* is the utter transcendence and inconceivability of God in Himself, that is, the divine essence. He writes,

> The first pole, on the recognition of God's essence: He is an eternal existent without beginning or end, one who is truly existent, not like the existence of things that abide through other things; rather, He is an existence that abides through itself. He is not a body, nor a substance, nor an accident, for substance is the locus of accidents, and nothing is a substance without being spatially located. Rather, He is incomparable with being interrelated with temporally originated things.[13]

Presented above is a standard discussion of God as an existence (*wujūd*) whose eternity is contrasted with "temporal origination" (*ḥudūth*), which applies only to created things. Rūzbihān thus points out that the first thing that can be said about God in His essence is that He exists and is entirely incomparable to creation.

The unknowability of God's essence is a widely accepted dictum in Muslim theological discourse, in association with which Muslims often quote the following ḥadīth (which exists in slightly different versions): "Reflect upon everything, but do not reflect upon God's essence."[14] Rūzbihān's commentary on a version of this ḥadīth is as follows:

> "Reflect upon God's creation, but do not reflect upon God." . . . When the Prophet saw the recognizer coveting the recognition of the depth of the essence, he commanded him to abandon reflecting upon [God's] essence, for he knew that the temporally originated does not perceive the eternal as it is in reality. Rather, by way of reflecting upon creation he reaches the station of the incapacity to recognize because of his being annihilated in God's unicity. His "incapacity to perceive is itself perception," as Abū Bakr said.[15]

In short, God's essence is the utterly transcendent aspect of God to which no creature has access. It is often said to be the referent of the verse, *There is nothing like Him* (Q 42:11), which Rūzbihān interprets to mean, "Whatever you agree upon from the throne to the earth, I am incomparable with that.'"[16] The phrase, "from the throne to the earth" is a common expression for the whole created realm.

Rūzbihān warns that if someone persists in thinking about God's essence, he would become utterly "bewildered at the first radiance of the majesty of the unicity. His understanding would be annihilated short of perceiving the assaults of tremendousness. So he will return from there to creation bewildered, annihilated, and incapable of perceiving the reality of the divinity."[17] The word *reality* (*ḥaqīqa*) designates the thing as it is in itself, so "the reality of the divinity" is the divine essence, God as He is in Himself and for Himself. It is so utterly beyond human comprehension that it is not only bewildering but also *annihilating* for the thinker. Annihilation (*fanāʾ*) is an important technical term in Sufism, indicating the obliteration of separative existence in the face of God's sheer oneness.

In *Mashrab al-arwāḥ* too, Rūzbihān discusses the manner in which God's essence annihilates those who seek Him. He explains that the reason why God's essence is unknowable to human beings is that anyone who has even a glimpse of it would simply be annihilated, for God's sheer oneness does not allow the duality of the knower and the known to remain.

In sum, there can be no true knower of God's essence except God Himself. Rūzbihān writes, "The Real discloses some of the lights of His essence unmixed to the secret core (*sirr*), so his secret core is drowned in the ocean of His essence. His locus there is the locus of annihilation....The recognizer says: The vision of the self-disclosure of the essence annihilates the sight of those who look."[18]

The idea that God alone knows His essence appears prominently in Rūzbihān's interpretation of certain Qur᾿ānic verses, such as *With Him are the keys of the unseen; none knows them but He* (Q 6:59). In his interpretation, the word *unseen* (*al-ghayb*) refers to God's essence, because its nature is *unseen,* that is, hidden and unknowable. His commentary reads: "None knows His attributes and essence in truth except He in Himself."[19]

In his Sufi works, Rūzbihān employs a number of alternative expressions to refer to "the divine essence," such as "unseenness" (*ghayba*), "treasure house" (*khizāna*), and "treasure" (*kanz*), among others.[20] Moreover, in a passage quoted earlier, he used the terms "depth" (*kunh*), "unicity" (*waḥdāniyya*), and possibly also "tremendousness" (*ʿaẓama*) in oblique reference to God's essence. Thus, what he calls God's "essence" in *Masālik al-tawḥīd* appears as "depth," "unseenness," and so on in his Sufi compositions.

There are still other Qur᾿ānic verses that Rūzbihān considers as indicating the unknowability of God's essence. A verse of particular importance in Rūzbihān's discussion of this idea is *Thou shalt not see Me* (Q 7:143),[21] God's famous reply to Moses's request on the mountain, *"Show me so that I may look upon Thee"* (Q 7:143), which was briefly discussed in the previous chapter. Below is another instance of Rūzbihān's interpretation of the verse: "[Moses] asked from [God] for one of His eyes (*ʿayn*) with which to see Him, that is, to see the source of the source (*ʿayn al-ʿayn*), the depth of the depth, the eternity of the eternity, the secret of the essence, the reality of the reality."[22]

All these phrases—"the source of the source," "the depth of the depth," "the eternity of the eternity," and "the reality of the reality" are used in apposition to "the secret of the essence," which means that they all signify the divine essence. The use of *ʿayn* to refer to the essence is apt given another sense of the word, "fountainhead" or "source," for all being emerges from the divine essence. Rūzbihān's use of the word *ʿayn* in the sense of "essence" can be found in his other works. For instance, in the *Mashrab* he writes, "Then He manifests the *ʿayn* in the *ʿayn,* I mean, the essence in the essence."[23] Thus, the above commentary shows Rūzbihān's view that what Moses requested from God in this Qurʾānic episode was the vision of God's essence. Rūzbihān explains God's reply, *"Thou shalt not see Me,"* as meaning "Thou shalt not perceive Me as I am (*kamā anā*),"[24] that is, "as I am in My essence."

Since the divine essence is the "God" that cannot be seen, known, or perceived in any way—i.e., the transcendent God—its discussion naturally leads to apophatic theology. However, in addition to engaging in apophatic theology, a strong point of many of the dogmatic theologians, Rūzbihān also engages in cataphatic theology. In other words, as much as he talks of God's unknowability in Himself, he also explains His knowability through His acts. This is typical of the Sufi approach, as Sufis maintain that excessive stress on God's undeniable otherness and unknowability cuts Him off from the also undeniable fact of His presence in all things through His creative acts, concerning which the Qurʾān talks extensively. Since the notion of divine acts must be first understood in order to understand the complex substructure of the divine attributes, the divine acts will be examined next.

Acts (*afʿāl*): The Beautiful Creations of God

God's "act" (*fiʿl*) is a term used in Muslim theological discourse that refers to every single thing in creation. The idea of every created thing as a divine act is a standard notion in Ashʿarite theology. Rūzbihān makes his allegiance to Ashʿarism clear in the following passage by supporting the view that human actions are God's creations and that human beings only "acquire" them without ever creating them, a signature doctrine of Ashʿarite theology called "acquisition" (*kasb*).

> Understand that from the throne to the earth is created by God, and everything except His existence is His act. He gave each act its existence from sheer nonexistence, and such is everything that is temporally originated in His kingdom. The acts of the servants are also created by God, even if they are acquired by the servants. God desired them in beginninglessness (*azal*) as a favor and mercy.[25]

At this point it is worth revisiting the ḥadīth, "Reflect upon God's creation, but do not reflect upon God." When we discussed it in the previous section, we focused on the latter half of this ḥadīth, which points out the unknowability of God's essence. Now, let us turn our attention to the first half of this ḥadīth: "Reflect upon God's creation." It suggests that it is worth thinking about God's acts, but why? Implicit in this saying is the idea that while God cannot be known as He is in Himself, He can be known indirectly through His act or creation.

Rūzbihān points out that creation indicates—by virtue of its existence—the existence of its Creator: "The creation is a pointer to the existence of the Creator, and the act points to the Actor."[26] To prove the above statement, Rūzbihān produces a standard rationalist argument in which he refutes the idea of infinite regress in the chains of causes, concluding that there must be a first cause that is eternal in order for there to be temporally originated things.[27] The same argument can be found, for instance, in a work of dogmatic theology by al-Qushayrī, a famous Sufi and defender of Ashʿarism whom Rūzbihān held in high regard. Al-Qushayrī writes, "The bringer-of-existence of the world is beginningless. The proof for this is that if it were [also] brought into existence, it would require another bringer-of-existence as well as the latter's bringer-of-existence, and it would go back in a chain ad infinitum, and that is impossible."[28] Having established the single, eternal existence of the first cause, Rūzbihān states, "Reflecting upon creation increases certitude in God's unicity."[29]

Aside from producing such rational arguments, Rūzbihān also refers to a standard idea that human beings are created with an innate nature (*fiṭra*) that recognizes God:

> God captured within the nature of the souls a luminous, intellective, and holy innate nature that testifies to its bringer-of-existence and recognizes that it has been conquered by the subjugation of its Artist (*ṣāniʿ*) and overpowered by the governing of its Creator; it is capable of making God recognized by way of the lights of His act and the glow of His artifacts. These guide the souls on the path of affirming God's existent and eternal essence, from which stem all things.[30]

Another thing that an act reveals about its Actor, according to Rūzbihān, is the Actor's characteristics, or attributes. He writes, "There is a manifestation of the essence in the clothing of the attributes, while the attributes become manifest in the clothing of the acts";[31] "His essence is the quarry of His attributes, and His attributes are the quarry of His act";[32] "If the acts and the attributes were recognized, the essence would [also] be recognized."[33] Thus, God becomes manifest and knowable in stages: He emerges out of the unknowable essence first by way of the knowable attributes and then by the knowable acts. Conversely, His acts, that is to say, the entire creation, reveal His attributes, which in turn reveal the unfathomable divine essence indirectly by "clothing" it, which is a signature term in Rūzbihān's writings, to be discussed in the subsequent chapters. Put another way, the acts and attributes are the beautiful clothes that cover up as well as reveal the invisible divine essence.

Likewise we should reconsider the verse, "*Thou shalt not see Me*" (Q 7:143), which, in Rūzbihān's interpretation, is God's reply to Moses's request to see God's essence. God's reply then continued like this: "*But look at the mountain: if it stays in its place, then thou shalt see Me.*" In the light of the foregoing analysis, if we translate this part of the verse, it might read: "Thou shalt not see My essence. But look at My act: if it stays in its place, then thou shalt see My essence." The verse ends in the following manner: *When his Lord disclosed Himself to the mountain, He made it crumble down, and Moses fell down in a swoon. When he awoke, he said, "Glory be to Thee! To Thee I have turned in repentance, and I am the first of the believers."* In other words, in response to Moses's request, God revealed His essence to His act (i.e., the mountain) instead of revealing it directly to Moses. Facing a direct revelation of God's essence, the mountain is annihilated, as no creature can bear such a direct manifestation of the divine essence. Moses had indirect witnessing of the divine essence through the intermediary of the divine act that was the mountain. However, even this sight of the mountain crumbling into dust was too strong for Moses to bear, even if he was a prophet. His "swooning" represents, one might say, the annihilation of ordinary consciousness.

Rūzbihān argues that Moses saw God's beauty in the mountain before falling unconscious: "Moses saw the beauty of eternity (*jamāl al-qidam*) in the mirror of the mountain, and then he fell down."[34] The "mirror"—which is a common image for creation in Sufism—is an especially apt symbol for the mountain, since it shows how divine acts function as mirrors of the invisible essence by displaying its attributes. Another key term in this discussion is *tajallī* or self-disclosure, which appeared in the verbal form in the verse Q 7:143: *his Lord disclosed Himself (tajallā) to the mountain*. If we use both mirror and self-disclosure to explain the verse, we can say that the mountain served as a mirror of God and the locus of His self-disclosure.

Thus, in Rūzbihān's interpretation, both the ḥadīth "Reflect upon God's creation, but do not reflect upon God" and the Qurʾānic verse, *Thou shalt not see Me. But look at the mountain: if it stays in its place, then thou shalt see Me* (Q 7:143) make the same two points: (1) God's essence cannot be known directly, so it should not be thought about; and (2) human beings should think about God's acts instead of His essence if they wish to know His essence, because His acts display His attributes, through which they can attain approximate knowledge of the divine essence.

The idea that divine attributes become manifest through divine acts also appears in Rūzbihān's interpretation of the following key ḥadīth and Qurʾānic verse, both mentioning *jamāl*: "[The Prophet] said, 'Indeed God is beautiful, and He loves beauty.' God said, *There is beauty in them* [i.e., the cattle] *for you when you bring them home to rest and when you drive them forth abroad to pasture* [Q 16:6]. This is the beauty that stems from the beauty of His act and His power."[35]

The Qurʾānic verse points out how beauty (*jamāl*) is apparent in the cattle, that is, a divine attribute becomes manifest in a divine act. The ḥadīth explains why beauty can be found in creation: because God is beautiful. What the beautiful Creator creates is also beautiful, as it reflects its Creator's attributes. This is also the point Rūzbihān makes in his interpretation of another Qurʾānic verse, *Blessed is God, the most beautiful (aḥsan) of creators* (Q 23:14), as we saw in the previous chapter.[36]

Attributes (*ṣifāt*): The Knowable, Beautiful God

The third term to be discussed is attributes (*ṣifāt*, sing. *ṣifa*), which derives from the root *w-ṣ-f*, meaning "to describe." The Arabic for "essence," *dhāt* has a close relationship with *ṣifāt*, because *dhāt* is a term that functions in conjunction with *ṣifāt*, for the root meaning of *dhāt* is "possessor of," implying the possessor of attributes. As one Ashʿarite theologian put it, *dhāt* is "what is described by the attributes" (*mawṣūfa bi-l-ṣifāt*),[37] which is analogous to saying "possessor of attributes." Such grammatical analysis of the word *dhāt* is not always present in theological texts, but this is most probably because it was so obvious for Arabic speakers. Thus, *dhāt* is a contentless word that only indicates *possession* of something, which is in fact fully in line with the idea of the unknowability of the divine essence: *dhāt* is unspecifiable in itself and can only be described indirectly by the attributes it possesses.

In order to investigate the place of *jamāl* and *ḥusn* in Rūzbihān's understanding of God, it helps to understand the close relationship between divine attributes and divine names. Both attributes and names describe the divine essence, and the difference between the two is grammatical. While divine attributes take the form of substantives (e.g., life, power, and majesty), divine names appear as adjectives, e.g., the Living (*al-ḥayy*) and the Majestic (*al-jalīl*); or as active participles, for example, the Powerful (*al-qādir*), the Exalter (*al-rāfiʿ*), and the Abaser (*al-khāfiḍ*); or as nouns, for example, the Light (*al-nūr*) and God (*Allāh*). In short, divine attributes are the qualities designated by the divine names that have come in the Qurʾān.

For this reason, if God is said to possess ninety-nine names, these names designate ninety-nine attributes at the same time.

At the beginning of *Masālik al-tawḥīd*, Rūzbihān introduces seven attributes of God in the following order: knowledge, power, hearing, sight, speech, life, and desire.[38] In the second chapter of the *Masālik*, entitled "The Second Pole: On the Knowledge of the Attributes,"[39] Rūzbihān discusses each of these seven attributes in detail while supporting his exposition with relevant passages from the Qurʾān and Ḥadīth. Since the affirmation of the distinct and eternal existence of these seven attributes of God is one of the centerpieces of early Ashʿarite theology in contradistinction to Muʿtazilism, which denied their eternal existence, Rūzbihān's presentation of divine attributes in the *Masālik* is also limited to those seven attributes typically discussed by the Ashʿarites. The above seven attributes are what Ashʿarites call "attributes of the essence" (*ṣifāt al-dhāt*) or "essential attributes" (*ṣifāt dhātiyya*), which they contrast with another category of attributes called "the attributes of the act" (*ṣifāt al-fiʿl*), which will be discussed later.

In the *Masālik*, Rūzbihān's subscription to Ashʿarism becomes clear from such statements as: "These [seven] attributes are in His essence beginninglessly and endlessly (*azaliyyatan abadiyyatan*),"[40] by which he opposes the Muʿtazilite denial of the existence of divine attributes. Muʿtazilites denied the existence of divine attributes in distinction to the divine essence, arguing that affirming their existence would imply multiplicity in God's being, which contradicts the principle of God's oneness. The Ashʿarite response to this criticism was to say that the attributes are neither the essence nor other than the essence (*lā hiya huwa wa-lā ghayruhu*).[41] In the *Masālik* Rūzbihān criticizes Muʿtazilites multiple times, and the main purpose of its second chapter seems to be to counter the Muʿtazilite denial of the existence of divine attributes by taking up the Ashʿarite position on the matter.

While these seven attributes are the most commonly discussed, Ashʿarites did not necessarily limit their discussion of the attributes of the essence to seven. For instance, some Ashʿarites (including al-Ashʿarī himself) consider subsistence (*baqāʾ*) as the eighth essential attribute.[42] Moreover, the Ashʿarites accept those anthropomorphic attributes mentioned in the Qurʾān, such as "hand," "face," and "foot" also as essential attributes therefore eternal. In the *Mashrab*, Rūzbihān confirms, "Hand is one of the specific attributes of the essence and is beginningless and endless and is the quarry of power."[43] In the subsequent two sections he also confirms God's "foot" and "face" as attributes of the essence.[44] These anthropomorphic attributes are also called "revealed attributes," for they are the attributes of God confirmed by the Qurʾān.[45]

While *Masālik al-tawḥīd* contains Rūzbihān's most focused discussion of divine attributes, it is certainly not the only place where he analyzes them. For example, in *Mashrab al-arwāḥ*, a much longer Arabic work, Rūzbihān gives a more extensive treatment of the subject than in the *Masālik*. At the beginning of the book's sixteenth chapter, he explains the seven essential attributes of God one by one while focusing on the experience of the human spirit traversing the path to God in the process of realizing the true meaning of each attribute.[46]

In his Qurʾān commentary, Rūzbihān discusses the seven attributes of the essence in association with the six days of creation as described in the verse, *Indeed your Lord is God who created the heavens and the earth in six days* (Q 7:54). He explains that out of the divine essence emerged the divine attributes, which appeared one by one over the six days of creation in the order of knowledge, power, hearing, sight, speech, and desire. Once these six attributes became manifest, God completed the process of creating the world by manifesting the seventh attribute, life. This is analogous to the process of creating Adam, which is completed by God's breathing of the living spirit into clay. Rūzbihān writes,

> Each of His days is the manifestation of one of His attributes from the rising place of eternity. Each arises in nonexistence so that a temporal being may come to be. These six days were the manifestation of six of His attributes. The first was knowledge, the second power, the third hearing, the fourth sight, the fifth speech, and the sixth desire. Things were

> perfected through the manifestation of the lights of the six attributes. When He completed them, the temporally originated things became like Adam's body without a spirit, which is one of the seven attributes, that is, His eternal, beginningless, and subsistent life, incomparable with the roaring of breaths, similarity, and analogy. Hence the things abide through His attributes, which abide through His essence.[47]

The attributes of the essence presented above constitute a category of the divine attributes that is contrasted with the attributes of the act. The basic difference between these two categories is that the first designates God in Himself and the second designates Him in relation to His creation. Thus, life, which is an attribute of the essence, designates God regardless of any act He may perform. In contrast, gentleness and severity, forgivingness and vengefulness, are attributes that become manifest through His activity.

A second important difference between the attributes of the essence and the attributes of the act is that the latter include pairs of complementary qualities such as gentleness and severity, forgiveness and vengefulness, and exaltation and abasement, showing the two opposing aspects of God's dynamic relationship with His creation. In contrast, essential attributes are not accompanied by their opposite qualities: God has life, knowledge, power, and so on, but never death, ignorance, or powerlessness. Over the course of time in Muslim intellectual history (especially in dogmatic theology and Sufism), these two subcategories of the active attributes came to be referred to as gentle and severe attributes, or beautiful and majestic attributes.[48] Thus, beauty and majesty are themselves two attributes of God's act as well as the names of the above two opposing subcategories of the attributes of act.

At the beginning of his Qurʾān commentary, in interpreting the very first verse of the Qurʾān, *In the name of God, the Merciful, the Compassionate,* Rūzbihān analyzes the word "God" (*Allāh*) in terms of beauty and majesty. First, he presents the Arabic tetragram, *A-L-L-H* to stand for five concepts: I-ness (*A*: *anāniyya*), unicity (*A: waḥdāniyya*), beauty (*L: jamāl*), majesty

(*L*: *jalāl*), and He-ness (*H*: *huwiyya*). He then calls the middle two concepts—*jamāl* and *jalāl*—as "two attributes" (*ṣifatān*) of God, by which he is referring to the whole range of the beautiful and majestic attributes. He-ness refers to the divine essence, whose unknowability is highlighted by the use of the third-person pronoun, *He,* which grammatically refers to what is absent, making it a common choice to symbolize the unknowable. Rūzbihān writes, "The [letter] *A* is an allusion to the I-ness (*anāniyya*) and unicity (*waḥdāniyya*)….In His name *Allāh* there are two *L*s: the first is an allusion to beauty (*jamāl*) and the second to majesty (*jalāl*). None recognizes these two attributes except the possessor of the attributes. The *H* is an allusion to His He-ness (*huwiyya*), which none recognizes except He."[49]

Names (*asmāʾ*): God as the Possessor of the Most Beautiful Names (*al-asmāʾ al-ḥusnā*)

Numerous Qurʾānic verses and ḥadīths refer to various names of God. On the basis of these, generations of Muslim scholars have compiled lists of divine names, often varying in the total number, while the most widely accepted number has been ninety-nine, largely due to the famous ḥadīth, "To God belong ninety-nine names."[50] Among the key Qurʾānic verses that address the notion of divine names is *Blessed is the name of thy Lord, possessor of majesty and generous giving* (Q 55:78). The main point Rūzbihān makes in interpreting this verse is the utter transcendence of God's essence, which he expresses by the term *majesty* (*jalāl*). Yet at the same time, he maintains that approximate knowledge of God's essence is attainable incrementally by way of His names, qualities, and finally attributes. This is where Rūzbihān recognizes the dilemma of the human situation: human beings need divine names to call upon God, yet these names are ultimately inadequate in addressing Him. Rūzbihān's Qurʾān commentary reads:

> His saying, *Blessed is the name of thy Lord, possessor of majesty and generous giving* (Q 55:78), is what we say about Him whose name is hallowed beyond the

> perception of imaginings and the allusion of intellects, since His name is a quality, while the qualities are attributes, and the attributes abide through the essence. How would he who is incapable of perceiving the reality of the name of the eternal object of description attain the knowledge of the existence of the named? He is more majestic than that thoughts can comprehend the holiness of His majesty or that formulas of remembrance can encompass an iota of His qualities. His majesty bewilders the intellects of the recognizers in the fields of His exaltedness. He drowns the spirits of those who profess oneness in the oceans of His tremendousness and annihilates the secret cores of those who arrive in the lofty mountains of His magnificence.[51]

The ultimate inadequacy of the divine names in addressing God is an idea that Rūzbihān, like Sufi teachers generally, sees as also underlying the following saying of the Prophet: "I do not count Thy laudations before Thee; Thou art as Thou hast lauded Thyself."[52] Rūzbihān writes, "The most eloquent of the worlds spoke about the reality of bewilderment and the courtyards of tremendousness: 'I do not count Thy laudations before Thee; Thou art as Thou hast lauded Thyself.' He remembered Him by remembering [His] majesty."[53] In other words, even the Prophet, who is the most eloquent human being, had to declare his incapacity to praise God adequately, for only God is capable of praising Himself in the true sense. In the above passage, Rūzbihān makes use of such terms as bewilderment, tremendousness, and majesty again to allude to the unfathomable, hidden, and transcendent nature of the divine essence. In his Ḥadīth commentary, he explains why even the Prophet's laudation is ultimately inadequate: it is because

> laudation stems from the fact of being temporally originated and [the Prophet] knows that laudation by a creature is fitting only for a creature. He saw the incomparability of the beginninglessness and said: "I do not count Thy laudation."...He added [God's own] laudation to it because He knows it but no

> one else does. Then he said, "Thou art as Thou hast lauded Thyself."[54]

Rūzbihān thus emphasizes the unfathomable gap between temporally created beings and the eternal, uncreated God, a gap that renders any creature's naming and lauding God inadequate. In the end,

> everything lauds God according to its capacity, and every rememberer remembers according to the measures of his capability, nature, knowledge, and understanding. Remembrance of the Real is outside the imaginings of humans, because laudation and recognitions are without limits. No one has truly lauded Him except He; no one has described Him with what is proper to Him except He. All the prophets are incapable of doing that such that the most majestic in capacity and loftiest in position among them said: "I do not count Thy laudations before Thee; Thou art as Thou hast lauded Thyself."[55]

Another important Qurʾānic verse on the subject of the divine names is *To God belong the most beautiful names, so call upon Him by them* (7:180). In his commentary on this verse, Rūzbihān subdivides divine names into four categories: (1) the names of the essence, (2) the names of the attributes, (3) the names of the acts, and (4) the specific (*khāṣṣa*) names or "the tremendous names" (*al-asmāʾ al-ʿiẓām*), which constitute a subcategory of the names of the essence. The idea of "God's most tremendous name" (*ism Allāh al-aʿẓam*) appears in some ḥadīths, in which the Prophet explains it as a name "by which if God is called, He answers."[56] Rūzbihān writes,

> He described Himself that He has the names of the essence, the names of the attributes, the names of the acts, and the specific names that report the wonders of His beginningless attributes to the hearts of the recognizers and that originate from His eternal essence, as He says: *And to God belong the most beautiful names, so call upon Him by them*. He reported to

> the people in search of those tremendous names that they will not attain them except through their unveilings. Those names will not be unveiled to them except through the unveilings of the specific attributes,[57] the keys to whose treasury are those names. Those attributes will not be unveiled except through the unveiling of the essence. Whoever is specified for these unveilings will be guided to His most tremendous name and be guided through His light to the meanings of the attributes and the lights of the essence. If he calls upon Him by [the most tremendous name], he will be answered.[58]

Rūzbihān seems to regard the first three categories of the divine names as commonly known to people, while the fourth category is only known to the elect,[59] as its knowledge leads to the knowledge of the most tremendous name, the secret and powerful name of God, invoking Him with which is guaranteed His response. In *Mashrab al-arwāḥ* Rūzbihān briefly discusses the most tremendous name of God and argues that it is also the name by which God calls the human being who has attained all the most beautiful names of God. "When all the [divine] names, qualities, and attributes are attributed to the recognizer while he is unified with the lights of the [divine] essence, has become God's bride in the beauty (*jamāl*) of intimacy, and has become holy in God's holiness, the Real names him with His most tremendous name just as He named Himself with His most tremendous name."[60] It is worth noting that Rūzbihān does not discuss this fourth category in his presentation of either the divine names or attributes in *Masālik al-tawḥīd*, which, as had been pointed out earlier, is a work of the Ashʿarite dogma. In contrast, in his works that are not specifically concerned with Ashʿarite theology, he talks about the attributes in a variety of ways, some of which would be beyond the pale of the standard Ashʿarism.

A further examination of the verse, *To God belong the most beautiful names* (Q 7:180), brings out yet another key aspect of divine beauty. The word for "most beautiful" is *ḥusnā,* which is a superlative from the adjective *ḥasan,* "good-and-beautiful." What this verse indicates is that each of the divine names is the most beautiful. Now, we might recall that God is the possessor of majestic (*jalīl*) and beautiful (*jamīl*) names and attributes. If God possesses both *jamāl* and *jalāl* in names and attributes and yet each and every one of His names is considered the most beautiful, it means that the most beautiful names encompass both *jamāl* and *jalāl*.[61]

Figure 3.1 A Venn diagram showing the interrelationship among *jamāl, jalāl,* and *ḥusnā/aḥsan*

Rūzbihān, like most other scholars, understands *jamāl* as an attribute of God's act, which is accompanied by its counterpart, *jalāl,* another attribute of God's act. He considers *ḥusn* an eternal attribute of God's essence, as God is good-and-beautiful (*ḥasan*) in Himself, independent of His acts. Rūzbihān writes in *Mashrab al-arwāḥ*: "God's *ḥusn* is one of His most specific descriptions";[62] and "Understand that *ḥusn* is one of the attributes of God and is eternal because His essence is eternal."[63] Possibly on the basis of these statements, Corbin asserted that beauty is not just one of the numerous attributes of God's act but rather an attribute of His essence.[64] This is a logical conclusion also in the light of the fact that God's *ḥusn* is not accompanied by its opposite, *qubḥ* ("ugliness"), which cannot be attributed to God as it contradicts God's nature by denoting deficiency and imperfection, a principle that applies to the rest of the attributes of the essence.

Summary

In sum, there are multiple senses to God's "beauty": (1) God is the possessor of *ḥusn,* which is an attribute of His essence; (2) God is the possessor of *jamāl,* which is an attribute of His acts, understood in contrast to *jalāl;* (3) God is the possessor of a number of attributes of acts categorized as beautiful (*jamāliyya*) and contrasted with majestic (*jalāliyya*); (4) all the names and attributes of God are the most beautiful (*ḥusnā*); (5) God is the most beautiful creator (*aḥsan al-khāliqīn*), whose creation is also beautiful. Thus, the transcendent, unfathomable God of *There is nothing like Him* (Q 42:11) and *Thou shalt not see Me* (Q 7:143) is countered by the knowable, approachable God of *To Him belong the most beautiful names* (Q 7:180). Rūzbihān understands creation as a gradual process of divine self-disclosure (*tajallī*) out of His unknowable essence, which corresponds to the process of the unfolding of the Hidden Treasure by way of the manifestation of the most beautiful (*ḥusnā*) names, attributes, and acts, including those of beauty (*jamāl*) and majesty. The driving force for God's creation of the world is God's love of His own beauty and His desire for this beauty to be recognized rather than remaining forever hidden and unknown.

The next chapter will shed light on Rūzbihān's understanding of the different degrees to which the divine attributes of *ḥusn* and *jamāl* become manifest in creation—the domain of divine acts—with a focus on the beauty of the human being and the world. We will also see how the ḥadīth of the Hidden Treasure connects to the purpose of human life in Rūzbihān's anthropology.

4

The Anthropology and Cosmology of Beauty

> Indeed We have created the human being in the most beautiful stature.
>
> —Qur'ān 95:4
>
> He who made beautiful everything He has created
>
> —Qur'ān 32:7

The Qur'ān calls God *the most beautiful creator* (Q 23:14), which signifies two things: God is beautiful Himself and what He creates is also beautiful. The present chapter investigates the latter: the beauty of creation. We have seen in the previous chapter how God in His love to be recognized begins to unfold His Hidden Treasure to show forth His most beautiful names and attributes. The unfolding continues by way of the divine acts, or creation. Key questions to be addressed in this chapter are: What is the role of beauty in the creation of the world and human beings? What makes anything beautiful? Why is perception of beauty pleasurable? What differentiates divine, human, and cosmic beauty? What purpose does beauty serve in human life? In addressing these questions, the chapter will trace the entire cycle of created existence, from its origin to return.

Rūzbihān presents the cycle of created existence, particularly human existence, in terms of the journey of the spirits from their creation by way of their embodied life on earth to their eventual return to God. He enumerates the key stages or stations (*maqāmāt*) that the spirits may go through in their journey to God in two of his Arabic works, namely *Mashrab al-arwāḥ* and *Sayr al-arwāḥ* ("The Journey of the Spirits"). *Mashrab al-arwāḥ* contains Rūzbihān's most elaborate and detailed presentation of these stations, which he counts as 1,001. In many of these stations, beauty has an important role to play.

The story of creation coincides with the story of the Hidden Treasure. In *Sharḥ-i shaṭḥiyyāt*, Rūzbihān explains that this ḥadīth indicates God's love for His own beauty in eternity, which is love that extends to His beautiful creation as well. Regarding God's love for creation, Rūzbihān distinguishes two kinds: general love and specific love. He maintains that God's general love is the driving force for the creation of all creatures, that is, all divine acts. In contrast, His specific love is connected to His essence, and with this specific love God creates the prophets and saints. The distinction between the general (*ʿāmm*) and the specific (*khāṣṣ*) is a recurring theme in Rūzbihān's discussion of both love and beauty, as will be seen.

> When [God] looked at the act through love, He created the universe with desire. This love is general. When He made the lover appear through this love, He looked at him through the eternal essence. This love is specific. He knows this love from Himself in His eternal knowledge; it is His love for the prophets and the saints. Know that *He loves them, and they love Him* [Q 5:54] pertains solely to eternal attributes. It is incomparable with the tenderness of nature and the changes of temporal origination.

> In eternity He became the lover of His own beauty (*jamāl*). Inevitably love, lover, and beloved were one. Since they are attributes, they do not have the defect of temporal origination. When He became His own lover, He wanted to create a creation so that it would become the place of His love and gaze, without alienation or intimacy. In His eternity He created

> the spirits of the lovers and made their eyes see His beauty (*jamāl*). He taught them that He was their lover before they came to be: "I was a Hidden Treasure so I loved to be recognized."[1]

Rūzbihān thus explains the mechanism of how God and His saints and prophets become mutual lovers: first God creates them out of love and then displays His beauty to them, which makes them love God in return.

At the beginning of *Sayr al-arwāḥ*, Rūzbihān enumerates the initial stages of creation, which comes forth from the hidden and unknowable essence in its process of self-disclosure. At the first disclosure of Himself to Himself in His hidden essence, God recognizes His own beauty (*jamāl*). Out of this recognition the multiple attributes emerge. Thereafter begins the process of creation per se, or the manifestation of His creative acts: He creates first His lovers and then the prophets and saints. Finally He creates the world by issuing the engendering command, *Be!* (*kun*), as in the Qur᾿ānic verse, *When He desires a thing, His command is to say to it "Be!"; then it is* (36:82), to which Rūzbihān alludes by the two letters *K* and *N* (which together spell *kun*). The command brings everything into existence except human beings, whose creation requires a more elaborate process.

> When [God] shone forth from the rising place of eternity and disclosed Himself to nonexistence through His knowledge, He did not see anything other than Himself. He marveled at His beauty (*jamāl*). His attributes spread apart from one another. Then He brought His lovers into existence so that they might take pleasure in union with Him and rejoice in His subsistence. Then He desired to create the spirits of His prophets and saints, just as He said, "I was a Hidden Treasure, so I loved to be recognized." Then He scooped up some water from the ocean of the letters *K* and *N*.[2]

The process of creation may be better understood if we also examine a parallel passage in *Mashrab al-arwāḥ*, where

Rūzbihān explains how God's self-disclosure takes place in stages. God discloses Himself first to His essence in its absolute unicity; second to His attributes in their multitude, which involves the dynamic tension between beauty and majesty; and finally to His command of love, "*Be!*" (Q 36:82). Rūzbihān says that the driving force for God's creation of the world is His love (*maḥabba*) for the beauty of "the self-disclosure of all the attributes and the essence," which directly connects to the wording of both the ḥadīth, "so I loved (*aḥbabtu*) to be recognized" and the Qur᾿ānic verse, *the most beautiful (ḥusnā) names*. In short, it is God's love for the *ḥusn* of His attributes—which embrace beautiful (*jamīl*) and majestic (*jalīl*) attributes—that leads to the creation of the world.

> When God wanted to bring the realm of being into existence, He exalted Himself in His magnificence and disclosed Himself to His essence through His essence and from His essence to His attributes, so beauty was subtilized for majesty and majesty for beauty. He Himself sought from Himself in knowledge of eternity the hiding places that He had recognized from Himself before the known objects. Desire responded to knowledge, knowledge to contentment, contentment to the decree, the decree to the ruling property, and the ruling property to the essence. The beauty (*ḥusn*) of the self-disclosure brought together all the attributes and the essence in the brilliance of love (*maḥabba*) such that the All itself became manifest in the love. He disclosed Himself from the love to the command, and He disclosed Himself from the command in the *K* and *N*, which are among the names and the qualities. From between the two became manifest a light, and that light became the non-compound intellect (*al-ʿaql al-basīṭ*).[3]

The "non-compound intellect" that emerges from the light in the above passage seems to be what the philosophers and Sufis commonly call "the universal intellect" (*al-ʿaql al-kullī*). Both "non-compound" (or "simple") and "universal" emphasize the fact that this is a singular intellect (i.e., not multiple) and has no parts (i.e., not composite), yet it is the germ of all created reality. The subsequent stages of creation, namely how multiple things emerge from the non-compound and singular intellect, are presented below.

Beauty in the Creation of Human Beings

The Birth of the Spirits

After God utters the engendering command, "*Be!*," the multi-stage formation of the human being begins. From the non-compound intellect spirits emerge in all their multiplicity. Rūzbihān describes the process thus: first there was a complete state of equilibrium of the attributes and the essence, but then there appeared agitation due to "the overpowering force of eternity. Then the equilibrium became dispersed. God then gathered together the dispersed things," and out of them He created the spirits that would eventually become embodied in human form.[4] Once God created the spirits, He taught or made them recognize the entirety of His most beautiful names. Rūzbihān writes that having created the spirits, God then "kept them in the veils of the unseen in order to make them recognize all the names, attributes, qualities, acts, and the majesty of the essence, and to show them the treasures of the marvels of the eternity of the essence and the wonders of the subtleties of the attributes, just as He said…'I was a Hidden Treasure, so I loved to be recognized.'"[5]

After the spirits are born in the very first of the 1,001 stations presented in *Mashrab al-arwāḥ*, they start enjoying God's self-disclosure, which is described by the subsequent three stations: the spirits taking pleasure in the direct perception of the divine act (the second station); their finding the direct self-disclosure of the divine attributes (the third station); and their vision of the self-disclosure of the divine essence (the fourth station).[6] In the fifth station, the spirits find servanthood in relation to God. Then the spirits gain preparedness for recognition (the sixth station) and then reach the station of standing still in presence (the seventh station). It is in the eighth station that the spirits hear the divine address, "*Am I not your Lord?*" (Q 7:172),[7] which is a key Qurʾānic event to which we will turn next. In sum, in the first seven stations of the spirits' journey, the spirits are born and then through exposure to God's essence and attributes gain the preparedness to encounter God on the Day of the Covenant.

The Day of the Covenant: The First Manifestation of God's Beauty, or a Covenant of Love

The notion of the covenant (*ʿahd, mīthāq*) is a major discussion in Sufi literature and important in the Qurʾān generally. A key verse reads: *When thy Lord took from the children of Adam, their seed from their loins and made them testify of themselves, "Am I not your Lord?" they said, "Yea, we testify"—lest you say on the Day of Resurrection, "Indeed, we were heedless of this"* (Q 7:172). Basic Muslim understanding of this verse is that it indicates human beings' primordial acknowledgment of God as their Lord, whom alone they promise to worship. If we turn to Sufi literature, we find that this covenant—often referred to by Sufis as *ʿahd-i Alast* ("the covenant of 'Am I not?'")—is a recurring theme and has special significance beyond the simple acknowledgment of monotheism.

Rūzbihān refers to the covenant in various places in his writings. He often uses the term (divine) *address* (*khiṭāb*)[8] to refer to it, emphasizing the auditory nature of the event. When he presents it as constituting the eighth station in the *Mashrab,* he writes that it is an event in which the spirits hear (*samāʿ*) the divine address of "*Am I not your Lord?*"[9] "Audition" (*samāʿ*) is an important practice in Sufism, referring to an auditory encounter with God by way of hearing His words. Audition and vision constitute the two key modes in which human beings may encounter God. In Rūzbihān's view, human audition of God originates in the covenant, for it was the human spirits' primordial audition of the divine address.[10] For this reason, he sometimes uses the term *samāʿ* by itself to allude to the covenant. Audition was the human experience of God's "address."

A striking feature of Rūzbihān's interpretation of the covenant is that he understands it as an occasion at which God manifested His beauty to the spirits for the first time. Moreover, since witnessing beauty causes passionate love, he argues that this in fact was a covenant of passionate love. Humans accepted God not only as their Lord but also as their beautiful Beloved. Rūzbihān writes, "The Real unveiled His beauty (*jamāl*) to the spirits of the passionate lovers in His first appearance after introducing Himself to them by saying, '*Am I not your Lord?*'"[11]; and "He unveiled to [the spirits] the beauty (*jamāl*) of [His] majesty, and spoke to them in a specific address."[12] He also says, "He made [the spirits] all become passionate lovers of [God's] beauty and majesty between the light of [His] attributes and the light of [His] essence."[13] While Rūzbihān is quite explicit in presenting the covenant as a covenant of love for divine beauty, he is hardly the first person to associate the event with beauty. For instance, ʿAyn al-Quḍāt (d. 1131) wrote, "Remember that day on which the beauty (*jamāl*) of '*Am I not your Lord*' was unveiled to you."[14]

Rūzbihān further explains that the covenant was an occasion on which God made the spirits recognize Him through the most beautiful attributes, both the beautiful and the majestic. He writes that the divine address of "*Am I not your Lord?*" was an expression of God's "making Himself recognized to them as well as self-disclosure to them through the quality of majesty and beauty (*jamāl*). When the spirits' faces became enraptured in eternity's face and when they became impassioned after the [divine] address and the vision of the beginningless and endless essence, they responded to the Real with '*Yea*' in love and recognition. This is one of the meanings of their immersion in the witnessing of the beauty (*jamāl*) of His exaltedness, magnificence, and subsistence."[15] Rūzbihān also writes, "The spirits were immersed in the oceans of the eternal beauty (*jamāl*) and became enraptured through the quality of passionate love in the deserts of recognition."[16]

In *ʿAbhar al-ʿāshiqīn*, Rūzbihān again discusses the two types of love for God (*maḥabbat-i ilāhī*): general and specific. General love for God derives from seeing God's beauty in creation, which people in general are able to do. In contrast, specific love belongs only to the elect, which originates in their witnessing of God, one of whose occasions is the covenant.

Rūzbihān then applies the distinction between the general and the specific to his categorization of God's attributes and acts.

> As for the specific love, it belongs to the elect after witnessing [God]. The folk of witnessing have three occasions of witnessing. One occurs to the spirits before the bodies, before human existence, in the presence of the [divine] glory. When He brought them together, He said to the chieftains of the spirits: *"Am I not your Lord?" They said "Yea"* (Q 7:172) voluntarily. The pleasure of the speech reached them. They asked for beauty (*jamāl*) from the Real so that recognition would become complete. The Real took off the veil of invincibility and presented to them the beauty (*jamāl*) of the majesty of the essence. The spirits of the prophets and saints became drunk from the effect of the listening and the beauty of the majesty. They fell in love with the eternal Witness (*shāhid*) without any trace of temporal origination. From that friendship (*walāyat*), their love (*maḥabbat*) increased in accordance with the degree of divine nurturing, because when the holy spirits appeared in the earthly form, all became sayers of *"Show me"* because of the ancient love-madness.[17]

The last sentence refers to Abraham and Moses, both of whom said *"Show me"* (*arinī*) to God on different occasions (Q 2:260 and 7:143, respectively) but who, in Rūzbihān's view, were in the state of intoxication or love-madness, a subject examined in detail in the next chapter.

It is also worth noting that in the above passage Rūzbihān presents the divine address as directed at some of the spirits rather than all: "When He brought them together, He said to the chieftains of the spirits: *'Am I not your Lord?'*" He argues that the specific love belongs to the elect, and it originates in the divine speech addressed exclusively to them. This argument is in line with Rūzbihān's view that while all human spirits saw God's first manifestation of beauty on the Day of the Covenant, only some of them said *"Yea"* (Q 7:172) in acknowledgment of God as their Lord.[18]

In sum, the Day of the Covenant proceeds in the following manner: God addresses the spirits while disclosing His beauty and majesty to them. The spirits hear that address and see the divine beauty. Consequently, they come to recognize and love God, not just to serve Him as their Lord. Finally, these human spirits reply to God by saying "*Yea*" to acknowledge God as their only Lord and Beloved. This covenant further indicates the primordiality of human love for God, which is a major theme in Sufi literature. A famous example is Aḥmad Ghazālī's *Sawāniḥ*, in which he extensively discusses the beginninglessness of *ʿishq* and its relation to *ḥusn*.[19] He also describes the covenant as an occasion for the human spirits to witness God's beauty thereby becoming His passionate lovers, which is in agreement with Rūzbihān's view.

The Birth of the Human Body

After presenting the primordial witnessing of God's beauty at the covenant as the eighth station in the *Mashrab*, Rūzbihān gives further accounts of the spirits' witnessing of God (the ninth to thirteenth stations).[20] Thereafter begins the spirits' gradual descent to earth, which culminates in the bodily birth of the spirits or their entrance into the human body. Rūzbihān's presentation in the *Mashrab* is elaboration on the Qurʾānic account of the bodily formation of human beings, which is concisely presented by Böwering as follows:

> The Qurʾān mentions four stages in the creation of humans…God created the first human being, Adam, from dust (*min turābin*, Q 3:59), procreating human beings through the sperm, shaping them individually to their complete figure, and finally making them male and female. "[God] created you of dust, then of a sperm-drop (*min nuṭfa*), then shaped you in the form of a man (*rajulan*)" (Q 18:37), and "then made you pairs" (Q 35:11), while other qurʾānic verses state that God created every animal of water (Q 24:45) and the jinn from a flame of fire (Q 55:15).[21]

In the *Mashrab*, the fourteenth station marks the spirits' entrance into the realm of sovereignty (*malakūt*). In the fifteenth station, they enter the world of form.[22] Thereafter, the spirits oversee the development of the clay, first in the form of a sperm drop (cf. Q 76:2) in the womb, then an embryo, and so on in the subsequent three stations. In the nineteenth station, the spirits gaze at the "beauty of the form" (*jamāl al-ṣūra*), which is then perfected in the twentieth station.[23] Thereafter the spirits enter the bodily form (the twenty-first station),[24] which is a process described by the verse, *I blew into him of My spirit* (Q 15:29; 38:72). This marks the birth of human beings proper; earlier there were only disembodied spirits and lifeless bodies. It must be noted that *Mashrab al-arwāḥ* focuses on human beings, and Rūzbihān does not discuss how God created other creatures such as the jinn and angels.

Blowing of God's Spirit and Shaping with His Two Hands

Rūzbihān maintains that God's blowing of His spirit into the bodily form signifies the impartation of the full range of the divine attributes, including those of the essence (one of which is life) and those of the acts (which encompass beautiful and majestic attributes). He writes, "*I blew into him of My spirit*, that is, I brought him into life through My life and spirit, which appeared from the manifestation of [My] majesty and beauty."[25] He also writes, "Blowing is the manifestation of the attribute in the act. Do you not see that He says regarding the reality of Adam, *When I shaped him and blew into him of My spirit* (Q 15:29)? The 'shaping' [refers to] the world of the divine act, while the 'blowing' [refers to] the world of the attribute."[26] Human existence encompasses two realms: bodily and spiritual. The bodily realm is visible and hence manifests God's activity, such as "shaping," while the spiritual realm pertains to the higher, inner dimension of the human being that is inseparable from the presence of the divine life and the rest of the attributes.

Rūzbihān often discusses the verse *I blew into him of My spirit* alongside another: *I created with My two hands* (Q 38:75). For instance, in *ʿAbhar al-ʿāshiqīn*, he presents these two verses as constituting the meaning of the ḥadīth, "God created Adam in His form."[27] In other words, he suggests that "God's form" in which Adam was created consists of the divine attributes, one group of which is represented by *spirit* and the other by the *two hands*. The first group is the attributes of the essence, one of which is life, symbolized by spirit here. The other group is the attributes of the act, which are divided into two types as discussed in the previous chapter: beautiful and majestic attributes. As Rūzbihān writes, "The self-disclosure of the essence is what He said: *I blew into him of My spirit*; the self-disclosure of the attributes is what He said: *I created with My two hands*."[28]

Other key verses describing the process of the formation of the human being are: *He formed thee and made your forms beautiful* (Q 40:64); *He who created thee then shaped thee and balanced thee and composed thee in whatever form He willed* (Q 82:7–8); and *Indeed We have created the human being in the most beautiful stature* (Q 95:4). The root utilized for describing the beauty of the human form (*ṣūra*) and stature (*taqwīm*) in the above two verses is *ḥ-s-n* rather than *j-m-l*. As already mentioned, *j-m-l* has a very limited application in the Qur᾽ān, whereas *ḥusn* designates all-encompassing beauty, including both *jamāl* and *jalāl*. Hence, *ḥusn* is a more fitting term to describe the beauty of the human being, for human beauty is nothing but a reflection of the full range of the divine attributes, which are altogether the most beautiful (*ḥusnā*). This point is clear from Rūzbihān's interpretation of the verse, "*He formed you and then made your forms beautiful* (Q 40:64): for I clothed you with the lights of My majesty and beauty (*jamāl*) and with My character."[29]

Elsewhere, he comments on the Qur᾽ānic notion of *creating* and *forming* the human being: "We created you through the acts and formed you through the attributes. Also, We created you through the command then formed you through the manifestation of the self-disclosure of the attributes to you."[30] He thus points out how the distinction between creating and forming parallels that between the body and the spirit, between the act and the attribute, which moreover corresponds to the distinction between *khalq* and *khuluq*, or creation and character. In other words, the human being is made up of a divine act ("*Be!*") that engenders the clay and the divine attributes ("*created with My two hands*," "*blew into him of My spirit*," etc.) that shape, nurture, and enliven the clay and give it the inner and outer form of beauty. The foregoing discussion may be summarized in the following chart.

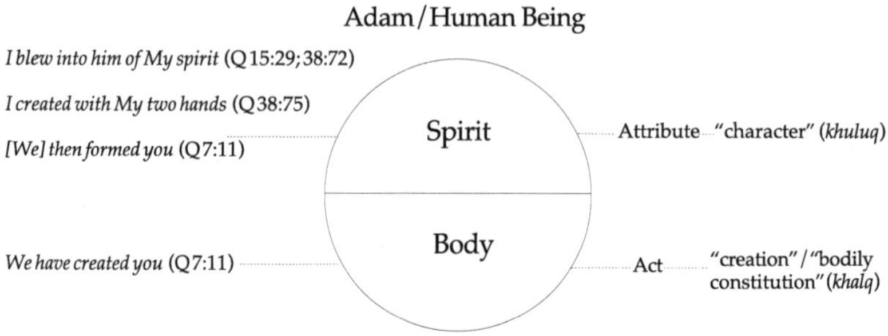

Figure 4.1 A diagram showing human constitution with corresponding Qur᾽ānic verses

Once human beings begin their life on earth, this also marks the beginning of their long journey back to God, which process takes the rest of the *Mashrab* for Rūzbihān to explain. Given the primordial covenant of love that the spirits made with their beautiful God before entering into their bodies, embodied life is a test of whether they can stay true lovers of God by seeking and finding signs of God's beauty in the world and in themselves. Whether or not they have kept the covenant will become clear on the Day of Judgment, a key Qur᾽ānic event in which beauty and majesty, according to Rūzbihān, have major roles to play.

The Day of Judgment: Vision of God's Beauty or Majesty in the Hereafter

We have seen in the previous chapter that whether humans can have a vision of God in this life and/or the next was a topic of major debate among dogmatic theologians in the early centuries of Islam. Their primary concern seems to have been whether it was possible to see God in this life and the next, not what could have happened *before* this life. As discussed earlier, Rūzbihān's presentation of the events on the Day of the Covenant is clear: humans not only heard but also *saw* or *witnessed* God: on that day, God addressed humans and disclosed His beauty to them. Moreover, Rūzbihān affirms the possibility of seeing God in this life and the next, though this does not imply that he thinks that all human beings will attain it.

Two key verses that refer to the vision of God in the afterlife are the following, which describe the Day of Judgment: *Some faces on that day shall be radiant, gazing upon their Lord* (Q 75:22–23) and *Some faces on that day shall shine, laughing and joyous* (Q 80:38–39). Rūzbihān comments on the first verse in this manner:

> They gaze upon [God's] beauty (*jamāl*). Then their faces come to gaze [upon it] radiantly, delightedly, and happily. This is due to the beauty (*ḥusn*) of the self-disclosure of His *jamāl*....Had they witnessed Him face-to-face through the description of majesty, tremendousness, and magnificence, then they would have perished at the first of His assaults, and their faces would have been baffled.[31]

With regard to the second Qur'ānic verse, *Some faces on that day shall shine, laughing and joyous* (Q 80:38–39), Rūzbihān comments, "That is due to the brilliance that reaches [the faces] from gazing at God's beauty (*jamāl*)."[32] In other words, their faces shine with delight because they are now allowed to see God's beauty.

In contrast, the Qur'ān describes the state of those who fail to attain that joyous state like this: *Some faces on that day shall be scowling* (Q 75:24). This is because they will be seeing God's majesty rather than His beauty. Moreover, Rūzbihān comments on the verse, *On that day there shall be dust on some faces, overspread with darkness* (Q 80:40–41) thus: "*Upon them there shall be dust* (*ghabra*) of separation on the day of meeting; and upon them there will be *darkness* (*qatara*) of the lowliness of the veil and the darkness of punishment—we seek refuge in God from rebuke."[33] Rūzbihān then interprets the "dust" as indicating three things: distance, darkness, and separation, following the commentaries of al-Sarī al-Saqaṭī (d. 865), Sahl al-Tustarī (d. 896), and al-Qushayrī (d. 1072), respectively.[34] These ideas point to God's majesty.

In short, Rūzbihān maintains that the human story begins with a vision and audition of the beautiful God and ends with a vision of either the beautiful God or the majestic God, depending on whether or not people have kept the covenant of love during their lives on earth. Those who have kept it will encounter God's beauty and mercy, and those who have not kept it will face God's majesty and wrath. The true test lies between the Covenant of "yesterday" and the Judgment of "tomorrow": this earthly existence that they face today. How human beings live today determines how they will re-encounter their Lord after death.

Search for Beauty in the World

Seeing human life as a search for divine beauty, Rūzbihān suggests that all beauty found in this world is a reminder of God's beauty as witnessed on the Day of the Covenant. For this reason, there is great benefit in seeking beauty on all levels, and Rūzbihān encourages people to do so whenever possible. He points out that in each human being there remains at least a vague memory of God's *jamāl* witnessed on the Day of the Covenant. In a key passage in *Mashrab al-arwāḥ*, he writes,

> In everyone who witnesses [the Unseen], there remains the sweetness of the address of eternity. When [those who have reached the station of audition] hear any goodly sound, see and witness anything comely and deemed beautiful, or smell any goodly fragrance in this world, they will hear it as an intermediary between the attribute and the essence through the quality of being prior to any act that emerges from the Real. It is as if one hears from the Real through the Real. Hence, every speck of engendered being has a specific tongue that speaks to him with the eternal speech.[35]

Thus, it turns out that for those who have reached the advanced station of being able to recognize God at all times, every *aesthetic* experience—i.e., a *sensory* encounter with a beautiful object—is a reminder of the Day of the Covenant as it evokes the same pleasure that they had experienced in beholding God's beauty on that day. In other words, every instance of beauty in the sensible world—be it a flower, a good smell, or a handsome face—triggers recollection of the beautiful God along with the pleasure this brings to its perceiver. Rūzbihān continues, "So, [this eternal speech] stirs him up away from his own existence toward the subsistence of the Real through the quality of annihilation [of everything other than Him]. God said, *Those who hear the speech and follow the most beautiful of it* [Q 39:18]."[36] For those who are able to hear God's speech, that speech is so loud that it annihilates creation from their awareness, making them turn away from creation toward God alone, or away from things' beauty toward God's beauty.

Seeking Intimacy with Every Instance of Beauty

There is a term of particular importance in Rūzbihān's discussion of beauty in general: *istiʾnās*, which means "to seek intimacy (with something)." In Rūzbihān's usage, this verb usually takes as its direct object something beautiful. Rūzbihān seems to have taken this expression from a saying of an enigmatic early Sufi, Dhū al-Nūn al-Miṣrī (d. 861), though Rūzbihān does not always mention the name. For example, in his Ḥadīth commentary, Rūzbihān explains the saying, "I saw my Lord in the most beautiful (*aḥsan*) form" in this manner: "It was [the Prophet's] seeking intimacy with the beautiful (*ḥasan*) face, just as it has been reported that he used to love beautiful faces, because 'Whoever seeks intimacy with God seeks intimacy with everything comely (*malīḥ*) and every handsome face.'"[37] Rūzbihān attributes the last statement to Dhū al-Nūn in *Mashrab al-arwāḥ*.[38] Dhū al-Nūn's statement serves as one basis for Rūzbihān's defense of the practice of loving beautiful human faces as a commendable activity for Muslims on the example of the prophet Muhammad. Elsewhere, Rūzbihān also observes rather matter-of-factly that it is natural for every "seeker of intimacy to seek intimacy with all things deemed beautiful."[39]

In *Manṭiq al-asrār* Rūzbihān explains that gazing on beautiful faces is commendable because seeking intimacy with beauty is a sign of strong yearning for the divine beauty to which every other beauty connects. Moreover, seeking intimacy with beauty in the world clarifies human beings' vision of reality, increasing their capacity to behold divine beauty. He writes: "Whoever seeks intimacy with the beauty (*jamāl*) of the beginninglessness seeks intimacy with the beauty of the forms of temporal origination by yearning for the quarry of holiness, because no one knows the degrees of intimacy with the Real except those who recognize the saying of the master of humanity: 'Gazing at a beautiful (*ḥasan*) face increases sight.'"[40] A fuller version of the ḥadīth is mentioned in *ʿAbhar al-ʿāshiqīn*: "Three things increase the power of sight: gazing at greenery, gazing at beautiful faces, and gazing at flowing water."[41]

While interpreting this ḥadīth, Rūzbihān points out the ontological difference between human beauty and cosmic or natural beauty. He argues that all creatures are beautiful insofar as they are divine acts, which is the general sort of beauty given to creation. This general beauty is the result of God's "general love" mentioned at the beginning of this chapter; likewise, the specific beauty is the result of God's specific love. Human beings have both general and specific beauty, the latter of which derives from the light of God's essence and attributes. Since all divine acts point to divine beauty, looking at them enhances human insight, which is the ability to recognize reality beyond appearances, but to a much lesser degree than gazing at beautiful human faces does, because they reveal God's essence and attributes. Rūzbihān writes, "In beauty (*ḥusn*) there is the light of the specific act in which the light of the essence and attributes is clothed, while in the purity of greenery and flowing water there is the light of the general act in which the Real manifests the light of the specific act by way of describing Himself."[42]

Rūzbihān further comments on the above ḥadīth: "This is from the station of the eye of gathering, and in this is an allusion to the station of becoming clothed."[43] "Eye of gathering" is a term that Rūzbihān uses to indicate the ability to see the created and the uncreated in a thing at the same time as if gathering the two in one vision. "Becoming clothed" (*iltibās*) is a unique term that appears in his writings. Ernst translates it as "clothing with divinity," which he contrasts with *kashf*, or unveiling.[44] Ballanfat notes the peculiar significance of *iltibās* in Rūzbihān's thought and devotes sixteen pages of his book to analyzing it.[45]

He translates the term as *amphibolie* (as Corbin does) and speculates on its etymological connection to *talbīs*. However, he casts a negative connotation on the term by emphasizing its connection to Iblīs, a connotation that I do not find in Rūzbihān's use of the term. I translate the term as "becoming clothed" to preserve the literal sense of the word. I do not include "divinity" in my translation of the term as Ernst does, because clothing seems to work both ways—creation becoming clothed by God and God becoming clothed by creation. With regard to the former, Rūzbihān writes, for instance, "the recognizer is clothed with the brilliance of the beauty (*jamāl*) of eternity."[46] As for the latter perspective, he writes, "Do you not see how Moses fled from his cane when tremendousness was clothed by it?" referring to the episode of his cane turning into a snake.[47] Here Rūzbihān takes the cane as the thing by which tremendousness, a word often referring to the divine essence, was clothed.

It is the human being in possession of the eye of gathering who is capable of seeing the uncreated Creator clothed by every created thing, for every instance of sensible beauty is a pointer to God, the source of all beauty. Since God's essence and attributes are intangible and too intense to be seen directly by humans, they appear as veiled or clothed by the human form. At the same time, beautiful human beings are clothed in the divine essence and attributes. It is the eye of gathering that can perceive both what is clothed (God) and what clothes (creation) or both what is clothed (creation) and what clothes (God) simultaneously. The opposite mode of perception is called the eye of separation (*tafriqa*), which sees the created apart from the Creator.[48]

Superiority of Human Beauty over Cosmic Beauty

Rūzbihān regards human beauty as far superior to cosmic beauty, because the former is a stronger reflection of divine beauty in that it carries the full range of the divine attributes. In other words, human beauty is specific beauty, whereas cosmic beauty is general beauty. We can see how the tripartite analysis of God in terms of essence, attributes, and acts as discussed in the previous chapter serves as a basis for Rūzbihān's examination of the difference between divine, human, and cosmic beauty.

Because human beings are able to reflect the full range of the divine attributes, it was said, "He who recognizes himself recognizes his Lord," the saying commonly attributed to the Prophet to which Rūzbihān alluded earlier. To know oneself may be sufficient for attaining knowledge of God because the human being can mirror the full range of the divine attributes. The world is a mirror of God, and so are individual human beings. To know God by observing the world is possible, but one must search through the entire world to discover the divine attributes scattered throughout. This suggests the greater "efficiency" of knowing oneself as a path to knowing God than studying the entire world. Rūzbihān ascribes to the common notion of the human being as a microcosm, because "the two worlds are kneaded within the human being." As he writes, "In the creation of the human being and in beautiful (*ḥisān*) faces the marks of His power are more than those found in the realm of being, because the two realms of being and the two worlds are kneaded within the human being. Within him [God's] work is known. If he recognizes himself, he will recognize his Lord."[49]

Rūzbihān also points out that although humans can become passionate lovers of both God and other humans, they can never become passionate lovers of *things*. In his view, human beauty is superior to cosmic beauty not only in that it reveals the beautiful attributes of God, but also in that it can serve as a window through which passionate lovers witness and adore the beautiful God. In contrast, cosmic beauty as found in non-human creatures can only be objects of due respect as God's beautiful creatures for those naive "ascetics," by which Rūzbihān seems to mean stiff-minded conservatives who condemn passionate love of God and the celebration of human beauty as a manifestation of divine beauty. They are suspicious of passionate love generally because it is not a Qur'ānic term. They are concerned about the potential harm that it may bring, such as leading people away from God. Rūzbihān explains the opposite approaches to beauty taken by the ascetics and the passionate lovers in this passage:

> As for the difference between Adamic beauty (*nīkū'ī*) and non-Adamic beauty among engendered beings and things in this world, it is that human beauty

> (*ḥusn*) has the specific characteristic of the lights of God's self-disclosure of the essence, while other things only have beauty from the freshness of the divine act. The vision of an engendered being is the *qibla* of ascetics, whereas the face of Adam is the *qibla* of the passionate lovers.[50]

Rūzbihān's use of the term "specific characteristic" (*khāṣṣiyyat*), which derives from the same root as "specific" (*khāṣṣ*), highlights Adamic beauty's connection to the divine essence, rendering it specific beauty rather than general beauty.

Rūzbihān further points out that while human beauty can cause love, cosmic beauty produces "mere" faith in God devoid of love for Him. In Rūzbihān's view, this is not enough for the ideal human life: one must not only have faith in God but also love Him, so that God's love for humans can be reciprocated, as the Qurʾān says, *He loves them, and they love Him* (Q 5:54). Rūzbihān writes,

> The immature in the Shariah carp at us and say, "The signs of the creation of the heavens are greater—why do you not look at them?" Yes indeed, there are signs in the heavens, and the signs are the path for the tight-hearted in the world. But in Adam's face is the emergence of the sun of the self-disclosure of the [divine] essence and attributes, because passionate love came out of Adam's beauty (*ḥusn*), while the light of faith came from the mold of the engendered being.[51]

Rūzbihān's contrast between cosmic beauty and human beauty and their association with faith and love, respectively, are also clear from his argument "the signs [i.e., the acts] are the locus of faith" but not of love, because "witnessing the beauty (*jamāl*) of eternity does not occur in the signs."[52]

Another implication of the above discussion is that the study of things in the world will not make humans passionate lovers of God, however much they may come to admire God as an amazing Creator of this complex world. Rūzbihān's warning toward "the immature in the Shariah" is firmly based on his ontological analysis of cosmic and human beauty, for they fail to understand the order of things. The more perfect a thing is, the more beautiful it is, because it is more similar to God. The more a thing reflects of God's beauty, the more admiration and love it deserves. The more admirable and lovable a thing is, the stronger its attractive force toward the source of all beauty—God. Therefore, Rūzbihān maintains that there is no reason to restrict human search for beauty in the created domain to non-human objects, ignoring the more obvious human beauty.

In fact, Rūzbihān argues that looking at beautiful human faces is a *means* to finding God—both His beauty and majesty. In his commentary on the ḥadīth, "Seek good in those with beautiful faces,"[53] Rūzbihān writes, "The beauty of the face is the garb of the light of God's majesty. He garbs it [i.e., beauty] on the face of everyone characterized by His character. Part of His lofty character is His munificence and generosity, so he who is qualified by His beauty is qualified by His munificence and generosity."[54] Moreover, this ḥadīth also means:

> Seek the purity of the Real's self-disclosure from the beautiful faces, for they are the locus of the appearance of the lights of [God's] beauty and majesty. Then you may come to love God by means of His act and you may recognize the realities of His art in the holy spirits and pure [bodily] frames. Thus you may attain to the recognition of the secrets of [God's] attributes and the realities of [His] essence.[55]

Rūzbihān also comments on a closely related ḥadīth: "Make use of beautiful (*ḥisān*) faces and the black pupil, for God is ashamed to chastise a comely face in the Fire."[56] He further writes, "When God distinguishes a servant with outer and inner beauty (*ḥusn*) and clothes him with the clothing of love for Him, He makes him a niche for the self-disclosure of His beauty and majesty, so His light appears from his light."[57]

Correspondence between Inner and Outer Beauty

Rūzbihān makes it clear that in speaking of beauty, he is referring not only to physical beauty, but also to a hidden correspondence between the outer and the inner. He refers to this correspondence by using two Arabic terms that are commonly contrasted: *khuluq* and *khalq*, or character and creation (or physical constitution), which derive from the same root. He argues that it is because of the correspondence between a person's character and creation that the Prophet said, "Let the most beautiful in face among you lead you, for he is more likely to be the most beautiful in character."[58] Rūzbihān writes, "[The Prophet] explained that beauty (*ḥusn*) of character follows upon beauty (*ḥusn*) of creation."[59] Thus, outward beauty is understood to be a reflection of inner beauty. In turn, the inner beauty of a human being mirrors divine beauty: "Whoever has more subtle existence has a finer body, a more noble spirit, and a more precious soul. In his [bodily] frame, the light of the [divine] quarry is more apparent from his substance."[60]

The idea that there is a connection between inner and outer beauty is also suggested by another ḥadīth: "'He who prays much by night—his face is beautiful by day," on which Rūzbihān comments, "God discloses Himself during the night to those who pray, and then garbs their faces with some of His light. Then their faces become the niche of the lights of the Real's self-disclosure, with the light of the [divine] self-disclosure glitters within them. The beauty (*ḥusn*) to which he alluded is a garb of the Real's light."[61]

Those Who Know God Are Loved by People

We have already seen that the more beautiful a thing is, the stronger the love it causes in its perceiver. Moreover, there is a relationship between knowledge and love, especially when it comes to God—the more humans know of God, the more they love Him, because they can see more of His beauty. Here are some of Rūzbihān's descriptions of such lovers/knowers of God:

> The truthful, loving recognizer is like roses and sweet basil because his body is created from the dust of the paradises and his spirit from the light of the sovereignty of the All-Merciful. All creatures love him and all things seek intimacy with him, for people find in him a breeze from the Real, and they

> perfume themselves with his scent. When someone is accepted by the people, their love for him is an indication of his recognition of God. When someone is not like that, their hatred for him is a mark of his misery—we seek refuge in God! Thus Abū Saʿīd al-Khudrī reported from the messenger of God: "Shall I not tell you who is the most beloved to God? They said, "Yes, O messenger of God," thinking that he would mention a man. He replied: "Surely the most beloved of you to God is the most beloved of you to the people." Then he said, "Shall I not tell you who is the most hated by God?" We said, "Yes, O messenger of God," thinking that he would mention a man. He replied: "Surely the most hated by God is the most hated of you by the people." He made us understand that the love that people's hearts have for a person is the testimony to God's love for him, because hearts incline toward whosoever has the garb of Lordship, they love whosoever has the reality of recognition, and they see God's gifts in the features of the recognizers. Indeed, when God loves a servant, He makes him lovable to the hearts of all creatures from His throne to the earth.[62]

If lovers of God are loved by other people, how do these lovers themselves see others and the world around them? On this, Rūzbihān remarks: "When the passionate lover's journey in passionate love is complete, he will not see anything deemed beautiful without seeing God's beauty (*ḥusn*) within it. This is why the passionate lover loves the beauty of every beautiful thing in existence."[63] Earlier, we saw how Rūzbihān encourages the practice of loving and seeking intimacy with beautiful things as a means to advance on the path to God. At the end of this path, human beings are able to see God's beauty behind all beautiful things, as if these things become transparent. Rūzbihān refers to this mode of perception by the already mentioned term *the eye of gathering*. He also uses the term *the eye of the spirit* in the same meaning. One of his poems reads: "Being became the mirror of the Real and the Real appeared from it. / With the eye of the spirit I gaze at the spirit in the mirror."[64] Elsewhere, Rūzbihān contrasts the eye of the spirit with the eye of the intellect. While the eye of the spirit sees the beauty of the Creator, the eye of the intellect sees the created object. Given that he uses the eye of the spirit synonymously with the eye of gathering, the eye of the intellect can be understood to correspond to the eye of separation.

Rūzbihān further discusses this idea while commenting on the ḥadīth, "God created Adam upon His form."[65] In discussing Adam's beauty, Rūzbihān recognizes the dilemma of whether to see creation (Adam) as "transparent"—which means to see only God with the eye of gathering—or to focus on the "opaqueness" of creation, which hides its Creator. Rūzbihān addresses this issue by calling God the "Artist" (*ṣāni*ʿ) and His creation "art" (*ṣun*ʿ). First, he describes the state in which he was once so overcome with the sheer creative power of the Creator such that he could only see the Creator, consequently falling in love with Him. While the eye of the spirit was fixed on God, his other eye, namely the eye of the intellect was fixated on His creation instead.

Faculty	**Object Perceived**
Eye of the Spirit	God
Eye of the Intellect	Creation

Figure 4.2 A chart showing the two inner eyes and the corresponding objects of their perception

Note that in the following passage, "intellect" refers to the partial intellect belonging to individual human beings, which is inferior to the spirit, as opposed to the universal or non-compound intellect discussed earlier, which is superior to the spirits as they derive from it. Rūzbihān writes,

> The bird of the garden of beginninglessness had become hidden in the nest of the acts with the curtain of the art of the pearl. It put on the clothing of *We have created the human being in the most beautiful stature* (Q 95:4) and was ornamented by the beauty

> (*jamāl*) of the meaning of "God created Adam upon His form" in the beauty (*ḥusn*) of *He made your forms beautiful* (Q 40:64, 64:3). The art of the Artist was lost in the Artist. I did not know what a rarity that was or what that was. Without choice the eye of my spirit lingered on that mirror, and the tumult of passionate love overcame me. The eye of the spirit remained on the Artist, and, in unbelief, the eye of the intellect on the artifact (*ṣanīʿat*). I saw the eternal beauty (*jamāl*) with the eye of the spirit, and the form of Adam with the eye of the intellect. It also took possession of me and said: "Look at the human world with the human eye."[66]

At the end of the above passage, Rūzbihān warns, "Look at the human world with the human eye." The passage is describing Rūzbihān's visionary encounter with God, who tells him to use the sober eye of separation to look at the human world rather than the intoxicated eye of gathering. This is because the latter induces a state of intoxication in which one would be unable to distinguish between the created and the uncreated.

In fact, Rūzbihān is aware of the danger of being stuck with either eye. If one is stuck with the eye of separation, one would be incapable of seeing anything beyond sensible phenomena, which is also problematic for seekers of God.[67] His defense of the love of beautiful human faces may even seem to suggest defense of *shāhid-bāzī*, literally meaning "witness-play," referring to an often-criticized practice of watching beautiful youths merely to enjoy the sight of them as manifestations of divine beauty. Later in Muslim history *shāhid-bāzī* became almost synonymous with homoeroticism in some circles and was vehemently denounced by jurists and theologians. Although Rūzbihān does not use the term *shāhid-bāzī* in his writings, he does use the term *shāhid* in a way that is consistent with much of earlier Sufi literature. For instance, Rūzbihān calls Adam *shāhid*, that is, a beautiful being through whom God is witnessed.

Instead of *shāhid-bāzī*, Henry Corbin uses another term to characterize Rūzbihān's approach to human beauty:

jamāl-parastī (or *zībāʾī-parastī*), meaning "adoration of beauty."[68] However, no Sufis who were later thought to belong to this trend of thought had used the phrase to label themselves in their own times, so this label is hardly perfect, especially since "adoration" may connote "worship," when the only proper object of worship is God, as Sufi teachers repeatedly affirm. Rūzbihān would support the adoration of the "beautiful" inasmuch as it reminds one of the divine beauty. Gradually, one can cultivate the eye to see that divine beauty disclosing itself in all things.

Summary

Rūzbihān's distinction between cosmic and human beauty is closely related to his discussion of God's essence, attributes, and acts. He argues that cosmos has general beauty insofar as it is a divine act, a divine creation. Human beings, in contrast, have specific beauty, consisting of the divine attributes, which in turn describe the divine essence. However, the degrees of their specific beauty vary and largely depend on their effort in beautifying their souls by eliminating vices or ugly qualities.

Rūzbihān presents the driving force for God's creation as *the most beautiful creator* (Q 23:14) to be His eternal desire to be recognized, as expressed by the ḥadīth of the Hidden Treasure. Beauty creates beautiful things, which seek to return to their origin. In other words, beauty is the origin and end of human existence as well as the means of returning to the origin. Hence, becoming beautiful and finding divine beauty in all things including oneself are the goal of human life. At the same time, they constitute the fulfillment of the covenant, because it was a covenant of love, promising to love only that beautiful God whom human beings witnessed on that primordial day. If they want to encounter that beautiful God again in this life and the next, that is possible only by beautifying their own souls by embodying the full range of the most beautiful names of God. This is a task too heavy for most human beings without guides on the path. And these guides are the prophets, who represent the most beautiful class of human beings.

5

The Prophetology of Beauty

Surely you have a beautiful example in God's messenger.
—Qur'ān 33:21

Human beauty is superior to cosmic beauty, but not all human beauty is equal. At the zenith of human beauty stand the prophets, who represent the highest degree of human perfection. Rūzbihān calls the prophets the mirrors of God and argues, "Adam, Joseph, Moses, Jesus, and Muhammad…are the quarries of the innate human nature of beauty that derives from the beauty of the beginningless, for God makes His beauty appear from them in the world. Hence, beauty (*ḥusn*) is inherited from them by the people of beauty (*jamāl*) in this world and the next, and they are at the center of God's beauty (*ḥusn*) in the world."[1] While all prophets are beautiful, five figures stand out in Rūzbihān's discussion: Adam, Joseph, Abraham, Moses, and Muhammad.[2] It is in the discussion of prophetic beauty that Rūzbihān's theory of beauty culminates. The very fact that creation is a realm of relativity seems to necessitate the variety of "perfections" represented by the multiple prophets. In fact, Rūzbihān's presentation of each instance of prophetic beauty has a different emphasis, as will be seen in the present chapter. Discussion of prophetic beauty is prominent in Rūzbihān's writings, which led Henry Corbin to declare "prophetology of beauty" to be one of the six themes that characterize the stages of inner journey in Rūzbihān's scheme.[3]

Adam: The Symbol of Universal Human Beauty

Adam is the first human being and the first prophet, so he occupies a place of prime importance in Rūzbihān's discussion of beauty. Emblematic is the following episode of Adam's life in paradise that Rūzbihān recounts: "Adam toured around paradise and returned to the [divine] presence, embarrassed. God asked him, 'What is this embarrassment?' He replied, 'Out of delight with my beauty (*jamāl*), because Thou hast not created any creature in paradise more beautiful (*aḥsan*) than I.'"[4] Rūzbihān constantly praises and admires Adam because he represents the beauty and perfection of the original human state. He emerges as a key figure in both *ʿAbhar al-ʿāshiqīn* and *Mashrab al-arwāḥ*, where Rūzbihān mentions Adam almost as often as Muhammad. In *ʿAbhar al-ʿāshiqīn*, a work of about 140 pages, Rūzbihān mentions Adam nearly seventy times. In the very last and highest station in the spirits' journey to God, namely the 1,001st station in *Mashrab al-arwāḥ*, Rūzbihān presents a crucial discussion of Adam. What is it about Adam that fascinated Rūzbihān so much? One useful way to examine this question is to investigate the contrast between Adam and the angels, discussed extensively in the Qurʾān and often commented upon by Rūzbihān.

We saw in the previous chapter that as the forefather of all humanity Adam symbolizes generic human beauty, for the Qurʾānic term *Ādam* refers both to Adam as an individual and to the human being (*insān*) generically, though a crucial difference remains: all are human, but not all are prophets. Most people are beautiful only potentially; their innate human nature of beauty (*fiṭrat al-ḥusn*) awaits rediscovery. In contrast, Adam and other prophets possess beauty in full actuality. In Rūzbihān's view, Qurʾānic verses and ḥadīths about Adam simply demonstrate the power of human beauty in full actualization. Key to his discussion of Adam's beauty is the Qurʾānic episode of God presenting Adam to the angels and commanding the latter to prostrate toward him:

> When thy Lord said to the angels, "Indeed, I am placing on earth a vicegerent," they said, "Wilt Thou place therein one who will do corruption there and shed blood, while we glorify Thee and proclaim Thee holy?" He said, "Indeed, I know what you do not know." And He taught Adam the names, all of them. Then He presented them unto the angels and said, "Now tell Me the names of these, if you speak truly." They said, "Glory belongs to Thee! We have no knowledge except what Thou hast taught us. Indeed Thou art All-Knowing, All-Wise. He said, "O Adam, tell them their names." When he told them their names, He said, "Did I not tell you that I know the unseen [things] of the heavens and the earth? I know what you display and what you were hiding. When We said to the angels, "Prostrate to Adam," they prostrated themselves except Iblīs; he refused and waxed proud, so he was one of the unbelievers. (Q 2:30–34)

In this Qurʾānic episode, the angels prostrate to Adam because of his knowledge of *the names, all of them* (Q 2:31), which they lacked. While this verse is often understood to mean that God taught Adam the names of *all things,* Rūzbihān also takes it to mean all the names of God, that is, the most beautiful names of God. He writes, "Adam became more knowledgeable than the angels because he knew all His most beautiful names, which are the keys to the doors of the treasuries of the [divine] attributes and the realities of the [divine] essence."[5] He explains elsewhere that *the names* that God taught to Adam were such that "in them was the announcement of all of the essence, attributes, qualities, and acts. He taught what was and what will be."[6]

Rūzbihān maintains that Adam did not simply have knowledge of the divine names, but they were deeply ingrained in his being. In interpreting another verse, *Verily God has chosen Adam and Noah* (Q 3:33), Rūzbihān argues that this is what made Adam superior to the angels.

> He chose Adam by the knowledge of the [divine] attributes. He unveiled the beauty (*jamāl*) of the

> [divine] essence before creating the world in the eternity of eternity. When He wanted to create [Adam's] spirit, He looked toward His majesty through His beauty and looked toward His beauty through His majesty. Then from these two looks appeared Adam's spirit, which He created with a specific attribute. He blew a spirit into his spirit, which is the knowledge of the [divine] attributes....Hence, through these attributes, he has precedence over the noble, dutiful angels.[7]

Rūzbihān also explains that God commanded the angels, "*Prostrate to Adam*" (Q 7:11), because God "disclosed Himself to [the angels] through the light of His beauty (*jamāl*) from the mirror of Adam's face."[8] In this process, Adam became "the *qibla* of the self-disclosure of the attributes and the essence."[9] Therefore, it was not toward Adam's humanity that God commanded the angels to prostrate; it was toward the divine beauty that was manifest in Adam. The only creature in this episode that did not prostrate to Adam at God's command was Iblīs because, Rūzbihān explains, "he was veiled from that majesty and beauty by his looking at himself, his making analogy, and his ignorance."[10]

One theme that emerges here is the close connection between beauty and knowledge or recognition (*maʿrifa*). The dividing line between those who prostrated to Adam and Iblīs was whether or not they were able to recognize God's beauty and majesty in Adam. Rūzbihān points out this connection more directly in the following passage: "The difference between things deemed beautiful and things deemed ugly is that God created what is deemed beautiful to be a mirror of gentleness and what is deemed ugly to be a mirror of severity. Severity came to be the locus of disavowal (*nakarat*), and gentleness the locus of recognition."[11] Recognition of reality leads to finding beauty and deeming things beautiful; disavowal of reality results in finding ugliness or deeming things ugly. The latter describes Iblīs's state in which he refused to bow down to Adam.

Rūzbihān makes a further point: it is wrong to deem God's majestic aspect ugly and only His beautiful (*jamīl*) aspect beautiful (*ḥasan*), for they together comprise God's *ḥusn*, while there is no ugliness in God.

> If an idle talker says that what appears in Adam's face is the same in a face deemed ugly, then he has not recognized the marvelous innate human nature and the extract of nearness. Do not listen to his sorcery, fraud, trickery and meaningless talk, because it is all nonsense. If he says that [i.e., what appears in Adam's face] is apparent in this [i.e., human face deemed ugly], these are purely foolish words. Those who profess oneness know that what is deemed ugly is one of the relative things, for in eternity itself, there is nothing ugly. But he [i.e., the idle talker] has supposed that His severe face is uglier.[12]

Here the distinction between *jamāl* and *ḥusn* becomes essential, because Rūzbihān is arguing that it is the mistaken identification of God's *jamāl* with *ḥusn* that leads to another mistaken identification of God's *jalāl* with *qubḥ*. It is true that in the created realm of relative things, things deemed ugly may reflect God's severity, as discussed in the previous quote. However, in the eternal realm of the absolute, there is nothing but *ḥusn*, with no room for ugliness, things deemed ugly, or even things deemed beautiful. This is because absolute ugliness is by definition nonexistence, and things deemed beautiful or ugly are relative things, therefore, do not belong to the realm of the absolute.

Rūzbihān notes that the angels were also ignorant when they protested to God, saying, "*Wilt Thou place therein one who will do corruption and shed blood, while we glorify Thee by praise and proclaim Thee holy?*" (Q 2:30). He writes, "When [the angels] did not know God truly and were incapable of perceiving the truth…they were turned away from the door of Lordship and God turned them toward Adam…because they were worshipping God in ignorance."[13] Here Rūzbihān presents the angels as ignorant worshippers of God. In a more nuanced presentation of the difference between the angels and human beings who share Adam's level of knowledge, he writes:

> The difference between the bearing witness (*shahāda*) of the angels and that of the folk of knowledge among the children of Adam is that the angels bore witness with respect to certitude and the possessors of knowledge with respect to witnessing (*mushāhada*). Also, the testimony of the angels was from the vision of the acts, and the testimony of the knowers was from the vision of the attributes. Moreover, the testimony of the angels was from the vision of tremendousness, but the testimony of the knowers was from the vision of beauty (*jamāl*). Hence fear was born from [the angels'] vision, but hope [was born] from the knowers' vision.[14]

Another difference between the angels and Adam is that God created the angels to worship Him, but He created Adam to love Him. Rūzbihān explains that God "did not see any pure lover in the realm of being as He would have desired. So He placed Adam for the sake of love, because He created the angels for the sake of worship. Upon consultation with the angels, He made them recognize that they are empty of love due to their preoccupation with Him by way of worship."[15] Since love is the inevitable response to seeing beauty, if the angels do not love God, it is because they are unable to see God's beauty.

The idea that the angels are compulsory worshippers of God who do not know passionate love is a common theme in Sufi literature. Even though the angels are usually placed above all other creatures in the hierarchy of being, when contrasted with the best of human beings—that is, those who have lived up to their innate nature—the angels become the same as the rest of nonhuman creatures in the sense that they are all static "end-products" of God's act of pronouncing "*Be!*" (Q 36:82), out of which they emerged. Both the angels and nonhuman creatures are incapable of disobeying God, for which reason they can never move "up" or "down" in relation to God. They are fixed in their own places, and God will neither reward nor punish them for their action because they do only what God commands them to do. They worship God out of compulsion, but never out of love, for love by nature is voluntary and can never be forced. In contrast, human beings constantly fluctuate in their relation to God, either by obeying or disobeying God. If they do obey, they do so out of love for Him. Rūzbihān shows that it is this possibility of love for God that puts humans above all other creatures, including the angels.

Adam's superiority over the angels is clear, but so is the superiority of the rest of the prophets over the angels. Then what fascinated Rūzbihān about Adam so much that he praised him much more often than most other prophets? There seems to be nothing special about Adam's beauty, because it is shared by all humanity in their innate nature. In fact, it is precisely the universality of Adamic beauty that seems to constitute its unique appeal for Rūzbihān. Adam symbolizes the original human perfection and beauty that all human beings are able to rediscover within themselves. Hence, Rūzbihān's celebration of Adam's beauty turns out to be the celebration of the beauty of innate human nature—what he calls *fiṭrat al-ḥusn*—which is waiting to be rediscovered by each human being. The human quest, then, is to recover the primordial state in which Adam existed in the full image of God, embodying all His most beautiful attributes. When people achieve that state, Rūzbihān says that they become "the second Adam"[16]—and that, Rūzbihān seems to suggest, is the goal of human life.

Joseph: The Beautiful Prophet

The prophet most commonly associated with the idea of beauty in Islam is undoubtedly Joseph. The twelfth chapter of the Qurʾān—Sūrat Yūsuf—is named after him and devoted to his story, providing ample evidence for his special beauty, both external and internal, that is, his attractive physical appearance and moral uprightness. The significance of Joseph's beauty is also noted in the Ḥadīth literature. In line with the Qurʾānic depiction of Joseph as an extremely beautiful human being, Muhammad is reported to have said, "Joseph was given half of [all] beauty" (*shaṭr al-ḥusn*).[17] The Qurʾān even calls Sūrat Yūsuf *the most beautiful of tales* (Q 12:3).

Rūzbihān comments: "How would it not be *the most beautiful of tales*? This tale is eternal without beginning or end. Every beauty (*ḥusn*) in the world goes back to it, and every beauty and everything deemed beautiful emerge from it."[18]

Rūzbihān's most concentrated treatment of Joseph is found in his Qurʾān commentary on Sūrat Yūsuf, even though the predominant theme there is not beauty per se but rather love (*ʿishq*), specifically the love of Jacob and Zulaykhā for Joseph. This is nothing unusual, as beauty is almost invariably discussed along with love, and love is a common discussion in Sufi texts, because it designates the true relationship between human beings and God.[19] In *ʿAbhar al-ʿāshiqīn*, Rūzbihān spends more time praising Adam's beauty than Joseph's, and the same applies to *Mashrab al-arwāḥ*, in which he mentions Joseph at various points but usually in passing. Thus, outside Rūzbihān's Qurʾān commentary, the figure of Joseph finds no concentrated treatment in Rūzbihān's works.

The relative dispersion of Rūzbihān's discussion of Joseph's beauty does not undermine his importance for Rūzbihān's understanding of prophetic beauty. In fact, he does not shy away from making such striking statements about Joseph as, "The entire world was not worth a single hair of Joseph";[20] and "our master [Muhammad] said that 'half of [all] beauty was given' to Joseph. His beauty (*ḥusn*) came as miracles and signs, for in him was the mark of God's beauty (*jamāl*)."[21] These are statements that Rūzbihān makes to highlight the true worth of Joseph in contrast to the *paltry price* (Q 12:20) for which the caravan sold him as a slave in Egypt.

In interpreting the verse, *When Joseph said to his father, "O father, indeed I saw eleven stars, the sun, and the moon prostrating to me"* (Q 12:4), Rūzbihān writes, "So the sun is like the essence, the moon the attributes, and the stars the descriptions, qualities, and names."[22] Elsewhere he explains the prostration of the sun, the moon, and the stars to Joseph in this manner:

> In the mirror of his beauty (*jamāl*) the countenance of the beginningless beauty appeared, so the planets of the heavens of messengerhood prostrated to him reverently, just as the angels did to Adam. This is because both were the Kaʿbas of the

> attributes as well as the rising places of the sun of beginningless things. Because of that, the sun worshippers of eternity prostrated to those two princes of nonexistence.[23]

The "sun" represents God Himself, who is the only proper object of worship and prostration by the creatures. Joseph and Adam were prostrated to because both displayed the divine attributes, through which the sun of the divine essence shines forth, even though they are "princes of nonexistence," that is, prophets created *ex nihilo* by God.

Rūzbihān recognizes that the beauty of both Joseph and Adam was due to an endowment of the divine attributes, but he seems to regard Joseph's beauty as superior to Adam's because angels prostrated to Adam, but Jacob and his sons prostrated to Joseph, and prophets are superior to angels.

> [Joseph] was the second Adam because he had the same garb of lordship that Adam had. When the angels saw what they saw upon Adam, they all prostrated to him. However, here noble prophets prostrated to him, and they are better than the angels. How should they not prostrate to these two when the holy lights and the majesty of the gloriousness shine forth from [their] faces?[24]

From the theological viewpoint, the prostration of creatures to another creature—even a prophet—poses a problem. Rūzbihān explains that it happened in the cases of Adam and Joseph because these were instances of becoming clothed (*iltibās*). Joseph became clothed in the divine attributes, which are what Jacob and his sons witnessed, causing them to prostrate.[25]

Rūzbihān often discusses Joseph's beauty as a mirror. He writes about him, "In the mirror of his beauty (*jamāl*) the face of eternal beauty was apparent";[26] "He was the mirror of the Real's beauty (*ḥusn*), and his beauty was an effect of the quarries of beginningless beauty."[27] Like the Kaʿba in an earlier passage, the mirror signifies the locus of divine self-disclosure. To be a mirror of God's beauty is to be clothed in His beauty: "The beauty (*ḥusn*) of the beginningless beauty (*jamāl*) clothed

[Joseph's] face, and in God's lands he was God's mirror from which the Real disclosed Himself to the worshippers."[28]

In the story as told in Sūrat Yūsuf, the first person to display intense affection for Joseph was his father, Jacob. Rūzbihān takes Jacob's love for Joseph as an indication of Jacob's strong love for God, as he writes about Jacob, "His love (*ʿishq*) for Joseph was nothing but love for the Real. Joseph's beauty (*jamāl*) was a means of approach to God's beauty in love. It was for this reason that our master [Muhammad] said, '[Joseph] was given half of [all] beauty.'"[29] Rūzbihān also writes, "[Joseph's] beauty was from that [divine] beauty, and the light of the attributes in his creation (*khalq*) and character (*khuluq*) was from that very perfection [of God]."[30]

After Joseph was separated from his father by his half-brothers' plot (cf. Q 12:9–18), the first person to discover Joseph was a water-carrier of the caravan that happened to pass by the well into which Joseph had been cast. Upon discovering Joseph in the well, the water-carrier says, "*Good news! Here is a boy*" (Q 12:19). Rūzbihān interprets this verse as meaning, "This is the one through whom eternity is witnessed (*shāhid al-qidam*)."[31] As discussed earlier, *shāhid* literally means "witness," a term that has gained a special connotation in later Sufi literature (especially in the Persianate world). It designates a beautiful person through whom divine beauty can be witnessed and contemplated upon.[32] Rūzbihān often calls Joseph a *shāhid,* for instance, in such phrase as "Jacob's passionate love for that *shāhid* of God,"[33] that is, the person through whom God is witnessed. However, the water-carrier from the caravan did not call Joseph a *shāhid* but merely referred to him as "a boy" (*ghulām*), which certainly does not do justice to either Joseph's extreme beauty or his status as a noble prophet. In other words, the water-carrier did not have full perception of Joseph's perfect qualities when he made the above statement. Rūzbihān explains that this is the reason why the caravan ends up selling Joseph *for a paltry price* (Q 12:20): "God had a secret in Joseph and He concealed His secret from them. If He had unveiled the reality of what He had put in him, they would have died. Do you not see how they said, '*Here is a boy*'? If they knew the traces of [divine] power in him, they would have said, 'This is a prophet and a righteous man.'"[34]

Rūzbihān also writes, "When they did not recognize him through the specific characteristics of prophecy and sainthood and did not see the traces of God's beauty (*jamāl*) upon him, they sold him *for a paltry price* (Q 12:20) due to their ignorance of him and of the treasures of power, the lights of witnessing, and the divinely-given knowledges of the unseen placed within him."[35] Thus, the connection between beauty and knowledge is again clear: people's perception of prophetic beauty depends on their level of understanding.

Another important character in Sūrat Yūsuf is Zulaykhā, the unnamed wife of the man from Egypt who buys Joseph in the Qurʾān (the biblical Potiphar), who is attracted to Joseph. She strikes a good contrast with Jacob, whose particular affection for Joseph was due to his awareness of prophetic qualities in Joseph. However, Sufi commentators on the Qurʾān did not hesitate to elevate Zulaykhā's love for Joseph to the love of God. This interpretation appears prominently in versions of the *Joseph and Zulaykhā* tale in Persian literature culminating in that by Jāmī (d. 1492). Rūzbihān takes a similar line of argument when he presents Zulaykhā's passionate love for Joseph as coming from a higher origin than *shahwa,* or sexual appetite. He interprets the verse, *She made for him and he would have made for her* (Q 12:24), as indicating the inseparability of beauty and love: "Zulaykhā's passionate love and Joseph's beauty (*jamāl*) are two attributes that stem from two beginningless quarries, and they are the attributes of beginningless beauty and beginningless love (*maḥabba*)."[36] Thus, Joseph and Zulaykhā symbolize beauty and love, which are joined for eternity and the inseparability of which is one of the common themes in Sufi literature.

Another group who witness Joseph's beauty in Sūrat Yūsuf are the women of Egypt. Upon seeing Joseph, they proclaim, *"God save us! This is no mortal; he is no other than a noble angel"* (Q 12:31). Their calling Joseph *a noble angel* indicates their realization that Joseph's beauty transcends ordinary human beauty, but like the water-carrier, they failed to see the truth about him: that he was a prophet—neither a mere young boy nor an angel. Rūzbihān writes, "They saw him in the attribute of holy angels…meaning: This is no person to delude anyone into having sexual appetite. He is hallowed beyond our world because upon him is the garb of the angels [made] of the beaming lights and the divine proof."[37]

Part of the evidence that the Egyptian women noticed something special about Joseph's beauty is that they cut their hands upon seeing him: "O possessor of intellect! Understand that when the female companions of Joseph saw Joseph, they saw the garb of Lordship upon the locus of servanthood. Hence, upon seeing him they fell into [the state] in which the angels fell, prostrating to Adam upon seeing him."[38] Such is the effect of perceiving divine beauty in the prophets. The fact that the women of Egypt cut their hands highlights their sense of bewilderment and awe.

Zulaykhā was the only person in the gathering who did not cut her hands. By focusing on this fact, Rūzbihān makes another point: Zulaykhā was superior to the women of Egypt in appreciating Joseph's beauty, as she was better prepared to bear the actual sight of its intensity: "Zulaykhā knew that [the women of Egypt] were too weak to bear the initial sights of Joseph, his beauty (*ḥusn*), beauty (*jamāl*), gentleness, and visage."[39] Since Zulaykhā had become accustomed to the beauty of Joseph over time, she was not bewildered to the point of cutting herself with a knife. Here emerges another important fact about human perception of beauty: one must have the receptivity and preparedness for bearing its sight. Otherwise one will be bewildered by its intensity and not be able to perceive it fully.

Just as Adam's superior beauty and knowledge caused Iblīs's envy, which became a major source of the trials of the children of Adam, Joseph's beauty became the source of tribulation for him and those around him. Joseph's beauty was so intense that it caused diverse reactions: intense affection and love (Jacob), envy (his half-brothers), passionate love (Zulaykhā), and bewilderment (the women of Egypt). The complex human attributes and psychological states that arose in reaction to Joseph's beauty have no doubt contributed to elevating Sūrat Yūsuf as one of the most extensively commented and elaborated upon *sūra*s in Muslim history.

While there are certain parallels between the Qurʾānic stories of Adam and Joseph, one key difference is that Rūzbihān understands Joseph's beauty to be special in the sense that it was not given to all humans, unlike Adam's beauty, which lies in each human being's innate nature. In contrast to the Adam story, which deals with the human situation across the board, the Joseph story focuses on his chosenness as a locus of the extraordinary manifestation of divine beauty. As the intensively beautiful human being, Joseph's life becomes the epicenter of the most intense love—one that eventually transforms his lover into a lover of God in the Sufi retelling. This seems to be what makes Joseph's story the "most beautiful" of stories.

Moses: The Witness to the Self-Disclosure of the Divine Beauty

For many Muslim thinkers, the most significant Qur'ānic episode of Moses is his encounter with God's self-disclosure (*tajallī*) on the mountain. He said, *"My Lord, show me so that I may look upon Thee."* God replied, *"Thou shalt not see Me, but look at the mountain. If it stays firmly in its place, then thou shalt see Me." When his Lord disclosed Himself to the mountain, He made it crumble into dust, and Moses fell down in a swoon* (Q 7:143). According to Rūzbihān, this was not the self-disclosure of "God" but rather of God's beauty. He interprets Moses's request this way: "If You were to show me Your beauty (*jamāl*), I would be able to look at You." Rūzbihān explains that Moses made this request not because he was unable to see God. Rather, "every atom of Moses saw God. When his intoxication became predominant and his yearning increased, the formalities of knowledge fell away from him, and only passionate love remained. Then the tongue of expansion got into motion in search of awareness of the Reality."[40]

God's reply to Moses's request was, *"Thou shalt not see Me."* Rūzbihān explains that this was the denial of the possibility for Moses as a creature to see God's essence directly. However, God does not simply leave Moses at that but suggests that he "see" God through the intermediary of creation, that is, the mountain. Rūzbihān writes, "The Real replied to him saying, *'Thou shalt not see Me'*—that is, 'You will not perceive Me just as I am, because you have the intermediary of temporal origination in the midst—even though you have from Me beginningless eyes and endless sight.' Then He turned him over to an intermediary by saying, *'Look at the mountain.'*"[41] Note the difference between "looking" (*naẓara*) and "seeing" (*ra'ā*): everyone can *look,* but only some will *see,* just as everyone who *listens* will not necessarily *hear* (cf., Q 7:198). When God finally disclosed Himself to the mountain, "Moses saw the beauty (*jamāl*) of eternity in the mirror of the mountain, and then he swooned."[42] Thus, Moses had an indirect vision of God.

Rūzbihān provides another commentary on God's reply to Moses, *"Thou shalt not see Me but look at the mountain"*:

> "As long as you are you, you will not see Me through the description of eternity, subsistence, the assaults of tremendousness, and magnificence. Look at your likeness in the realm of temporal origination, that is, the mountain. Look at the mountain, because in you is the defect of temporal origination, and you will not see Me except through the intermediary of temporal origination." So He made the mountain a mirror of His acts and then disclosed Himself through His attribute to His specific act and then to the mountain. Then Moses saw the beauty of eternity in the mirror of the mountain. He *fell down in a swoon,* because he reached his goal to the extent of his state. Had He disclosed Himself solely to Moses, then Moses would have become dust; and had He disclosed Himself solely to the mountain, the mountain would have been burnt down to the seventh earth, for He disclosed Himself to the mountain from the source of exaltedness and the glories of beginninglessness.[43]

There is an unfathomable gap between the Creator and the created, the eternal and the temporal. Creatures—even prophets—can never see God in Himself (i.e., in His essence) but only His attributes as manifest in creation (i.e., divine act). That is why God disclosed His attribute, beauty, to Moses through the intermediary of a divine act, that is, the mountain functioning as a mirror. In the preceding sections on Adam and Joseph, we have seen that Rūzbihān calls both Adam and Joseph "mirrors" of God for others to see God. One difference here is that it is an inanimate object, the mountain, that serves as a mirror to display God to Moses (as opposed to Adam for the angels).

Other Qur'ānic verses also indicate Moses's connection to beauty, such as, *"I threw love upon thee from Me and that thou mightest be made upon My eyes"* (Q 20:39). This is a verse commonly cited by Muslim thinkers primarily to indicate the connection between Moses and the notion of love. And if God loves Moses, he must be beautiful. This is a point that Rūzbihān also makes:

> Adam was the *qibla* of the angels, because he was God's means of approach [placed] between Him and His angels, for on him was the garb of His majesty and beauty. Thus [the Prophet] said, "God created Adam upon His form," meaning that He threw upon him the beauty (*ḥusn*) of His attributes and the light of witnessing Him. Likewise, God said with regard to the reality of Moses, *"I threw love upon thee from Me."* And *love* is a specific property of His beginningless attributes.[44]

While Moses had a similar function to that of Adam and Joseph in that he was a mirror to display God's beauty, Rūzbihān does not call Moses a *qibla* because in contrast to Adam and Joseph he was never an object of prostration in the Qur'ān. If Adam received his beauty by being created upon God's form, then it was God's throwing love upon Moses that made him beautiful. Both the form and the love consist of the most beautiful divine attributes. In other words, God's casting love upon Moses meant endowing him with the most beautiful attributes.

In discussing the same verse in *Mashrab al-arwāḥ*, Rūzbihān explains that the "love" (*maḥabba*) that God cast upon Moses consisted in "comeliness" (*malāḥa*):

> The recognizer said—God bless his spirit—"Love and beauty (*ḥusn*) are two beginningless attributes,

> neither of which emerges in the truthful servant without the other, because there is no division in the attributes." This meaning is well known from God's speech in which He said concerning His speaking companion, Moses: *I threw love upon thee from Me and for thee to be made upon My eyes* [Q 20:39]. Qurʾān commentators said, "There is comeliness in your eyes, so no one sees you without loving you."[45]

In the above passage we can also see the recurring theme of the inseparability of love and beauty and the idea that seeking intimacy (*istiʾnās*) is a natural effect of beauty. In his commentary on Q 20:39 in the *ʿArāʾis*, Rūzbihān makes the connection with intimacy more explicit: the verse "means that whoever saw him loved him and sought intimacy with him."[46] In sum, Rūzbihān presents Moses both as a lover of God who seeks a vision of His beauty and as a beautiful prophet embodying the divine attributes.

Abraham: The Seeker of Intimacy with Divine Beauty

While Rūzbihān discusses Adam, Joseph, and Moses as beautiful in themselves, he presents Abraham primarily as a seeker of beauty, or to use Rūzbihān's expressions, a *mustaḥsin* (literally, "one who deems beautiful") and a *mustaʾnis bi-l-mustaḥsanāt* (one who seeks intimacy with things deemed beautiful). Rūzbihān's understanding of him as a *mustaḥsin* is largely due to the famous Qurʾānic event of Abraham saying about the stars, moon, and sun, "*This is my Lord*" (Q 6:76; 6:77; 6:78).

The passage begins with the verse, *Thus We were showing Abraham the sovereignty of the heavens and the earth* (Q 6:75). Rūzbihān explains that God "tested him with the vision of the sovereignty to distract him from witnessing eternity by the sweetness of seeing it."[47] This was Abraham's first test, followed by the second test: *When night outspread over him, he saw a star and said, "This is my Lord"* (Q 6:76). Rūzbihān explains that Abraham mistakenly regarded the star as his Lord because he was fascinated by the beauty of the star as a divine act. Abraham was then in the station of "becoming clothed," for he saw the star clothed in divine attributes:

> In the same way He tested him at his beginning with the station of becoming clothed when the star of the self-disclosure of the light of the specific act became manifest in the form of Sirius. He gazed at it *when* the *night* of testing *outspread over him*. Then he saw with the eye of desire the light of His specific act, whose drinking place is the lights of the attribute. Then he said with the tongue of wonder, "*This is my Lord.*"[48]

In a way, Rūzbihān's notion of "becoming clothed" (*iltibās*) encompasses the two opposing symbols of the world as a sign and a veil (*ḥijāb, sitr*), pointing out the ambivalent status of God's creation that reveals and hides God at the same time. While the fact it hides and covers up God may be taken as a "bad" thing for the seekers of God, it is obvious to Rūzbihān that God needs to be veiled in order to be seen, for His essence can never be seen directly by creatures. Abraham's seeing the star clothed in divine attributes intensifies his wonder and desire for his Lord, who he realizes is not the star that sets.

The next stage of Abraham's search for God is described in the subsequent verse: *When he saw the moon rising, he said, "This is my Lord." But when it set, he said, "If my Lord does not guide me, surely I will be of the people gone astray"* (Q 6:77). At this stage, Abraham sees divine attributes in the moon:

> *When* the *night* of separation from the first station *outspread over him*, the light of the attribute appeared from the quarry of the essence. It became manifest to him in the moon from the light of the specific act. He looked at it and saw the witnessing of the attribute in the act. Then He said with the tongue of yearning, "*This is my Lord*." Then the turn of intimate friendship turned around him. He nurtured him with the light of joining and made him reach the station of passionate love. He made him taste the flavor of the

> reality of the joy of his secret core, and his yearning to seek increase was incited.[49]

Abraham says *"This is my Lord"* (Q 6:78) for the third time in reference to the sun. Rūzbihān explains that the sun here represents the divine essence, manifesting itself in a divine act:

> Then the lights of the essence appeared in the attributes, and the lights of the attributes and the essence appeared in the specific acts. Then its lights appeared in the sun. When his present moment became limpid and pure and the darkness of the night of separation was enveloped, the sun shone upon his moment. So he looked at and saw the witnessing of the majesty of eternity in the mirror of the sun. Then he spoke with the tongue of passionate love, *"This is my Lord."* So the jealousy of eternity reached him and disengaged him from seeing the intermediaries while seeing eternity, for he saw the setting of the signs with the attribute of their annihilation in the tremendousness of the lights of eternity. Then eternity itself was unveiled to him.[50]

Through his encounter with the star, moon, and sun, Abraham underwent a three-stage transformation from a desirer to a yearner to a passionate lover of God, for he "spoke with the tongue of passionate love" when he said *"This is my Lord"* for the third time. Hence, Rūzbihān seems to maintain that at this third stage, Abraham no longer regarded a created thing (the sun) as his Lord, but he was actually seeing God's *essence* when he said about the sun, *"This is my Lord."* Hence, Abraham declares in the subsequent verse (Q 6:79): *"I have turned my face to Him who originated the heavens and the earth, as a man of pure faith. I am not of the idolaters,"* which is a declaration of his faith in the one and only God.

Rūzbihān also discusses Abraham's threefold vision in *Mashrab al-arwāḥ* in the section entitled "On deeming things beautiful," because it was Abraham's deeming the stars, moon, and sun beautiful that made him say, *"This is my Lord."* The eye that deems things beautiful is the eye of contentment.

Rūzbihān writes, "When the eye of contentment is opened in the face of trust [in God] through the light of truthfulness, and when the dust of nature is taken away by the limpidness of sincerity and the light of election, one sees the quiddity of existence and the beauty of God's production appearing from it in all atoms."[51] Such a person will "deem beautiful all the things decreed by the unseen in the clothing of the [divine] acts....For him the vision of beauty and ugliness will be equal because he is in [the midst of] the vision of tremendousness, where the traces of temporally originated things no longer remain, and the acts of severity and gentleness are equal."[52] As examples of those who are in this state, Rūzbihān mentions Abraham for saying *"This is my Lord"* and Muhammad for saying "Lord, show us things as they are."[53] In fact, Rūzbihān writes that the latter saying was Muhammad's "asking for what the intimate friend had seen."[54]

To deem things beautiful is to transcend the distinction between *jamāl* and *jalāl* and to see *ḥusn* in each thing, which is a pointer to the overall beauty and goodness of God. Those capable of finding *ḥusn* in every thing will be capable of recognizing God behind each thing. Hence, Rūzbihān concludes, "Deeming things beautiful does not occur to anyone except one who sees Him who brings things into existence in the things."[55] As discussed in the previous chapter, there are two complementary ways of perceiving reality: the eye of gathering and the eye of separation. Between the two, it is the eye of gathering that "sees Him who brings things into existence in the things," thereby bringing together the Creator and the created in a single perception. Hence, the eye of gathering deems things beautiful, and this is the mode of perception that Abraham had in saying *"This is my Lord,"* recognizing God's *ḥusn* in the celestial objects.

Elsewhere in the *Mashrab al-arwāḥ*, Rūzbihān comments on Abraham's words, *"This is my Lord,"* in the following manner: "This station pertains to the station of being clothed and the passionate lover's seeking intimacy with the vision of the Real in everything that is deemed beautiful."[56] In other words, the star, moon, and sun were deemed beautiful by Abraham because they were clothed in the divine attributes and essence. Since he was able to recognize God in them, he fell in love and sought intimacy with them in order to gain access to God. Rūzbihān draws the general conclusion that people seek intimacy with everything deemed beautiful because the thing reflects the divine beauty. As Rūzbihān writes, "What is deemed beautiful is deemed beautiful due to the appearance of God's beauty (*ḥusn*) within it. That is the beauty of His self-disclosure, just as He disclosed Himself to Moses in the mountain."[57] Similarly, in an account of his visions Rūzbihān writes, "I saw Abraham among the mountains where the lights of the star [of] the acts had arisen, and the acts are the mirror of the self-disclosure of the essence and the attributes. [Abraham] was seeking the Real and was saying, '*This is my Lord*.'"[58]

Rūzbihān also points to a "subtle allusion" in Abraham's statement. He writes, "'*This is my Lord*' is an excuse for the angels and the prophets in their prostration to Adam and Joseph, because in that case the Real disclosed Himself from the celestial bodies whose quarries are the [divine] acts, and in this case the Real disclosed Himself from the attributes."[59] In other words, since prostrating to what is other than God (i.e., creatures) goes against the principle of monotheism, if there is any excuse for the angels to have prostrated to Adam or Jacob to Joseph, it has already been stated by Abraham: "*This is my Lord.*" Both Adam and Joseph were loci of divine self-disclosure, clothed in the divine attributes.

In interpreting another key verse involving Abraham, Rūzbihān again presents him as a seeker of beautiful visions of God. He explains Abraham's words, "*Show me how Thou bringest the dead back to life*" (Q 2:260), as his request for "beauty (*jamāl*) in seeing those through whom God can be witnessed (*shawāhid*),"[60] that is, beautiful creatures in whom divine beauty is manifest and witnessed. Here Rūzbihān cites Ibn Khafīf as having said that "the requests by Moses and Abraham were the same except that Abraham's was more subtle in beautiful manners when he asked to see the dead being brought back to life."[61] Nonetheless, both Moses and Abraham were asking for some vision of God, and their requests were fulfilled to a certain degree, both by way of an intermediary.

In *ʿAbhar al-ʿāshiqīn*, Rūzbihān explains that Abraham made this request (mentioned in Q 2:260) only after he had seen *the sovereignty of the heavens and the earth* (Q 6:75). His statement, *Show me how Thou bringest the dead back to life* (Q 2:260) was his another attempt at finding God through observation of the world, having been dissatisfied with his attempt to find Him in the star, the moon, and the sun, "because in them there was no trace of beauty (*jamāl*)."[62] It is worth noting that this is an alternative reading of the verses about Abraham's gazing at the sky, as Qurʾān commentators, not least Rūzbihān, often offer multiple interpretations of a given verse.

In response to Abraham's request, "*Show me how Thou bringest the dead back to life*," God responds, "*Or dost thou not have faith?*" (Q 2:260). Rūzbihān explains that this "answer came because the signs [i.e., all created things, or the divine acts] are the locus of faith," but "witnessing the beauty (*jamāl*) of eternity does not occur in the signs."[63] Abraham had faith in God because he was able to see the world as His act and recognize Him as the Creator. However, Abraham wanted to see more than God's act—His attribute, and specifically His beauty. Here, Rūzbihān's interpretation of the Abraham story comes close to that of the Moses story, in which Moses asks God, *My Lord, show me so that I may look upon Thee* (Q 7:143).

Later in the same work, Rūzbihān takes another perspective and highlights differences between Abraham and Moses. Abraham asked for an indirect vision of God by way of creation becoming clothed by Him; in contrast, Moses asked for a direct vision of God. Rūzbihān associates Abraham with sobriety and *iltibās*, and Moses with intoxication and "sheer witnessing" (*mushāhada-yi ṣirf*), by which he means "witnessing of the Real without intermediary."[64]

Although Rūzbihān offers various interpretations of Abraham's and Moses's encounters with God as depicted in the Qurʾān, he consistently highlights the unbridgeable gap between God and the human being, the uncreated and the created. As Rūzbihān writes, "God replied to His intimate friend by saying, '*Or dost thou not have faith?*, for surely you did not perceive Me with the conditions of eternity's secret, since you are a created thing, imprisoned by the qualities of temporal origination.'"[65]

Muhammad: The Most Beautiful Prophet

How then does the beauty of Islam's last and most important prophet compare with that of the four prophets discussed above? Rūzbihān has no doubts as to Muhammad's superior beauty. In one passage, for example, he compares them to indicate their different degrees of beauty: "If Abraham had seen Joseph and Adam, he would have seen in them much more than what he saw in the celestial bodies.... If all of them had seen the beauty (*jamāl*) of the master of the prophets and messengers, they would have fallen into rapture in the wastelands and deserts."[66]

Muhammad's superior beauty is connected to his superior knowledge of God, for as mentioned, human beauty entails experiential knowledge of the divine. Rūzbihān contrasts Adam with Muhammad and points out that only Muhammad can have a vision of God's essence.

> Adam's heart is the closest heart to God except for Muhammad's heart, so no heart in all of God's creation compares to [Muhammad's] heart, because his heart is the depository of the secret of the secrets, the realities of the lights, and the vision of the sheer essence. The Real did not open up any heart other than Muhammad's heart to the God-given knowledge, the unknown knowledge, and the realities of recognition, *tawḥīd,* unveiling, witnessing, secrets, and lights, because his heart was the oceans of [divine] self-disclosure and approach.[67]

Rūzbihān highlights the difference between Joseph and Muhammad by associating Joseph's beauty with that of the divine attributes and Muhammad's beauty with that of the divine essence.

> [The Prophet] said, "God said, 'O Muhammad, I garbed the beauty of Joseph's face with the light of the Footstool, and I garbed the light of thy face with the light of My Throne.'" God discloses Himself to the Footstool from the light of His attributes,

> and He discloses Himself to the Throne from the light of His essence. Hence, the Footstool is illuminated by the light of the attributes, and the Throne is illuminated with the light of the essence.[68]

In the same passage he writes, "The light of the Throne is specific to the beauty of the master of the messengers and gives him superiority over Joseph. When he was asked, 'Are you more beautiful (*aḥsan*) or is Joseph?' He replied, 'I am comelier (*amlaḥ*) than Joseph.'"[69]

Rūzbihān maintains that Muhammad's superior beauty is connected to his character, as suggested by the verse, *Verily thou art upon a tremendous character* (Q 68:4). Rūzbihān explains: "[T]hat is, 'I have clothed you with My character. You are upon My character, and My character is tremendous,'"[70] for "tremendous" is one of the divine names. He then quotes al-Wāsiṭī: "This is the clothing of the attributes and being characterized by His character traits." And, quoting al-Wāsiṭī again, "God manifested His power in Jesus, His penetration in Āṣaf, and His anger in Moses's cane, while He manifested His character traits and qualities in Muhammad, as He said, *Verily thou art upon a tremendous character*."[71]

On a related ḥadīth, "Assume the character traits of the All-Merciful," Rūzbihān comments: "This is a description of someone whom God garbed in the brilliance of the holiness of the beginningless beauty (*jamāl*) and the endless majesty before the clay of the mortal human being came into being."[72] In Rūzbihān's vocabulary, "to garb" (*kasā*) means the same as "to clothe" (*albasa*) and indicates that a creature displays God's attributes. Muhammad is beautiful because God clothed him with all the most beautiful (*ḥusnā*) attributes, not least those of beauty and majesty. No other creature surpassed Muhammad in the assimilation of the divine attributes, for his spirit was "the closest creature to God."[73]

In Rūzbihān's presentation, Muhammad's superior beauty has a double significance: he is not only the most beautiful human being, but he also has the most intense vision of God's beauty. Rūzbihān discusses the Prophet's vision of God in his commentary on the verse, *The heart did not swerve in what it saw*

(Q 53:11), explaining that the Prophet saw God's beauty with his eye and heart.

> God mentioned the vision of the Prophet's heart, not the eye, because the vision of the eye is a secret between him and his Beloved. It was because of jealousy that He did not mention it, for the vision of the heart is general, but the vision of the eyesight is specific. He showed His beauty (*jamāl*) to the Prophet face-to-face, so he saw Him with his eyesight, which had been daubed with the kohl of the light of His essence and attributes. What God had willed remained in his vision through seeing face-to-face. All of his body became merciful eyes, and he saw the Real through them altogether. Then the vision joined to the heart, and his heart saw the beauty (*jamāl*) of the Real and it saw what he saw with his eye. There was no difference between what he saw with his eye and what he saw with his heart.[74]

A ḥadīth of import for Rūzbihān's discussion of Muhammad's vision of God's beauty is "I saw my Lord in the most beautiful form." Rūzbihān explains this saying in various ways in his writings. In his Ḥadīth commentary, he says, "This is from excessive love. When the servant loves his Lord, he sees Him in a beautiful form so as to have the full enjoyment of witnessing in his vision."[75] In *Mashrab al-arwāḥ* he argues that when the Prophet made the above statement he was seeing with the eye of gathering, which Rūzbihān explains here as "that which sees the lights of the attributes in the clothing of the acts."[76] Rūzbihān then compares the Prophet's statement to a Sufi saying, "I have not looked at anything without seeing God within it," and the verse, *Thou didst not throw when thou threwest, but God threw* (Q 8:17), both of which indicate the mode of perception dictated by the eye of gathering.[77]

Rūzbihān gives another reading of this ḥadīth in *ʿAbhar al-ʿāshiqīn*, where he uses it to contrast Muhammad's state with those of Abraham and Moses. He writes,

> Sobriety in passionate love was the station of Abraham. For that reason, he made a request in becoming clothed: *My Lord, show me how Thou bringest the dead back to life* (Q 2:260). Intoxication was the station of Moses. He wanted the sheer absolute. He said, *My Lord, show me so that I may look upon Thee* (Q 7:143). Both stations were preserved for Muhammad. In the station of sobriety, he said, "Show us things as they are." In the station of intoxication, he said, "I saw my Lord in the most beautiful form."...When he passed beyond temporal origination with the eye of the drunken spirit, he saw the beginningless being and said, "I do not count Thy laudations."[78]

Muhammad is not only the most beautiful prophet and the most perfect perceiver of God's beauty, but he is also the most passionate lover of beauty. Rūzbihān cites a number of ḥadīths to make this point, including "Gazing at a beautiful face increases sight"[79] and its variants, such as "Greenery and beautiful faces made him marvel";[80] "Three things increase the power of sight: gazing at greenery, gazing at beautiful faces, and gazing at flowing water";[81] and "Gazing at faces increases sight; gazing at greenery and flowing water increases sight."[82]

Rūzbihān explains the last of these sayings like this: "In the beauty (*ḥusn*) [of the face] is the light of the specific act in which the light of the essence and the attributes is clothed. In the limpidness of greenery and waters is the light of the general act within which the Real discloses the light of the specific act by its being attributed to Him."[83] Moreover, he writes, "This is from the station of the eye of gathering and within it is an allusion to the station of becoming clothed."[84] Rūzbihān understands the Prophet's love of beautiful things in the world as an indication of his vision of reality through the eye of gathering and his recognition of the world as clothed in divine attributes. In other words, the Prophet saw God in every instance of beauty in the world, so he took pleasure in looking at beautiful things.

Rūzbihān also discusses another ḥadīth, "Three things from your world were made lovable to me: good fragrance and women, and my delight is in prayer."[85] He explains that the Prophet "is seeking the lights of witnessing in the mirror of the attribute of the act—and here is no accusation of indwelling. Rather, the Real discloses Himself to those who seek to witness Him in the beautiful and the deemed beautiful."[86] Indwelling (*ḥulūl*), sometimes translated as incarnation, is a heretical belief that some theologians ascribe to some Sufis. Rūzbihān explains that finding God's beauty in a thing does not mean that God "dwells" in the thing. Rather, it constitutes God's self-disclosure, His showing of Himself, and every instance of His self-disclosure will be deemed beautiful.

The Prophet as a lover of beauty is also indicated by his act of kissing the first fruit of the season (*bākūra*), which is mentioned in the Ḥadīth literature.[87] Rūzbihān writes, "When he saw a first fruit, he would kiss it and place it upon his eyes. One of the recognizers said, 'I have not looked at anything without seeing God in it.'"[88] In *ʿAbhar al-ʿāshiqīn*, Rūzbihān explains further: "His kissing was the spirit's contact with the eternal act from love's appetite. His putting it upon his eyes was nearness's wanting nearness."[89] Here the first fruit is deemed beautiful by the kisser, who is nothing but the appreciator of its beauty and the seeker of intimacy with the beautiful. Rūzbihān explains that kissing a beautiful thing is a natural reaction for human beings.

> In everything deemed beautiful, there is the effect of that Beauty (*ḥusn*), because every particle of engendered being has a spirit from the Real's act, in which it is in direct contact with the quality of the attributes and the self-disclosure of the essence. In particular, things deemed beautiful have no eye except the eye of the Real. Whatever is closer to the quarry of beauty (*jamāl*) is closer to the covenant of love.... Whatever came forth newly in the garden of divine decrees from the Beloved, he would immediately kiss it and place it upon his eyes.[90]

Rūzbihān also refers to the rose to make a similar point, in keeping with a saying ascribed to the Prophet, "The red rose is from the splendor of God. Whenever someone wants to look at God's splendor, let him look at the red rose."[91] Rūzbihān explains:

> This is an allusion to self-disclosure and the eye of gathering, that is, the self-disclosure of the Real through the quality of splendor in the Garden, for the Garden makes the red rose grow. [The Prophet] also said, "The red rose is the master of the aromatic plants of the Garden after the myrtle," for the lights of the essence's self-disclosure penetrated the rose. The Real made it into a mirror for the beauty (*ḥusn*) of His splendor for the folk of His intimacy and His love. In the same way the red rose is the most beloved of the aromatic plants to His friends, so much so that [the Prophet] used to love it, kiss it, place it upon his eyes, and say, "This is freshly acquainted with its Lord."[92]

In sum, Muhammad is beautiful as a mirror of God, someone clothed in His attributes; he loves beauty found in things in the world because he can see, with the eye of gathering, that these things are clothed in God's beauty; and he loves beautiful things in the world because he sees God's beauty in them, further enhancing his ability to see God. It follows that to love beauty in creation is a commendable practice for humans. To do so is simply to follow the most perfect human being, who has set down for humankind a beautiful model: *Surely you have a beautiful example in God's messenger—for those who hope for God and the Last Day, and who remember God much* (Q 33:21).

Rūzbihān's discussion of beauty culminates in the prophets' beauty not only because they are the most beautiful beings in creation but also because they are the greatest lovers of beauty, which means the greatest lovers of the beautiful God, the source of all beauty. By imitating the prophets, human beings can become beautiful themselves and increase their chances of encountering God's beauty and gentleness rather than His majesty and severity in this life and the next. Love of beauty is the way of the prophets, which is nothing but their longing for the divine, with whom they have made the covenant of love. This is the longing famously encapsulated by Rūmī in one of the beginning verses of his *Mathnawī*:

> Whoever remains far from his origin
> seeks again for the days of his union.[93]

Beauty, therefore, is the origin and the end of human existence. If human beings live this life beautifully, their beauty will be the means whereby they return joyfully to their beautiful God.

NOTES

Introduction

1. Sharaf al-Dīn Ibrāhīm b. Ṣadr al-Dīn Abī Muḥammad Rūzbihān Thānī, *Tuḥfat al-ʿirfān fī dhikr sayyid al-aqṭāb Rūzbihān*, in Muḥammad Taqī Dānishpazhūh, *Rūzbihān-nāma* (Tehran: Intishārāt-i Anjuman-i Āthār-i Millī, 1347sh/1969), 110. This passage is discussed in Carl Ernst, *Rūzbihān Baqlī: Mysticism and the Rhetoric of Sainthood in Persian Sufism* (Richmond: Curzon, 1996), 4; and in Henry Corbin, *En Islam iranien: Aspects spirituels et philosophiques*, vol. 3 (Paris: Gallimard, 1971–72), 28.
2. Edward Farley, *Faith and Beauty: A Theological Aesthetic* (Aldershot: Ashgate, 2001), 117.
3. Kathleen Raine, "The Use of the Beautiful," in *Defending Ancient Springs* (London: Oxford University Press, 1967), 157.
4. The editors' introduction provides a useful survey of the shifts in scholarly discourse on beauty over the centuries.
5. As the author himself notes, Cyrus Zargar's *Sufi Aesthetics: Beauty, Love, and the Human Form in the Writings of Ibn 'Arabi and 'Iraqi* (Columbia: University of South Carolina Press, 2011) is not, despite its title, about aesthetics or beauty as such, but rather about visions of God in a beautiful human form (p. 2), which is a specific discussion in connection with beauty.
6. *The Oxford Dictionary of Art* (Oxford: Oxford University Press, 1988), s.v. "Aesthetics."
7. *The Concise Oxford Dictionary of Art Terms*, ed. Michael Clarke (Oxford: Oxford University Press, 2001), s.v. "Aesthetics."
8. *The Oxford Dictionary of Philosophy*, ed. Simon Blackburn (Oxford: Oxford University Press, 1994), s.v. "Aesthetics."
9. Nazif Hoca, "Das arabische Werk *Kitāb mašrab al-arwāḥ*," *Akten des VII. Kongresses für Arabistik und Islamwissenschaft, Göttingen, 15. bis 22. August 1974*, ed. Albert Dietrich, Abhandlungen der

Akademie der Wissenschaften in Göttingen, Philologischhistorische Klasse, Dritte Folge, no. 98 (Göttingen: Van-denhoeck und Ruprecht, 1976), 211.

10. Henry Corbin is one of the first Western scholars to discuss this term. See Corbin, "Introduction," in *Le jasmin des fidèles d'amour; Kitâb-e 'abhar al-'âshiqîn*, ed. H. Corbin and M. Muʿīn (Tehran: Département d'iranologie de l'Institut franco-iranien 1958), 6ff.
11. The best resource to familiarize oneself with representative texts from these authors is ʿAlī Akbar Afrāsiyābpūr's *Zībāʾī-parastī dar ʿirfān-i islāmī* (Tehran: Intishārāt-i Ṭahūrī, 1380sh / 2001).
12. Cf. Ernst, *Rūzbihān Baqlī: Mysticism and the Rhetoric of Sainthood in Persian Sufism* (Richmond: Curzon, 1996), 1–2; Firoozeh Papan-Matin, *The Unveiling of Secrets* Kashf al-Asrār*: The Visionary Autobiography of Rūzbihān al-Baqlī (1128–1209 A.D.)* (Leiden: Brill, 2006), 5–6.
13. Rūzbihān, *Kashf al-asrār*, ed. Papan-Matin, in *The Unveiling of Secrets*, 7–10; Ernst, trans., *The Unveiling of Secrets: Diary of a Sufi Master* (Chapel Hill: Parvardigar Press, 1997), 9–11; Ernst, *Rūzbihān Baqlī*, 2; Paul Ballanfat, "Une mystique de la ruse: Remarques sur la pensée de Rûzbehân Baqlî Shîrâzî,"in *Quatre traités inédits de Rûzbehân Baqlî Shîrâzî* (Tehran: Institut français de recherche en Iran, 1998), 58–59.
14. Ballanfat, *Quatre traités*, 64.
15. Ibid. Cf. Ernst, *Rūzbihān Baqlī*, 12n5.
16. Papan-Matin, *The Unveiling of Secrets*, 6; Ballanfat, *Quatre traités*, 68–70. His trip to Alexandria is disputed. See Papan-Matin, *The Unveiling of Secrets*, 6n6.
17. Ballanfat, *Quatre traités*, 71.
18. Ibid., 72–73.
19. Ibid., 75.
20. Ernst has compiled a handy list of works attributed to Rūzbihān in "Appendix A: The Writings of Rūzbihān Baqlī: A Checklist," in *Rūzbihān Baqlī*, 151–59.
21. An English translation of various passages from *Mashrab al-arwāḥ* can be found in Javad Nurbakhsh, *Sufi Symbolism: The Nurbakhsh Encyclopedia of Sufi Terminology*, 16 vols. (London: Khanqah-i Nimatullahi Publications, 1987–).
22. Cf. Massignon's edition of *Kitāb al-ṭawāsīn* by al-Ḥallāj (Paris: Libraire Paul Geuthner, 1913).
23. Wladimir Ivanow, "A Biography of Ruzbihan al-Baqli." *Journal and Proceedings of the Asiatic Society of Bengal* N.S. XXIV (1928): 353–61; "More on Biography of Ruzbihan al-Baqli." *Journal of the Bombay Branch of the Royal Asiatic Society* VII (1931): 1–7.

24. Muḥammad Taqī Dānishpazhūh, *Rūzbihān-nāma* (Tehran: Intishārāt-i Anjuman-i Āthār-i Millī, 1347sh/1969).
25. Paul Nwyia, ed., "Waqāʾiʿ al-Shaykh Rūzbihān al-Baqlī al-Shīrāzī: Muqtaṭafāt min kitāb *Kashf al-asrār wa mukāshafat al-anwār*," *al-Mashriq* LXIV, no. 4–5 (1970): 385–406. For a brief overview of the scholarship until 1996, see Ernst, *Rūzbihān Baqlī*, xi–xiii.
26. Corbin and Muʿīn, eds., *Le jasmin des fidèles d'amour; Kitâb-e 'abhar al-'âshiqîn* (Tehran: Département d'iranologie de l'Institut franco-iranien 1958).
27. In Henry Corbin, ed., *Commentaire sur les paradoxes des soufis (Sharh-e Shathîyât)* (Paris: Adrien-Maisonneuve, 1966).
28. Nazif Hoca, ed., *Rūzbihān al-Baḳlī ve Kitāb Kaşf al-asrār'ı ile Farsça bāzi Šiirleri* (Istanbul: Edebiyat Fakültesi Matbaası, 1971).
29. Nazif Hoca, ed., *Kitāb maşrab al-arvāḥ va huva'l-maşhūr bi-hazār u yak maḳām (bi-alfi maḳāmin va maḳāmin)* (Istanbul: Edebiyat Fakültesi Matbaasi, 1974).
30. Jawād Nūrbakhsh, ed., *ʿAbhar al-ʿāshiqīn* (Tehran: Intishārāt-i Yaldā-Qalam, 1380/2001).
31. Jawād Nūrbakhsh, ed., *Risālat al-quds wa risāla-yi ghalaṭāt al-sālikīn* (Tehran: Khānqāh-i Niʿmat Allāhī, 1351sh/1972).
32. Dānishpazhūh, *Rūzbihān-nāma* (Tehran: Intishārāt-i Anjuman-i Āthār-i Millī, 1347sh/1969).
33. See for example Schimmel's *Mystical Dimensions of Islam* (Chapel Hill: University of North Carolina Press, 1975).
34. See Ballanfat, ed., *Quatre traités*.
35. *Le dévoilement des secrets et les apparitions des lumières: Journal spirituel du maître de Shîrâz* (Paris: Seuil, 1996). Ernst published his English translation of *Kashf al-asrār* at around the same time in *The Unveiling of Secrets: Diary of a Sufi Master* (Chapel Hill: Parvardigar Press, 1997).
36. See chapter 5 of Ballanfat's introduction to *Quatre traités*.

Chapter 1. Discourse on Beauty

1. Cf. Muslim, *Kitāb al-ṣaḥīḥ* (Beirut: Dār al-Kutub al-ʿIlmiyya, 1992), 2.74; Aḥmad b. Ḥanbal, *Musnad al-imām Aḥmad* (Beirut: Dār Iḥyāʾ al-Turāth al-ʿArabī, n.d.), V.120, V.121, V.149.
2. Cf. Valérie Gonzalez, *Beauty and Islam: Aesthetics in Islamic Art and Architecture* (New York: I. B. Tauris, 2001), 19–25. Jamal Elias has an extensive discussion of Ibn al-Haytham's aesthetic theory in *Aisha's Cushion: Religious Art, Perception, and Practice*

in Islam (Cambridge: Harvard University Press, 2012), 156–60. Ḥasan Bulkhārī presents the notion of beauty in optics according to Ibn al-Haytham and Kamāl al-Dīn Fārisī in *Maʿnā wa mafhūm-i zībāʾī dar al-Manāẓir wa Tanqīḥ al-manāẓir* (Tehran: Farhangistān-i Hunar, 1387sh/2008).

3. Deborah Black, "Aesthetics in Islamic philosophy," *Routledge Encyclopedia of Philosophy*, http://www.rep.routledge.com/article/H020 (accessed May 6, 2016).
4. Aaron W. Hughes, "'God Is Beautiful and Loves Beauty': The Role of Aesthetics in Medieval Islamic and Jewish Philosophy," in *The Texture of the Divine: Imagination in Medieval Islamic and Jewish Thought* (Bloomington: Indiana University Press, 2004), 161.
5. Al-Fārābī, *Al-Farabi on the Perfect State: Abū Naṣr al-Fārābī's* Mabādiʾ ārāʾ ahl al-madīna al-fāḍila, trans. R. Walzer (Oxford: Clarendon Press, 1985), 83–85.
6. Al-Fārābī, *Perfect State*, 85.
7. Ibn Sīnā, *al-Najāt*, ed. M. Fakhrī (Beirut: Dār al-Āfāq al-Jadīda, 1985), 281. Gonzalez discusses this passage in *Beauty and Islam*, 15.
8. Al-Ghazālī, *Iḥyāʾ ʿulūm al-dīn* (Beirut: Dār al-Maʿrifa, n.d.), 4.299. Richard Ettinghausen discusses a parallel passage in *Kīmīyā-yi saʿādat* in "Al-Ghazzālī on Beauty," *Art and Thought: Issued in Honour of Dr. Ananda K. Coomaraswamy on the Occasion of His 70th Birthday*, ed. K. Bharatha Iyer (London: Luzac, 1947), 163. For further discussion of al-Ghazālī's view on beauty, see Carole Hillenbrand, "Some Aspects of al-Ghazālī's Views on Beauty," in *Gott ist schön und Er liebt die Schönheit: Festschrift für Annemarie Schimmel zum 7. April 1992 dargebracht von Schülern, Freunden und Kollegen*, ed. Alma Giese and J. Christoph Bürgel (Bern: Peter Lang, 1994), 249–65; Jamal Elias, *Aisha's Cushion*, 162–68; and Binyamin Abrahamov, *Divine Love in Islamic Mysticism: The Teachings of al-Ghazâlî and al-Dabbâgh* (London: RoutledgeCurzon, 2003), 47–56. Abrahamov argues that Ibn al-Dabbāgh, the author of *Kitāb mashāriq anwār al-qulūb wa-mafātīḥ asrār al-ghuyūb*, largely follows al-Ghazālī's understanding of beauty though with some points of divergence; for Ibn al-Dabbāgh's view on beauty's connection to perfection and pleasure, see Abrahamov, *Divine Love*, 105–13.
9. For a history of Muslim writings on the divine names, see Daniel Gimaret, *Les noms divins en Islam: Exégèse lexicographique et théologique* (Paris: Les editions du cref, 1988). For a general survey on the subject, see J. W. Redhouse, *On "the Most Comely*

Names," i.e. *The Laudatory Epithets, or The Titles of Praise, Bestowed on God in the Qur'ān or by Muslim Writers* (London: Trübner, 1880).

10. For details see chapter 3.
11. Cf., Parwīz Sulaymānī, *"Jalāl wa jamāl," Dānishnāma-yi jahān-i islām* [*The Encyclopedia of the world of Islam*], ed. Ghulām Riḍā Ḥaddād ʿĀdil, et al. (Tehran: Bunyād-i Dāʾirat al-Maʿārif-i Islāmī, 1996–present), vol. 10, #442, http://rch.ac.ir/article/Details/9813.
12. Ibn Sīnā, *The Metaphysics of the Healing: A Parallel English-Arabic Text,* trans. M. E. Marmura (Provo: Brigham Young University Press, 2005), 291. Al-Fārābī's analysis of the divine attributes such as life, knowledge, etc., can be found in *Perfect State,* chapter 1, 57ff.
13. See Amnon Shiloah, *The Epistle on Music of the Ikhwan al-Safa (Baghdad, 10th century)* (Tel-Aviv: Tel-Aviv University, Faculty of Fine Arts, School of Jewish Studies, 1978).
14. Ikhwān al-Ṣafāʾ, *Rasāʾil Ikhwān al-Safāʾ wa-Khullān al-Wafāʾ*, ed. Buṭrus al-Bustānī (Beirut: Muʾassasat al-ʿIlmī li-l-Maṭbūʿāt, 2005), vol. 1, 201. Cf. Hughes, *Texture of the Divine,* 163; Shiloah, *The Epistle on Music,* 69.
15. Ikhwān al-Ṣafāʾ, *Rasāʾil Ikhwān al-Safāʾ*, vol. 1, 201.
16. Plotinus, *Plotinus,* vol. 1 (*Ennead* I. 1–9), trans. A. H. Armstrong (Cambridge: Harvard University Press, 1966), 235. It must be noted, however, that the *Ennead* I did not form part of the Plotinian corpus that was available in medieval Arabic translation.
17. It is worth noting that Plotinus describes the experience of human encounter with something ugly as finding something to be "out of tune." Cf. Plotinus, *Plotinus,* vol. 1, 235 (*Ennead* I.6.2).
18. Though not considered as "sound" by Ḥadīth scholars, this divine saying is quoted frequently in Sufi and other texts. A major Sunni scholar, Fakhr al-Dīn al-Rāzī (d. 1209), for instance, mentions it in *Tafsīr al-Rāzī* (Dār Iḥyāʾ Turāth al-ʿArabī), 28.188 (in his commentary on the verse Q 51:56).
19. Rashīd al-Dīn Maybudī, *Kashf al-asrār wa-ʿuddat al-abrār*, ed. ʿAlī Aṣghar Ḥikmat (Tehran: Amīr Kabīr, 1381sh/2002), vol. 5, 668 (Q 18:13).
20. Al-Ghazālī, *al-Maqṣad al-asnā fī sharḥ maʿānī asmāʾ Allāh al-ḥusnā*, ed. Fadlou Shehadi (Beirut: Dār al-Mashriq, 1971), 162. See also its fourth chapter, which is called "Explaining that the servant's perfection and happiness lie in being characterized by the character traits of God and adorned by the meanings of His attributes and His names in the measure that can be conceived

of for him," ibid., 42. I translate words derived from the Arabic root *ʿ-r-f* consistently as follows: "to recognize" (*ʿarafa*), "recognition" (*maʿrifa*), and "recognizer" (*ʿārif*). I am fully aware of some scholars' criticism against using "recognition," a term less commonly used than "gnosis" to translate *maʿrifa*. The truth is that no perfect translation exists for this critical term in Sufism. I prefer to use "recognition" to "gnosis" to avoid the latter's two key problems: being suggestive of Gnosticism, which is a separate tradition, and the lack of a verbal form to translate *ʿarafa*, which makes one bound to use two etymologically unrelated English words to translate *ʿarafa* and *maʿrifa*. In the end, it is a question of translation philosophy: some prefer to alter the translation of a single term depending on the context; some prefer to stick to a single translation for each term for the sake of consistency. Each method has its advantages and disadvantages, and I belong to the second camp. I translate *ʿilm* as "knowledge" and *maʿrifa* as "recognition" throughout this book. While *ʿārif* was a synonym for a Sufi (i.e., someone who has *maʿrifa*) during Rūzbihān's time, it came to acquire different connotations over the subsequent centuries. For the history of its related terms, *ʿirfān* and *taṣawwuf*, and the polemics surrounding them, see Ata Anzali's forthcoming work, *Mysticism in Iran: The Safavid Roots of a Modern Concept* (University of South Carolina Press). Also, for Chittick's rationale for translating *maʿrifa* as "recognition," see his *Divine Love: Islamic Literature and the Path to God* (New Haven: Yale University Press, 2013), 230–32.

21. Ibn Sīnā, *Risāla fī al-ʿishq*, in *Traités mystiques d'Abū ʿAlī al-Ḥusain ibn ʿAbdallāh ibn Sīnā ou d'Avicenne*, ed. August Ferdinand Mehren (Frankfurt am Main: Institute for the History of Arabic-Islamic Science, 1999), 3:5–22; Emil L. Fackenheim, "A Treatise on Love by Ibn Sina," *Mediaeval Studies* 7 (1945): 215–25.
22. Black, "Aesthetics in Islamic philosophy."
23. Aḥmad Ghazālī, *Sawāniḥ*, in *Majmūʿa-yi āthār-i fārsī-yi Aḥmad Ghazzālī (ʿārif-i mutawaffā-yi 520 A.H.)*, ed. Aḥmad Mujāhid (Tehran: Dānishgāh-i Tihrān, 1370sh/1991), 135. Cf. Pourjavady, Sawāniḥ*: Inspirations from the World of Pure Sprits, the Oldest Persian Sufi Treatise on Love* (London: KPI, 1986), 33; Hellmut Ritter, *The Ocean of the Soul: Man, the World, and God in the Stories of Farīd al-Dīn ʿAṭṭār*, trans. O'Kane (Leiden: Brill, 2003), 416; Joseph Lumbard, "Aḥmad al-Ghazālī (d. 517/1123 or 520/1126) and the Metaphysics of Love," PhD dissertation (Yale University, 2003), 275. Ḥishmat-Allāh Riyāḍī presents Aḥmad Ghazālī's view on love and beauty in relation to

various other Sufis' views on the subject in *Āyat-i ḥusn wa ʿishq*, 2 vols. (Tehran: Ḥaqīqat, 1381sh/2002), see esp. vol. 1, 195ff.

24. Al-Fārābī, *Perfect State*, 85.
25. Ibid.
26. Ibn Sīnā, *al-Najāt*, 282. Gonzalez discusses this passage in *Beauty and Islam*, 15.
27. Shihāb al-Dīn Yaḥyā Suhrawardī, "On the Reality of Love," trans. W. M. Thackston, *The Philosophical Allegories and Mystical Treatises* (Costa Mesa, CA: Mazda Publishers, 1999), 58–76.
28. Michael Sells, *Approaching the Qurʾān: The Early Revelations* (Ashland: White Cloud Press, 1999), 23.

Chapter 2. The Language of Beauty

1. Annemarie Schimmel, *Mystical Dimensions of Islam* (Chapel Hill: University of North Carolina Press, 1975), 298. To demonstrate her point of the impossibility of translating Rūzbihān's flowery language, Schimmel provides a sample translation of Rūzbihān's Persian work, *Sharḥ-i shaṭḥiyyāt*: "Look well, for the heart is the marketplace of His love, and there the rose of Adam on the branch of Love is from the color of manifestation [*tajallī*] of His Rose. When the nightingale 'spirit' becomes intoxicated by this rose, he will hear with the ear of the soul the song of the bird of *Alast* ['Am I not your Lord?'] in the fountainplace of preeternity."
2. Ernst, *Rūzbihān Baqlī*, 10.
3. Cf. ibid. I have modified his wording ("in the state of overpowering and ecstasy") here in accordance with a newer edition of Jāmī's *Nafaḥāt al-uns*, ed. Maḥmūd ʿĀbidī (Tehran: Sukhan, 1386sh/2007), 261. Ernst's own assessment of Rūzbihān's "elliptical style"—with a special attention to the question of "fidelity" and "infidelity" in Rūzbihān's writings—can be found in his *Words of Ecstasy in Sufism* (Albany: State University of New York Press, 1985), esp. 85–94. There, Ernst notes that Rūzbihān's difficult language is partly responsible for the limited general circulation of his works: "His works were less commonly read than `Ayn al-Qudat's because of their greater difficulty, but they were influential among learned Sufis," 85.
4. Ibn Fāris, *Tartīb maqāyīs al-lugha* (Tehran: Pazhūhishgāh-i Ḥawza wa Dānishgāh, 1387sh/2007), s.v. *ḥusn*; Al-Jawharī, *Tāj al-lugha wa-siḥāḥ al-ʿarabiyya* (Beirut: Dār Iḥyāʾ Turāth al-ʿArabī, 1999), s.v. *ḥusn*; Ibn Manẓūr, *Lisān al-ʿarab* (Beirut: Dār Iḥyāʾ al-Turāth al-ʿArabī, 1988), s.v. *ḥusn*.

5. See al-Jawharī, *Tāj al-lugha wa-siḥāḥ al-ʿarabiyya*, s.v. *ḥusn*.
6. See for instance, Ibn Manẓūr, *Lisān al-ʿarab*, s.v. *ḥusn*, where he contrasts *ḥusnā* (the adjectival form of *ḥusn* in the feminine superlative) with *sūʾā* ("the worst," "the most evil"). In addition, he contrasts *ḥasana* (a substantive form) with *sayyiʾa* ("bad/evil deed").
7. Edward William Lane translates *sūʾ* as "evil, ill; iniquity, injury, offence, calamity, misfortune" and explains the verb, *sāʾa* thus: "to be or become bad, evil, foul, wicked; to become worse, deteriorate (condition); to grieve, sadden, afflict, hurt, vex, torment, trouble, offend, pain, make sorry, displease," *Arabic-English Lexicon* (New York: F. Ungar, 1955–56), s.v. *sūʾ* and *sāʾa*, respectively.
8. Ibid., s.v. *ḥusn*.
9. If we turn to contemporary Persian scholarship, we see that Nasrollah Pourjavady regards *nīkūʾī* (not *zībāʾī*, which is the more common Persian word for "beauty" today) as the most accurate Persian translation of *ḥusn*. He therefore translates *ḥusn* as *nīkūʾī* and *jamāl* as *zībāʾī* in Persian. See Pourjavady, "Maʿnī-yi ḥusn wa ʿishq dar adabiyāt-i ʿirfānī [The meaning of *ḥusn* and *ʿishq* in Sufi literature]," *Sophia Perennis* 2, no. 1 (1976): 43. In another article on the topic of beauty, Pourjavady explains that the word *zībāʾī* comes from *zībanda būdan*, i.e., to be "befitting," "becoming," for which reason he considers *zībāʾī* inadequate as a full rendering of *ḥusn*—see Pourjavady, "Ḥusn wa marātib-i idrāk-i ān: Nigāhī bih naẓar-i ḥukamā wa ʿurafā [*Ḥusn* and the levels of its perception: An observation on the views of the philosophers and Sufis]," in *Ishrāq wa ʿirfān: Maqālahā wa naqdhā* [Illumination and Sufism: Articles and critiques] (Tehran: Markaz-i Nashr-i Dānishgāhī, 1380sh/2001), 178. Also see Pourjavady, "*ḥusn*," *Dānishnāma-yi jahān-i islām*, vol. 13, #384, http://rch.ac.ir/article/Details/12004.
10. See Aḥmad Ghazālī, *Sawāniḥ*, 132; Suhrawardī, *Fī ḥaqīqat al-ʿishq* [On the reality of passionate love], in *The Philosophical Allegories and Mystical Treatises*, ed. W. Thackston (Costa Mesa, CA: Mazda, 1999), 58.
11. Abū Ḥāmid al-Ghazālī, *Kīmiyā-yi saʿādat* (Tehran: Shirkat-i Intishārāt-i ʿIlmī wa Farhangī, 1386/2007), vol. 2, 575.
12. Toshihiko Izutsu, *Ethico-Religious Concepts in the Qurʾan* (Montreal: McGill-Queen's University Press, 2002), 224.
13. See chapter 11, "Good and Bad," in Izutsu, *Ethico-Religious Concepts in the Qurʾān*, esp. 221ff. Cf. Murata and Chittick, *The Vision of Islam*, 108–11 and 268.

14. Well-known versions of the ḥadīth of Gabriel are found in al-Bukhārī, *Ṣaḥīḥ,* 4.1792 and Muslim, *Ṣaḥīḥ,* 1.134, 1.143. Its variations as well as partial reports are found in numerous collections including: al-Tirmidhī, *Sunan* (Beirut: Dār al-Kutub al-ʿIlmiyya, 1994), 7.331; Abū Dāwūd, *Kitāb al-sunan* (Mecca: Dār al-Istiqāma, 1997), 12.459; Ibn Mājah, *Sunan,* 1.24, 1.25; Ibn Ḥanbal, *Musnad,* 1.46, 1.84, 1.86, 1.524, 3.159, 5.169, 5.113, among others. Murata and Chittick explain the ḥadīth of Gabriel in *The Vision of Islam,* xxv–xxxiv.

15. While this is a well-known saying of the Prophet, in this exact form it appears only outside the six books of standard Sunni Ḥadīth: al-Dārimī, *al-Musnad* (Riyadh: Dār al-Mughnī, 2000), II.1366; Abū Yaʿlā Mawṣilī, *al-Musnad* (Damascus: Dār al-Maʾmūn li-l-Turāth, 1984), IV.475; Ṭabarī, *Jāmiʿ al-bayān fī taʾwīl al-qurʾān,* ed. Aḥmad Muḥammad Shākir (Cairo: Dār al-Maʿārif, 1420/2000), 22.507; and Ibn Khuzayma, *Kitāb al-tawḥīd wa-ithbāt ṣifāt al-rabb* (Riyadh: Maktab al-Rushd, 1994), I.201, II.533, II.539, among others. Variations of this saying, however, do appear in major Ḥadīth collections, including Ibn Ḥanbal's *Musnad,* which records "My Lord—exalted and majestic is He—came to me at night in the most beautiful form," I.607; V.13; VI.522. Essentially the same ḥadīth (except for the glorification formula for God—*tabāraka wa-taʿālā* in place of *ʿazza wa-jalla*) is also found in al-Tirmidhī's *Sunan,* 9.84. Variations are often found in Sufi literature. A good example—especially in connection to the subject of beauty—is found in ʿAyn al-Quḍāt Hamadānī's (d. 1131) writing: "From 'I saw my Lord'—God—'in the most beautiful form, a beardless youth' a group has appeared who worship *jamāl.*" See *Nāmahā-yi ʿAyn al-Quḍāt Hamadānī,* ed. ʿAlī-Naqī Munzawī and ʿAfīf ʿUsayrān (Tehran: Intishārāt-i Asāṭīr, 1377sh/1998), I.156.6–7 (Letter #18). On the Prophet's seeing God in the most beautiful form as reported in these ḥadīths, also see Corbin, *Creative Imagination in the Ṣūfism of Ibn ʿArabī,* trans. R. Manheim (Princeton: Princeton University Press, 1969), 272–81; Schimmel, *Mystical Dimensions,* 290.

16. For a study of color symbolism in Rūzbihān's *Kashf al-asrār,* see Antoni Gonzalo Carbó, "El cielo teñido de rojo: La visión del color en el Diarium spirituale de Rûzbihân Baqlî (m. 606/1209)," *Convivium: Revista de Filosofia* 13 (2000): 31–59.

17. While discussing the significance of camels to Bedouin life in *The Bedouins and the Desert: Aspects of Nomadic Life in the Arab East,* Jubrail Jabbur emphasizes that the word for camel, *jamal,* shares

the same root as *jamāl* and that the sense of *jamāl* as "beauty" may even have derived from *jamal*. He writes, "The lexicographical compendia held that the camel's name, *jamal*, is derived from the word *jamāl*, 'beauty,' since the Bedouins consider the camel a fine beautiful animal. In a Prophetic tradition it is said: 'He brought a fine beautiful (*jamlāʾ*) she-camel,' and in another we read: 'Then a fine beautiful (*jamlāʾ*) woman appeared before him.' And who knows, perhaps the word *jamāl* ('beauty') is itself derived from *jamal* ('camel'), since the latter is the source of goodness and life for the Bedouin. Desert life decreed that the Bedouin woman should be of slender build, due to the great amounts of moving about, traveling, and working that she did, which kept her something short of plumpness and corpulence. Hence, if she became plump and soft-bodied, like a camel (*jamal*) fills out when it becomes fat, then they would refer to her as *jamīla* and *jamlāʾ*, 'beautiful,'" in Jabbur, *Bedouins and the Desert*, trans. Lawrence Conrad (Albany: State University of New York Press, 1995), 237.

18. Although as a lexicographer Lane lists a number of meanings for *jamāl*, the first meaning he mentions is "beauty," and the first he mentions for *ḥusn* is "goodness or goodliness." His entry on *jamāl* reads as follows: "Beauty, goodliness, comeliness, or pleasingness"; "goodness in action, or actions, or behaviour"; "elegance, or prettiness; i.e., delicacy, or minuteness, of beauty." Lane, *Arabic-English Lexicon*, s.v. *jamāl*.
19. See Daniel Gimaret, *Les noms divins en Islam*, 215–17. Gimaret also notes that both al-Qushayrī and al-Ghazālī associate *al-jamīl* with its counterpart, *al-jalīl* ("the Majestic"), ibid., 216. However, it is worth noting that while al-Qushayrī does so in his *al-Taḥbīl fī al-tadhkīr*, he does not mention *al-jamīl* in the short list of divine names found in his much shorter treatise on Ashʿarite dogma, *al-Fuṣūl fī al-uṣūl*. See Richard Frank, "Two Short Dogmatic Works of Abū l-Qāsim al-Qushayrī. Second Part: Edition and Translation of 'Al-Fuṣūl fī-Uṣūl,'" *Melanges* 16 (1983): 66–70. For Rūzbihān's discussion of *jamīl* as a divine name, see the next chapter on his theology of beauty.
20. Ibn Ḥanbal, *Musnad*, V.120, V.121, V.149.
21. Muslim, *Ṣaḥīḥ*, 2.74. A later Ḥadīth scholar, al-Bayhaqī (d. 1066), who lived a century before Rūzbihān, also records this version of the ḥadīth in his *Shuʿab al-īmān* (Beirut: Dār al-Kutub al-ʿIlmiyya, 2000), #6201, V.162. After Rūzbihān's time, another variation of this ḥadīth can be found in both Sunni and Shiite collections: "Indeed God is beautiful and He loves beauty, and He loves to have the trace of His blessing seen

upon His servant" (*Inna Allāh jamīl yuḥibb al-jamāl wa-yuḥibb an yurā athar niʿmatihi ʿalā ʿabdihi*). This is found, for instance, in al-Haythamī's (d. 1404) *Majmaʿ al-zawāʾid*, a secondary collection of unique ḥadīths occurring in the six books of Sunni Ḥadīth (Beirut: Dār al-Fikr, n.d.), #8582, V.232; #8589, V.234; al-Suyūṭī's (d. 1505) *Jāmiʿ al-masānīd wa-l-marāsīl* (Beirut: Dār al-Fikr, 1994, #5324, II.269; #6716, II.475); as well as the Shiite Ḥadīth collection by ʿAllāma al-Majlisī (d. 1698), *Biḥār al-anwār* (Beirut: Muʾassasat al-Wafāʾ, 1984), 10.92.

22. Rūzbihān Baqlī, *Kitāb maşrab al-arvāḥ va huva'l-maşhūr bi-hazār u yak maḳām (bi-alfi maḳāmin va maḳāmin)*, ed. Naşreden Nazif M. Hoca (Istanbul: Edebiyat Fakültesi Matbaasi, 1974). Henceforth referred to as *Mashrab* (in standard Arabic transliteration).
23. Ibid., 132.
24. Ibid., 132–33.
25. *Al-Maknūn fī ḥaqāʾiq al-kalim al-nabawiyya*, ed. ʿAlī Ṣadrāʾī Khuʾī, in *Kitābkhāna-yi madrasa-yi fiqāhat* (N.p.: n.d.), http://lib.eshia.ir/27484/1/293, #62, vol. 1, 293–94.
26. *Mashrab*, 133.
27. Ibid.
28. Ibid.
29. It is in the sense of "to approve" that *istaḥsana* is considered the antonym of *istahjana*, "to disapprove," cf. Dakramanjī, *Qāmūs al-aḍdād al-kabīr*, s.v. *ḥ-s-n*.
30. Lane translates its verbal form (with an added objective pronoun, *hu*), *istaḥsanahu*, as "He counted, accounted, reckoned, or esteemed, him, or it, حسن [i.e., good, goodly, beautiful, comely, pleasing, &c.; he approved, thought well of, or liked, him, or it]," in *Arabic-English Lexicon*, s.v. *ḥ-s-n*.
31. Rūzbihān paraphrases al-Daylamī's book in several works, especially in discussions of *ʿishq*. A few scholars have pointed out al-Daylamī's "influence" on Rūzbihān, the earliest of which is Jean-Claude Vadet, who published the first critical edition of the *ʿAṭf* (1962). He examines al-Daylamī's influence on Rūzbihān in his introduction to the French translation of the *ʿAṭf* (1980), *Le traité d'amour mystique d'al-Daylami* (Geneva: Droz, 1980), 12–17. The most important and detailed study of the connection between al-Daylamī and Rūzbihān is Masataka Takeshita's "Continuity and Change in the Tradition of Shirazi Love Mysticism," *Orient* XIII (1987): 113–31. Carl Ernst compares the two thinkers' views on various stages of love in "The Stages of Love in Early Persian Sufism from Rābiʿa to Rūzbihān," *Classical Persian Sufism from its Origins to Rumi*, ed.

Leonard Lewisohn (London: Khaniqahi Nimatullahi, 1994), 435–55. Joseph Norment Bell and Ḥasan Maḥmūd al-Shāfiʿī discuss Rūzbihān's familiarity with al-Daylamī's *ʿAṭf* in the introduction to their English translation of the *ʿAṭf, A Treatise on Mystical Love*, esp. lxvi–lxix. Nasrollah Pourjavady touches on this subject in his study of love and argues that the first major influence of al-Daylamī's *ʿAṭf* on subsequent Sufism is found in the works of Rūzbihān: "The book *ʿAṭf* was written in Shiraz at the end of the fourth or the beginning of the fifth century [A.H.]. However important this book may be in the history of Sufism in general, it did not have an extensive influence on Sufi writers in the fifth and sixth centuries. In fact it seems that the first person in Shiraz to follow Daylamī's work by writing a book on *ʿishq* is Rūzbihān Baqlī." Pourjavady, *Bāda-yi ʿishq: Pazhūhishī dar maʿnā-yi bādah dar shiʿr-i ʿirfānī-yi fārsī* [The Wine of passionate love: Study on the meaning of wine in Persian Sufi poetry] (Tehran: Nashr-i Kārnāma, 1387/2008), 54–55.

32. Chapter 5 in *ʿAbhar al-ʿāshiqīn*, ed. J. Nūrbakhsh (Tehran: Intishārāt-i Yaldā-Qalam, 1380/2001), 35–44. All subsequent references to the *ʿAbhar* in this study will be to the Nūrbakhsh edition, which has eliminated many of the textual problems in the previous Corbin-Muʿīn edition (Tehran: Intishārāt-i Manūchihrī, 1383sh/2004, originally published in 1958).
33. All "beauty" in this passage translates *ḥusn*.
34. Al-Daylamī, *ʿAṭf*, 10 (ed. Vadet); 23 (ed. Bell and al-Shāfiʿī). Translation is mine, in order to keep the translation of technical terms consistent. For Bell's translation, see *Treatise on Mystical Love*, 15.
35. As Bell and al-Shāfiʿī note, al-Daylamī rarely names the sources of the sayings that he has compiled in the *ʿAṭf*. Similar discussions with the use of such philosophical terms as emanation (*fayḍ*) can be found, for instance, in Ibn Sīnā's *al-Risāla fī al-ʿishq*. See Fackenheim, "A Treatise on Love," 212, 213, 223, 224; Frithiof Rundgren, "Avicenna on Love: Studies in the 'Risāla fī māhīyat al'išhq' I," *Orientalia Suecana* 27–28 (1978-1979): 56.
36. *ʿAbhar*, 41.
37. *Mashrab*, 134.
38. Ibid., 132.
39. Ibid., 134.
40. Rūzbihān, *Ghalaṭāt al-sālikīn*, 101, in *Risālat al-quds wa risāla-yi ghalaṭāt al-sālikīn*, ed. Jawād Nūrbakhsh (Tehran: Yaldā Qalam, 1381sh/2002).
41. Ibid., 101–102.

42. *Mashrab*, 73. I am reading *maʿārif* in the first sentence as *ʿurafāʾ* to make sense of the passage. Elsewhere, Rūzbihān attributes virtually the same sentence found in the middle of this passage to another Sufi: "al-Nūrī said, 'Things deemed beautiful are beautiful through His self-disclosure, and things deemed ugly are ugly through His being veiled,'" in *Mashrab*, 134.
43. See, for instance, al-Qushayrī, *Al-Qushayri's Epistle on Sufism*, trans. Alexander Knysh (Reading: Garnet, 2007), 205–207. In a parallel discussion of *riḍā*, Rūzbihān quotes part of this discussion by al-Qushayrī, whom he consistently refers to as "the Teacher," in *Mashrab*, 33.
44. *ʿArāʾis al-bayān* II.29 (Q 9:66).
45. *Mashrab*, 72–73.
46. Ibid., 73.
47. The word is *ḥadathān*, from *ḥudūth*, "temporal origination" or "new arrival," which is the opposite of *qidam*, "eternity." The Persian equivalent for *ḥadathān* that Rūzbihān employs is the unusual word, *naw-āmadagān* ("newly arrived things"), cf., *Sharḥ-i shaṭḥiyyāt*, 18.
48. *Mashrab*, 73.
49. Cf. Murata and Chittick, *The Vision of Islam*, 40–42.
50. *Mashrab*, 72–73.

Chapter 3. The Theology of Beauty

1. The poem cited in the epigraph is recorded by Rūzbihān's great-grandson, ʿAbd al-Laṭīf b. Ṣadr al-Dīn Abī Muḥammad Rūzbihān Thānī (d. 705/1305), in *Rawḥ al-jinān fī sīrat al-shaykh Rūzbihān*, ed. M. Dānishpazhūh, *Rūzbihān-nāma* (Tehran: Bahman, 1347sh/1969), 340–41. The verse continues thus: "O far removed from understanding, estimation, and imagination, / speaking in description of You is impossible. / In Your beauty (*jamāl*) the intellect is mad, / in Your majesty the spirit is a moth."
2. Though widely known among Muslims and popular especially among Sufis, this saying is not part of the standard six collections of Sunni Ḥadīth but found for instance in al-Majlisī, *Biḥār al-anwār*, 84.198; 84.344. Slightly after Rūzbihān's time, Najm al-Dīn Dāya Rāzī (d. 1256) centrally features the saying in *Mirsād al-ʿibād*, where he presents it to be God's response to the prophet David when he asked Him why He created the world. According to Chittick, "Early authors do not suggest that it

came from the Prophet's mouth, but attribute it rather to the corpus of stories handed down about the prophet David." He finds an early citation in the *Rasāʾil* of Ikhwān al-Ṣafāʾ from the tenth century, while noting that Ibn al-ʿArabī is the first author he knows of who explicitly attributes the saying to the prophet Muhammad. See Chittick, *Divine Love*, 439n6.

3. Michael Sells, *Mystical Languages of Unsaying* (Chicago: University of Chicago Press, 1994).
4. One must note that intermixture of the technical terminology of *kalām, falsafa,* and Sufism is nothing new, which may be best represented by the works of Abū Ḥāmid al-Ghazālī (d. 1111) before Rūzbihān's time, and after him by the works of Ibn al-ʿArabī (d. 1240). However, one major difference between Rūzbihān and these two thinkers—who may be considered "Sufi theoreticians"—is that he makes no explicit attempt at systematizing his ideas through extensive importation of technical terms from *kalām* and *falsafa* nor does he make any visible effort to make the task of reading his writings easier by defining his terms. For a useful survey of the interaction between dogmatic theology and Sufism, see Toby Mayer, "Theology and Sufism," in *The Cambridge Companion to Classical Islamic Theology*, ed. Tim Winter (Cambridge: Cambridge University Press, 2008), 258–87. A case study of the complex nature of Sufi language can be found in Martin Nguyen, *Sufi Master and Qur'an Scholar: Abū Qāsim al-Qushayrī and the* Laṭāʾif al-ishārāt (Oxford: Oxford University Press, 2012).
5. Masataka Takeshita, "Continuity and Change in the Tradition of Shirazi Love Mysticism": 113–31. For an example of parallel discussions in al-Daylamī's *ʿAṭf* and Rūzbihān's writings, see the section on *mustaḥsan* in the previous chapter.
6. Mayer, "Theology and Sufism," 272.
7. Ernst, *Rūzbihān Baqlī*, 39.
8. The position of *Masālik al-tawḥīd* in relation to the rest of Rūzbihān's compositions is similar to that of al-Qushayrī's *Lumaʿ fī al-iʿtiqād* and *al-Fuṣūl fī al-uṣūl*, two works of Ashʿarite dogma, in relation to his other (mostly Sufi) works. Cf. Richard Frank, "Two Short Dogmatic Works of Abū l-Qāsim al-Qushayrī. First Part: Edition and Translation of 'Luma' fī l-i'tiqād,'" *Melanges* 15 (1982): 53–74; and "Two Short Dogmatic Works of Abū l-Qāsim al-Qushayrī. Second Part: Edition and Translation of 'Al-Fuṣūl fī l-Uṣūl,'" *Melanges* 16 (1983): 59–94. Ibn Khafīf, another Ashʿarite Sufi, whom Rūzbihān holds in great respect through the intermediary of Abū al-Ḥasan al-Daylamī's transmission of his ideas, has a work of similar nature, namely a

work of dogma called *Muʿtaqad Ibn Khafīf*, edited by Schimmel in the appendix to al-Daylamī's *Sīrat al-shaykh al-kabīr Abū ʿAbd Allāh Muḥammad b. al-Khafīf al-Shīrāzī*. While both Ibn Khafīf and al-Qushayrī exerted influence on Rūzbihān's thought, the content of his *Masālik al-tawḥīd* is closer to al-Qushayrī's *Lumaʿ* than to Ibn Khafīf's *Muʿtaqad*.

9. Rūzbihān, *Kitāb masālik al-tawḥīd*, ed., Ballanfat, *Quatre traits inédits de Rûzbehân Baqlî Shîrâzî*, 167–90. Henceforth referred to as *Masālik*.
10. Ballanfat, *Quatre traits inédits de Rûzbehân Baqlî Shîrâzî*, 38–39.
11. *Masālik*, 171.
12. Ibid.
13. Ibid., 170.
14. *Tafakkarū fī kulli shayʾin wa-lā tafakkarū fī dhāti Allāh*. This ḥadīth in this exact wording is not included in the standard six books of Sunni Ḥadīth. Among the early sources that record it are: Hannād b. al-Sarī al-Kūfī, *Kitāb al-zuhd*, ed. ʿAbd al-Raḥmān ʿAbd al-Jibār al-Farīwāʾī (Kuwait: Dār al-Khulafāʾ li-l-Kitāb al-Islāmī, 1986), II.469; Abū al-Muẓaffar Manṣūr b. Muḥammad al-Samʿānī, *al-Intiṣār li-aṣḥāb al-ḥadīth*, ed. Muḥmmad b. Ḥusayn b. Ḥasan al-Jīzānī (N.p.: Maktabat Aḍwāʾ al-Manār, n.d.), I.9; Shīrawayh b. Shahrdār al-Daylamī al-Hamadhānī, *al-Firdaws bi-maʾthūr al-khiṭāb*, ed. al-Saʿīd b. Basyūnī Zughlūl (Beirut: Dār al-Kutub al-ʿIlmiyya, 1986), II.56. Among the well-known scholars of Ḥadīth in the later generations, Jalāl al-Dīn al-Suyūṭī (d. 1505) records this ḥadīth in slight variations. In his *Jāmiʿ al-masānīd wa-l-marāsīl*, al-Suyūṭī records, "Reflect upon every thing, but do not reflect upon God's essence" (4:112); "Reflect upon God's creation, but do not reflect upon God" (4:111, 112, 114); "Reflect upon God's bounties, but do not reflect upon God" (4:111). The second version is also recorded by Shiites, e.g., al-Majlisī in *Biḥār al-anwār*, 54:348.
15. *Al-Maknūn*, http://lib.eshia.ir/27484/1/355, #183, vol. 1, 355. The print edition is incomplete and omits some of the sentences (surrounding the saying of Abū Bakr) translated above; cf. *ʿArāʾis al-ḥadīth aw al-maknūn fī ḥaqāʾiq al-kalim al-nabawiyya*, ed. ʿAlī Ṣadrāʾī Khuʾī (Tehran: Sāzmān-i Tablīghāt-i Islāmī, 1389sh/2010), #188, 241–43.
16. *ʿArāʾis al-bayān*, III.261 (Q 42:11). Henceforth abbreviated as *ʿArāʾis*.
17. *Al-Maknūn*, http://lib.eshia.ir/27484/1/355, #183, vol. 1, 355. This part is also omitted in the printed edition; cf. *ʿArāʾis al-ḥadīth aw al-maknūn fī ḥaqāʾiq al-kalim al-nabawiyya*, #188, 242.

18. *Mashrab*, 215.
19. *ʿArāʾis*, I.368 (Q 6:59).
20. Cf., *ʿArāʾis*, I.368 (Q 6:59) and *Mashrab*, 6.
21. This echoes the biblical verse, *No one shall see me and live* (Exodus 33:20).
22. *Arāʾis*, I.465 (Q 7:142).
23. *Mashrab*, 150. In addition, Rūzbihān uses *ʿayn* interchangeably with *dhāt* when he writes "*ʿayn, ṣifa,* and *fiʿl*," with *ʿayn* replacing *dhāt*, the more standard term in such a list, in *Mashrab*, 162.
24. *Arāʾis*, I.465 (Q 7:142).
25. *Masālik*, 171.
26. Ibid., 173.
27. Ibid., 170–71.
28. My translation. Richard Frank, "Two Short Dogmatic Works of Abū Qāsim al-Qushayrī. Second Part: Edition and Translation of 'Al-Fuṣūl fī l-Uṣūl," 60. For Frank's translation, see ibid., 76.
29. *Al-Maknūn*, http://lib.eshia.ir/27484/1/355, #183, vol. 1, 355.
30. *Masālik*, 174.
31. *ʿArāʾis*, I.268 (Q 4:94).
32. Ibid., I.345 (Q 6:1).
33. Ibid., I.516 (Q 8:10).
34. Ibid., I.465 (Q 7:142).
35. *Mashrab*, 133.
36. See the section on *mustaḥsan* in chapter 2 and *Mashrab*, 132.
37. Fakhr al-Dīn al-Rāzī, *al-Maṭālib al-ʿāliyya fī al-ʿilm al-ilāhī*, ed. al-Saqqā (Beirut: Dār al-Kitāb al-ʿArabī, 1987), vol. 3, 246. He writes, "The fifth name: *dhāt*. Know that this expression was put down to indicate the specification of a thing by another thing. They say 'a woman possessing (*dhāt*) money' and 'possessing beauty'....It is impossible to define [the essence] except by its attributes....It is what the attributes are attributed to (*hiya mawṣūfa bi-l-ṣifāt*)."
38. *Masālik*, 170.
39. Ibid., 178ff.
40. Ibid.,170.
41. See Gimaret, *La Doctrine d'al-Ashʿarī*, 260 and 276-81. For a concise discussion of the history of the problem of *taʿṭīl*, or divesting God of attributes, see Josef van Ess, "*Tashbīh wa-Tanzīh*," *Encyclopaedia of Islam*, 2nd ed.
42. Gimaret, *La Doctrine d'al-Ashʿarī* (Paris: Editions du Cerf, 1990), 259.
43. *Mashrab*, 269.
44. Ibid., 270.

45. See Gimaret, *La Doctrine d'al-Ash'arī*, 323–28.
46. *Mashrab*, 258–59.
47. *ʿArāʾis*, I.441 (Q 7:54).
48. In a useful survey of the history of *jamāl* and *jalāl* as terms in Muslim theological discourse, Parwīz Sulaymānī points out how these terms were understood by early dogmatic theologians and were further developed by Sufis, in *Dānishnāma-yi jahān-i islām*, s.v. "*Jalāl wa jamāl*," http://rch.ac.ir/article/Details/9813. The complementarity of God's beauty and majesty is the central subject of Sachiko Murata's *The Tao of Islam: A Sourcebook on Gender Relationships in Islamic Thought* (Albany: State University of New York Press, 1992).
49. *ʿArāʾis*, I.16 (Q 1:1).
50. This ḥadīth is widely accepted and reported by numerous Ḥadīth scholars, including such major scholars as al-Bukhārī, Muslim, Ibn Ḥanbal, and al-Tirmidhī. Ninety-nine is also the number of beads in the Muslim rosary for the purpose of invoking (*dhikr*) God's names. While Rūzbihān did not write a treatise enumerating the divine names, some preceding Sufi-theologians did, such as al-Qushayrī and al-Ghazālī; cf. al-Qushayrī, *al-Taḥbīr fī al-tadhkīr li-Abī al-Qāsim ʿAbd al-Karīm b. Hawāzin al-Qushayrī*, ed. Muḥammad Amīn b. ʿAbd al-Hādī al-Fārūqī (Ḥimṣ: Dār al-Maʿārif, n.d.); al-Ghazālī, *al-Maqṣad al-asnā fī sharḥ maʿānī asmāʾ Allāh al-ḥusnā* (Beirut: Dār al-Mashriq, 1971).
51. *ʿArāʾis*, III.381 (Q 55:78).
52. Muslim, *Ṣaḥīḥ*, 4.170; Abū Dāwūd, *Sunan*, 3.132, 4.302; al-Tirmidhī, *Sunan*, 9.372, 9.375, 10.10; Ibn Ḥanbal, *Musnad*, 1.155, 1.243, 7.87, 7.287; Mālik b. Anas, *Muwaṭṭaʾ*, 2.37.
53. *ʿArāʾis*, III.381 (Q 55:78).
54. *Al-Maknūn*, http://lib.eshia.ir/27484/1/276, #22, vol. 1, 276.
55. *ʿArāʾis*, III.381 (Q 55:78).
56. This ḥadīth is found in Ibn Ḥanbal, *Musnad*, 3.632; Abū Dāwūd, *Sunan*, 4.363; al-Nasāʾī, *Sunan al-Nasāʾī bi-sharḥ al-Suyūṭī wa-l-Sindī*, ed. al-Sayyid Muḥammad Sayyid, et al. (Cairo: Dār al-Ḥadīth, 1999), 1.386 and 3.59, among others. A brief discussion of *al-ism al-aʿẓam* can be found in Chittick, *Sufism: A Short Introduction* (Oxford: Oneworld, 2000), 56.
57. The Arabic is *ṣifāt al-khāṣṣa*, which I am reading as *al-ṣifāt al-khāṣṣa*.
58. *ʿArāʾis*, I.498 (Q 7:180).
59. For this reason, it is also possible to regard this fourth category of names as "the names known to the elect," reading *khāṣṣa* as a noun ("the elect") rather than an adjective ("specific").

60. *Mashrab*, 232.
61. The idea that *ḥusn* is a wider notion of beauty than *jamāl* by encompassing both *jamāl* and *jalāl* solves the conundrum discussed by Elaine Scarry regarding Kant's bifurcation of the sublime and the beautiful in her book, *On Beauty and Being Just* (83–85), where the sublime seems to correspond roughly to *jalāl* and the beautiful to *jamāl*. Scarry laments: "The sublime occasioned the demotion of the beautiful" (84); and "The sublime (an aesthetic of power) rejects beauty on the grounds that it is diminutive, dismissible, not powerful enough" (85). Had the notion of *ḥusn* been put into the picture, there would have been nothing to lament about, as *ḥusn* is by definition that which *is* and transcends the dichotomy between the beautiful / *jamīl* and the sublime / *jalīl* that belongs only to the temporal realm.
62. *Mashrab*, 132.
63. Ibid.
64. Corbin, *En Islam iranien*, vol. 3, 21.

Chapter 4. The Anthropology and Cosmology of Beauty

1. Rūzbihān, *Sharḥ-i shaṭḥiyyāt*, 166.
2. Rūzbihān, *Kitāb sayr al-arwāḥ*, ed. P. Ballanfat, *Quatre traits inédits de Rûzbehân Baqlî Shîrâzî* (Tehran: Institut français de recherche en Iran, 1998), 6.
3. *Mashrab*, 6.
4. Ibid.
5. Ibid.
6. Ibid., 7.
7. Ibid., 9.
8. See, for instance, ibid., 306.
9. Ibid., 9.
10. Ibid., 85. Rūzbihān devotes the seventh chapter of *Risālat al-quds* to discussing the purpose and effect of *samāʿ*, which has been translated into English as "On Listening to Music," in Ernst, *Teachings of Sufism* (Boston: Shambhala, 1999), 97–103.
11. *Mashrab*, 10.
12. Ibid., 43. I have translated *khiṭāb al-khāṣṣ* as "a specific address" as Rūzbihān often drops the first *al-* in an adjectival phrase, e.g., *al-khiṭāb al-khāṣṣ*. However, if the *iḍāfa* construction was intentional, then the phrase would mean "an address for the elect."
13. Ibid., 85.

14. ʿAyn al-Quḍāt Hamadānī, *Tamhīdāt*, ed. ʿAfīf ʿUsayrān (Tehran: Manūchihrī, 1380sh/2001), 106.
15. *Mashrab*, 28.
16. Ibid. Cf. *ʿAbhar*, 9.
17. *ʿAbhar*, 129.
18. *Mashrab*, 307.
19. Aḥmad Ghazālī, *Sawāniḥ*. Also see Pourjavady, "*ʿIshq-i azalī wa bāda-yi Alast*" ["Eternal passionate love and the wine of *Alast*"], in *Bāda-yi ʿishq*, 215–38; and Chittick, *Divine Love*, 32–35 and 43–49, on the ideas of beginningless love and the Covenant according to Anṣārī, Samʿānī, and Maybudī.
20. *Mashrab*, 9–10.
21. *Encyclopaedia of the Qurʾān*, s.v. "God and his Attributes." Rūzbihān's commentary on the above verses can be found in the corresponding sections in his Qurʾān commentary, *ʿArāʾis al-bayān*.
22. *Mashrab*, 10.
23. Ibid., 11.
24. Ibid., 12.
25. *ʿArāʾis*, III.199 (Q 38:72).
26. *Mashrab*, 176.
27. *ʿAbhar*, 38.
28. *Al-Maknūn*, http://lib.eshia.ir/27484/2/46, #225, vol. 2, 46.
29. *ʿArāʾis*, III.239 (Q 40:64).
30. Ibid., I.418 (Q 7:11).
31. Ibid., III.470 (Q 75:22–23).
32. *Al-Maknūn*, http://lib.eshia.ir/27484/2/63, #261, vol. 2, 63.
33. *ʿArāʾis*, III.487 (Q 80:40–41).
34. Ibid.
35. *Mashrab*, 85. A similar idea is expressed in the biblical tradition: "from the greatness and beauty of created things comes a corresponding perception of their Creator" (Wisdom of Solomon 13:5), cited by Frank Burch Brown in *Good Taste, Bad Taste, and Christian Taste: Aesthetics in Religious Life* (New York: Oxford University Press, 2000), 100.
36. *Mashrab*, 85.
37. *Al-Maknūn*, http://lib.eshia.ir/27484/1/327, #137, vol. 1, 327.
38. *Mashrab*, 133. Rūzbihān's likely source for Dhū al-Nūn's saying is al-Daylamī's *Aṭf*, 135, where this statement is presented as Dhū al-Nūn's response when he was asked "about the recognizers' state of seeking intimacy." Al-Daylamī's teacher, Ibn Khafīf also seems to have had a similar inclination toward appreciating beauty in creation, as he is reported to have said,

"The spirit's pleasure lies in three things: good smell, beautiful voice, and gazing," in Abū al-Ḥasan al-Daylamī, *Sīrat al-shaykh al-kabīr Abū ʿAbd Allāh Muḥammad b. al-Khafīf al-Shīrāzī*, 214. This passage is discussed in Leonard Lewisohn, "Sufism's Religion of Love, from Rābiʿa to Ibn ʿArabī," in *The Cambridge Companion to Sufism*, ed. Lloyd Ridgeon (Cambridge: Cambridge University Press, 2015), 162–63; and Bell and Shafie, *A Treatise on Mystical Love*, xxxix. Thus, it is possible to trace Rūzbihān's strong appreciation of beauty in creation to al-Daylamī (ca. 1000), Ibn Khafīf (d. 981), and Dhū al-Nūn al-Miṣrī (d. 859), all of whom Rūzbihān held in great respect.

39. *Al-Maknūn*, http://lib.eshia.ir/27484/1/304, #88, vol. 1, 304.
40. Rūzbihān, *Manṭiq al-asrār*, ed. Mojtaba Shahsavari, unpublished critical edition, 57, paragraph 112. I am grateful to the editor for sharing this extremely important unpublished text. The saying by the Prophet is also quoted in *Mashrab*, 133.
41. *ʿAbhar*, 37. The closest that comes to this saying is recorded by a later author, al-Suyūṭī: "Three things clear up sight: gazing at greenery, flowing water, and beautiful faces," in *Jāmiʿ al-masānīd wa-l-marāsīl*, IV.157. Lewisohn presents a similar discussion in Rūzbihān's *Sharḥ-i shaṭḥiyyāt* (150), in Lewisohn, "Sufism's Religion of Love, from Rābiʿa to Ibn ʿArabī," 155–56.
42. *Al-Maknūn*, http://lib.eshia.ir/27484/1/322, #124, vol. 1, p. 322.
43. Ibid.
44. Ernst, *Rūzbihān Baqlī*, 35.
45. Ballanfat, *Quatre traités*, 184–201.
46. *Mashrab*, 208.
47. Ibid., 236.
48. See for instance Rūzbihān's discussion of *tafriqa* in *Mashrab*, 149.
49. *ʿArāʾis*, III.173 (Q 36:78).
50. *ʿAbhar*, 42. Corbin discusses the extended passage in *En Islam iranien*, vol. 3, 96.
51. *ʿAbhar*, 42. Elaine Scarry argues against various attempts at banishing beauty from modern human life and refutes a similar attack on the contemplation of human beauty in modern discourse in *On Beauty and Being Just*, 72ff. A common theme that runs through both Scarry's contemporary example and Rūzbihān's is the fear that some people feel toward beautiful people—either because they are susceptible to being harmed or because they impart harm to their perceivers, through the sustained gaze. Underlying this fear is the recognition that beauty has power: either to guide or misguide people.

52. *ʿAbhar*, 42.
53. *Uṭlubū al-khayr ʿinda ḥisān al-wujūh.* This saying is not found in the six books of the canonical Sunni Ḥadīth, but it is recorded in a number of secondary Ḥadīth collections after Rūzbihān's time, such as al-Haythamī, *Majmaʿ al-zawāʾid*, #13730, VIII.355; #13732, VIII.356; and al-Suyūṭī, *Jāmiʿ al-masānīd wa-l-marāsīl*, #3204, I.462; #3205, I.463. Also see Doris Behrens-Abouseif, *Beauty in Arabic Culture* (Princeton: Markus Wiener Publishers, 1999), 64.
54. *Al-Maknūn*, http://lib.eshia.ir/27484/1/337, #156, vol. 1, 337.
55. Ibid.
56. Ibid., http://lib.eshia.ir/27484/2/39, #208, vol. 2, p. 39.
57. Ibid., http://lib.eshia.ir/27484/1/337, #156, vol. 1, 337.
58. Ibid., http://lib.eshia.ir/27484/2/46, #225, vol. 2, 46.
59. Ibid.
60. *ʿAbhar*, 41.
61. *Al-Maknūn*, http://lib.eshia.ir/27484/2/63, #261, vol. 2, 63.
62. Ibid., http://lib.eshia.ir/27484/1/345, #162, vol. 1, 345–46.
63. *Mashrab*, 133.
64. Muḥammad Taqī Mīr, *Sharḥ-i ḥāl wa āthār wa ashʿār-i shaykh Rūzbihān-i Baqlī-yi Fasāʾī-yi Shīrāzī* (Shiraz: Intishārāt-i Dānishgāh-i Pahlawī, 1354sh/1975), 88.
65. Cf. Muslim, *Ṣaḥīḥ*, 14.142; Ibn Ḥanbal, *Musnad*, 2.483, 2:496, 2:620, 3:224, 3:326.
66. *ʿAbhar*, 12. I am taking the alternative reading of *bāl* as *bāgh*.
67. Although Rūzbihān does not discuss "two eyes" per se, his contrast between the eye of gathering and the eye of separation seems more or less analogous to Ibn al-ʿArabī's discussion of the two eyes, consisting of imagination and intellect, that is, one that combines and another that separates, or one that sees *tashbīh* and another that sees *tanzīh*. Cf., Chittick, *The Sufi Path of Knowledge: Ibn 'Arabi's Metaphysics of Imagination* (Albany: State University of New York Press, 1989), 356–81.
68. Henry Corbin and Muḥammad Muʿīn, introduction to *Le jasmin des fidèles d'amour (Kitâb-e 'Abhar al-'âshiqîn): Traité de soufisme en person* (Tehran: Institut français de recherche en Iran, 1987), 97ff.

Chapter 5. The Prophetology of Beauty

1. *Mashrab*, 133.
2. Rūzbihān does mention Jesus's beauty but does not discuss it extensively. This is probably because of his attention to Jesus's strong association with spirit, which highlights his incomparability (*tanzīh*) more than his similarity (*tashbīh*) to the rest of

creation. However, Rūzbihān's discussion of prophetic beauty primarily focuses on the prophets' imitability for the rest of humanity as their role models.

3. Corbin, *En Islam iranien*, vol. 3, 81.
4. *Mashrab*, 87.
5. Ibid., 156.
6. *ʿArāʾis*, I.412 (Q 7:1).
7. Ibid., I.143 (Q 3:33).
8. Ibid., I.419 (Q 7:11).
9. Ibid., I.418 (Q 7:11).
10. Ibid., I.419 (Q 7:11).
11. *ʿAbhar*, 43.
12. Ibid.
13. Ibid., 42. Cf., *ʿArāʾis*, I.41 (Q 2:30).
14. *ʿArāʾis*, I.132 (Q 7:18).
15. Ibid., I.41 (Q 2:30).
16. Cf., *ʿAbhar*, 119; *ʿArāʾis*, II.148 (Q 12:4).
17. Cf. Muslim, *Ṣaḥīḥ*, 2:170; Ibn Ḥanbal, *Musnad*, 3:616; 4:203.
18. *ʿArāʾis*, II.147 (Q 12:3).
19. For a study of the theme of love in the story of Joseph in Sufi interpretation, see Jalāl Sattārī, *Dard-i ʿishq-i Zulaykhā: Pazhūhishī dar qissa-yi Yūsuf* (Tehran: Intishārāt-i Tūs, 1373sh / 1994).
20. *ʿAbhar*, 36.
21. Ibid.
22. *ʿArāʾis*, II.148 (Q 12:4).
23. *ʿAbhar*, 36.
24. *ʿArāʾis*, II.148 (Q 12:4).
25. *Risālat al-quds*, 24.
26. *ʿAbhar*, 36.
27. *Arāʾis*, II.147 (Q 12:3).
28. Ibid., II.146 (Q 12:3).
29. *ʿAbhar*, 36.
30. Ibid., 37. For various thinkers' approaches to interpreting Joseph's beauty, see Afrāsiyābpūr, *Zībāʾī-parastī dar ʿirfān-i islāmī*, 66ff.
31. *ʿArāʾis*, II.155 (Q 12:19).
32. See, for instance, Ritter, "Chapter Twenty-Six: Religious Love of a Beautiful Person," *The Ocean of the Soul*, 448–519.
33. *ʿAbhar*, 36.
34. *ʿArāʾis*, II.155 (Q 12:19). Rūzbihān makes this point by way of quoting a certain Jaʿfar.
35. Ibid., II.155 (Q 12:20).
36. Ibid., II.160 (Q 12:24).

37. Ibid., II.168–9 (Q 12:31).
38. Ibid., II.169 (Q 12:31).
39. Ibid., II.168 (Q 12:31).
40. Ibid., I.465 (Q 7:143).
41. Ibid.
42. Ibid.
43. Ibid.
44. Ibid., I.174 (Q 3:96).
45. *Mashrab*, 133.
46. *ʿArāʾis*, III.84 (an interpretation of Q 20:39 provided under Q 28:25).
47. Ibid., I.376 (Q 6:76).
48. Ibid.
49. Ibid.
50. Ibid., I.376–77 (Q 6:76).
51. *Mashrab*, 72–73.
52. Ibid., 73.
53. Ibid. This is a supplication often ascribed to Muhammad in Sufi literature.
54. Ibid.
55. Ibid.
56. Ibid., 134.
57. Ibid.
58. *Kashf al-asrār*, 35 (section 67). Cf., *al-Maknūn*, http://lib.eshia.ir/27484/1/283, #33, vol. 1, 283, whose incomplete excerpt is found in ʿAbd al-Laṭīf Rūzbihān Thānī, *Rawḥ al-jinān*, 262.
59. *ʿArāʾis*, II.148 (Q 12:4).
60. *Mashrab*, 66. Cf., *Mashrab*, 73; *ʿArāʾis*, I.106.
61. *Mashrab*, 66.
62. *ʿAbhar*, 42.
63. Ibid.
64. Ibid., 125.
65. *ʿArāʾis*, I.107 (Q 2:260).
66. Ibid., II.148–49.
67. *Kitāb al-ighāna*, 108–109.
68. *Al-Maknūn*, http://lib.eshia.ir/27484/2/50, #237, vol. 2, 50.
69. Ibid.
70. *ʿArāʾis*, III.444 (Q 68:4).
71. Ibid., III.445 (Q 68:4).
72. Ibid., I.159 (Q 3:79).
73. *Sayr al-arwāḥ*, 33.
74. *ʿArāʾis*, III.358–59 (Q 53:11).
75. *Al-Maknūn*, http://lib.eshia.ir/27484/1/327, #137, vol. 1, 327.

76. *Mashrab*, 149.
77. Ibid.
78. *ʿAbhar*, 126.
79. *Mashrab*, 133.
80. *ʿAbhar*, 37.
81. Ibid.
82. *Al-Maknūn*, http://lib.eshia.ir/27484/1/322, #124, vol. 1, 322.
83. Ibid.
84. Ibid.
85. Versions of this ḥadīth are found in al-Nasāʾī, *Sunan*, 5:280; Ibn Ḥanbal, *Musnad*, 3:581, 4:54, 4:201.
86. *Al-Maknūn*, http://lib.eshia.ir/27484/1/328, #137, vol. 1, 328.
87. This ḥadīth is found in secondary collections such as Abū Dāwūd, *al-Marāsīl* (Riyadh: Dār al-Ṣamīʿī, 1422/2001), 499 and 500; and Haythamī, *Majmaʿ al-zawāʾid*, 5.39.
88. *Mashrab*, 134. Cf., *al-Maknūn*, http://lib.eshia.ir/27484/1/328, #137, vol. 1, 328; al-Daylamī, *A Treatise on Mystical Love*, trans. Bell and Shafie, 16; al-Ghazālī, *Iḥyā*, 2.165.
89. *ʿAbhar*, 41.
90. Ibid.
91. *Al-Maknūn*, http://lib.eshia.ir/27484/1/345, #162, vol. 1, 345.
92. Ibid.
93. Jalāl al-Dīn Rūmī, *Mathnawī-yi maʿnawī*, verse 4 (Tehran: Nashr-i Būta, 1381sh/2002), vol. 1, 7.

SELECTED BIBLIOGRAPHY

Part I. Primary Sources

Abū Dāwūd, Sulaymān b. al-Ashʿath al-Azdī al-Sijistānī. *Kitāb al-sunan*. 4 vols. Mecca: Dār al-Istiqāma, 1997.

———. *al-Marāsīl*. Riyadh: Dār al-Ṣamīʿī, 1422/2001.

Baqlī, Rūzbihān. See under Rūzbihān b. Abī Naṣr.

al-Bayhaqī, Abū Bakr Aḥmad b. Ḥusayn b. ʿAlī al-Khusrawjirdī. *Shuʿab al-īmān*. 17 vols. Beirut: Dār al-Kutub al-ʿIlmiyya, 2000.

al-Bukhārī, Abū ʿAbd Allāh Muḥammad b. Ismāʿīl. *Kitāb al-jāmiʿ al-ṣaḥīḥ*. 9 vols. Beirut: Dār Iḥyāʾ al-Turāth al-ʿArabī, n.d.

al-Dārimī, Abū Muḥammad ʿAbd Allāh b. ʿAbd al-Raḥmān al-Samarqandī. *al-Musnad*. 4 vols. Riyadh: Dār al-Mughnī, 2000.

al-Daylamī, Abū al-Ḥasan ʿAlī b. Muḥammad. *Kitāb ʿaṭf al-alif al-maʾlūf ʿalā al-lām al-maʿṭūf*. Edited by Jean-Claude Vadet. Cairo: Maṭbaʿat al-Maʿhad al-ʿIlmī al-Faransī li-l-Āthār al-Sharqiyya, 1962; Edited by Joseph Norment Bell and Ḥasan Maḥmūd al-Shāfiʿī. Cairo: Dār al-Kutub al-Miṣrī, 2007; French translation: *Le traité d'amour mystique d'al-Daylami*. Translated by Jean-Claude Vadet. Geneva: Droz, 1980; English translation: *A Treatise on Mystical Love*. Translated by Joseph Norment Bell and Ḥasan Maḥmūd al-Shāfiʿī. Edinburgh: Edinburgh University Press, 2005.

———. *Sīrat al-shaykh al-kabīr Abū ʿAbd Allāh Muḥammad b. al-Khafīf al-Shīrāzī: Tarjama-yi fārsī, Rukn al-Dīn Yaḥyā b. Junayd Shīrāzī*. Edited by Annemarie Schimmel-Tari. Tehran: Intishārāt-i Bābak, 1363sh/1984.

al-Fārābī, Abū Naṣr. *Al-Farabi on the Perfect State: Abū Naṣr al-Fārābī's* Mabādiʾ ārāʾ ahl al-madīna al-fāḍila. Translated by Richard Walzer. Oxford: Clarendon, 1985.

Fasāʾī, Ḥasan b. Ḥasan. *Fārs-nāma-yi Nāṣirī*. Edited by Manṣūr Rastgār Fasāʾī. Tehran: Amīr-Kabīr, 1367sh/1988.

al-Ghazālī, Abū Ḥāmid Muḥammad. *Iḥyāʾ ʿulūm al-dīn*. 4 vols. Beirut: Dār al-Maʿrifa, n.d.

———. *Kīmiyā-yi saʿādat*. Edited by Ḥusayn Khadīw-Jam. 2 vols. Tehran: Shirkat-i Intishārāt-i ʿIlmī wa Farhangī, 1386sh/2007.

———. *al-Maqṣad al-asnā fī sharḥ maʿānī asmāʾ Allāh al-ḥusnā*. Edited by Fadlou Shehadi. Beirut: Dār al-Mashriq, 1971. English translations: R. J. McCarthy, trans., *The Furthest Goal in the Commentary on the Meanings of the Most Beautiful Names of God*. In *Deliverance from Error*. Louisville: Fons Vitae, 1980; David Burrell and Nazih Daher, trans., *The Ninety-Nine Beautiful Names of God*. Cambridge: Islamic Texts Society, 1992.

———. *The Niche of Lights*. Translated by David Buchman. Provo: Brigham Young University Press, 1998.

Ghazālī, Aḥmad. *Sawāniḥ*. In *Majmūʿa-yi āthār-i fārsī-yi Aḥmad Ghazzālī (ʿārif-i mutawaffā-yi 520 A.H.)*, edited by Aḥmad Mujāhid, 93–189. Tehran: Dānishgāh-i Tihrān, 1370sh/1991; English translation: Sawāniḥ, *Inspirations from the World of Pure Spirits*. Translated by Nasrollah Pourjavady. London: KPI, 1986.

al-Ḥallāj, Ḥusayn b. Manṣūr. *Dīwān al-Ḥallāj wa-maʿahu Akhbār al-Ḥallāj wa-Kitāb al-ṭawāsīn*. Edited by Muḥammad Bāsil ʿUyūn al-Sūd. Beirut: Dār al-Kutub al-ʿIlmiyya, 2002.

———. *Kitāb al-ṭawāsīn*. Edited by Louis Massignon. Paris: Libraire Paul Geuthner, 1913.

al-Hamadānī, ʿAyn al-Quḍāt Abū Naṣr Muḥammad. *Nāmahā-yi ʿAyn al-Quḍāt Hamadānī*. Edited by ʿAlī-Naqī Munzawī and ʿAfīf ʿUsayrān. 3 vols. Tehran: Intishārāt-i Asāṭīr, 1377sh/1998.

al-Haythamī, ʿAlī b. Abī Bakr b. Sulaymān. *Majmaʿ al-zawāʾid wa-manbaʾ al-fawāʾid*. 10 vols. Beirut: Dār al-Fikr, n.d.

Ibn al-ʿArabī, Abū Bakr Muḥammad al-Ḥatamī. *Kitāb al-jalāl wa-l-jamāl*. In *Rasāʾil Ibn al-ʿArabī*. Hyderabad: Maṭbaʿat Dāʾirat al-Maʿārif al-ʿUthmāniyya, 1948; English translation by Rabia Terri Harris as "On Majesty and Beauty: The *Kitâb Al-Jalâl Wa-l Jamâl* of Muhyiddin Ibn 'Arabi." *Journal of the Muhyiddin Ibn 'Arabi Society* 8 (1989): 5–32.

Ibn Fāris, Abu al-Ḥusayn Aḥmad al-Rāzī. *Tartīb maqāyīs al-lugha*. Tehran: Pazhūhishgāh-i Ḥawza wa Dānishgāh, 1387sh/2007.

Ibn Ḥanbal, Aḥmad. *Musnad al-imām Aḥmad*. 7 vols. Beirut: Dār Iḥyāʾ al-Turāth al-ʿArabī, n.d.

Ibn Khafīf. *Muʿtaqad Ibn Khafīf*. In al-Daylamī, *Sīrat al-shaykh al-kabīr Abū ʿAbd Allāh Muḥammad b. al-Khafīf al-Shīrāzī: Tarjama-yi fārsī, Rukn al-Dīn Yaḥyā b. Junayd Shīrāzī*, edited by Annemarie Schimmel-Tari, 284-308. Tehran: Intishārāt-i Bābak, 1363sh / 1984.

Ibn Khuzayma. *Kitāb al-tawḥīd wa-ithbāt ṣifāt al-rabb*. Riyadh: Maktab al-Rushd, 1994.

Ibn Mājah, Abū ʿAbd Allāh Muḥammad al-Qazwīnī. *Sunan Ibn Mājah*. 2 vols. Beirut: Dār Iḥyāʾ al-Turāth al-ʿArabī, n.d.

Ibn Manẓūr, Abu al-Faḍl Muḥammad. *Lisān al-ʿarab*. Beirut: Dār Iḥyāʾ al-Turāth al-ʿArabī, 1988.

Ibn Sīnā. *The Metaphysics of the Healing: A Parallel English-Arabic Text*. Translated by Michael E. Marmura. Provo: Brigham Young University Press, 2005.

———. *al-Najāt*. Edited by Majīd Fakhrī. Beirut: Dār al-Āfāq al-Jadīda, 1985.

———. *al-Risāla fī al-ʿishq*. In *Traités mystiques d'Abū ʿAlī al-Ḥusain ibn ʿAbdallāh ibn Sīnā ou d'Avicenne*, edited and translated into French by August Ferdinand Mehren. Vol. 3. Frankfurt am Main: Institute for the History of Arabic-Islamic Science, 1999; English translation: Emil L. Fackenheim. "A Treatise on Love by Ibn Sina." *Mediaeval Studies* 7 (1945): 208–28.

Ibn Taymiyya and Ibn Qayyim al-Jawziyya. *al-Jamāl: Faḍluhu ḥaqīqatuhu aqsāmuhu*. Edited by Ibrāhīm b. ʿAbd Allāh al-Ḥāzimī. Riyadh: Dār al-Sharīf li-l-Nashr wa-l-Tawzīʿ, 1413 / 1992.

Ikhwān al-Ṣafāʾ. *Rasāʾil Ikhwān al-Safāʾ wa-Khullān al-Wafāʾ*. Edited by Buṭrus al-Bustānī. 4 vols. Beirut: Muʾassasat al-ʿIlmī li-l-Maṭbūʿāt, 2005.

ʿIrāqī, Fakhr al-Dīn Ibrāhīm. *Divine Flashes: Fakhruddin ʿIraqi*. Translated by William C. Chittick and Peter Lamborn Wilson. New York: Paulist Press, 1982.

Jāmī, ʿAbd al-Raḥmān. *Mathnawī-yi haft awrang-i Nūr al-Dīn ʿAbd al-Raḥmān Aḥmad Jāmī Khurāsānī*. Tehran: Kitābfurūshī-yi Saʿdī, 1337sh / 1958.

———. *Nafaḥāt al-uns min ḥaḍarāt al-quds*. Edited by Maḥmūd ʿĀbidī. Tehran: Sukhan, 1386sh / 2007.

al-Jawharī, Ismāʿīl b. Ḥammād. *Tāj al-lugha wa-ṣiḥāḥ al-ʿarabiyya*. Beirut: Dār Iḥyāʾ Turāth al-ʿArabī, 1999.

al-Kūfī, Hannād b. al-Sarī. *Kitāb al-zuhd*. Edited by ʿAbd al-Raḥmān ʿAbd al-Jibār al-Farīwāʾī. 2 vols. Kuwait: Dār al-Khulafāʾ li-l-Kitāb al-Islāmī, 1986.

al-Majlisī, ʿAllāma Muḥammad-Bāqir. *Biḥār al-anwār al-jāmiʿa li-durar akhbār al-aʾimma al-aṭhār*. 111 vols. Beirut: Muʾassasat al-Wafāʾ, 1404 / 1983.

Mālik b. Anas. *Kitāb al-muwaṭṭaʾ*. 2 vols. Beirut: Dār al-Kitāb al-ʿArabī, 1988.

al-Mawṣilī, Abū Yaʿlā Aḥmad. *al-Musnad*. 16 vols. Damascus: Dār al-Maʾmūn li-l-Turāth, 1984–94.

Maybudī, Rashīd al-Dīn. *Kashf al-asrār wa-ʿuddat al-abrār*. Edited by ʿAlī Aṣghar Ḥikmat. 10 vols. Tehran: Amīr Kabīr, 1381sh/2002.

Muslim b. al-Ḥajjāj. *Kitāb al-ṣaḥīḥ*. 2 vols. Beirut: Dār al-Kutub al-ʿIlmiyya, 1992.

Muṣṭafā, Ibrāhīm, et al. *al-Muʿjam al-wasīṭ*. Tehran: Muʾassasat al-Ṣādiq li-l-Ṭibāʿa wa-l-Nashr, 1386sh/2007.

al-Nasāʾī, Abū ʿAbd al-Raḥmān Aḥmad. *Sunan al-Nasāʾī bi-sharḥ al-Suyūṭī wa-l-Sindī*. Edited by al-Sayyid Muḥammad Sayyid et al. 5 vols. Cairo: Dār al-Ḥadīth, 1999.

Plotinus, *Plotinus I:* Enneads *I. 1–9*. Translated by Arthur Hilary Armstrong. Cambridge: Harvard University Press, 1966.

Qazwīnī, Ḥamd Allāh Mustawfī. *The* Ta'ríkh-i-guzída*: or, "Select History" of Hamdulláh Mustawfí-i-Qazwíní, Compiled in A.H. 730 (A.D. 1330), and Now Reproduced in Facsimile from a Manuscript Dated A.H. 857 (A.D. 1453)*. Edited by Edward G. Browne. Leiden: Brill, 1910.

Kāshānī, ʿAbd al-Razzāq. *Iṣṭilāḥāt al-ṣūfiyya*. Tehran: Hawza-yi Hunarī, 1376sh/1997; English translation: *A Glossary of Sufi Technical Terms*. Translated by Sabil Safwat. London: Octagon Press, 1991.

al-Qushayrī, Abu al-Qāsim. *al-Fuṣūl fī al-uṣūl*. In "Two Short Dogmatic Works of Abū l-Qāsim al-Qushayrī. Second Part: Edition and Translation of 'Al-Fuṣūl fī l-Uṣūl,'" edited by Richard Frank. *Melanges* 16 (1983): 59–94.

———. *Lumaʿ fī al-iʿtiqād*. In "Two Short Dogmatic Works of Abū l-Qāsim al-Qushayrī. First Part: Edition and Translation of 'Luma' fī l-i'tiqād,'" edited by Richard Frank. *Melanges* 15 (1982): 53–74.

———. *al-Risāla al-Qushayriyya fī ʿilm al-taṣawwuf*. Edited by Muḥammad ʿAbd al-Raḥmān al-Marʿashalī. Beirut: Dār Iḥyāʾ al-Turāth al-ʿArabī, 1998; English translation: *Al-Qushayri's Epistle on Sufism*. Translated by Alexander Knysh. Reading: Garnet Publishing, 2007.

———. *al-Taḥbīr fī al-tadhkīr li-Abī al-Qāsim ʿAbd al-Karīm b. Hawāzin al-Qushayrī*. Edited by Muḥammad Amīn b. ʿAbd al-Hādī al-Fārūqī. Ḥimṣ: Dār al-Maʿārif, n.d.

al-Rāzī, Fakhr al-Dīn Abū ʿAbd Allāh Muḥammad. *al-Maṭālib al-ʿāliyya fī al-ʿilm al-ilāhī*. 7 vols. Edited by Aḥmad Ḥijāzī al-Saqqā. Beirut: Dār al-Kitāb al-ʿArabī, 1987.

———. *Tafsīr al-Rāzī*. 32 vols. Beirut: Dār Iḥyāʾ Turāth al-ʿArabī, n.d.

Rāzī, Najm al-Dīn Dāya. *Mirṣād al-ʿibād min mabdaʾ ilā al-maʿād*. Edited by Muḥammad Amīn Riyāḥī. Tehran: Intishārāt-i ʿIlmī wa Farhangī, 1373sh / 1994; English translation: *The Path of God's Bondsmen from Origin to Return*. Translated by Hamid Algar. Delmar, NY: Caravan Books, 1982.

Rūmī, Jalāl al-Dīn Muḥammad Balkhī. *Mathnawī-yi maʿnawī*. 2 vols. Tehran: Nashr-i Būta, 1381sh / 2002.

Rūzbihān Baqlī. *ʿAbhar al-ʿāshiqīn*. Edited by Henry Corbin and Muḥammad Muʿīn. *Le jasmin des fidèles d'amour; Kitâb-e 'abhar al-'âshiqîn*. Tehran: Département d'iranologie de l'Institut franco-iranien 1958; an improved edition: *ʿAbhar al-ʿāshiqīn*. Edited by Jawād Nūrbakhsh. Tehran: Intishārāt-i Yaldā-Qalam, 1380sh / 2001.

———. *ʿArāʾis al-bayān fī ḥaqāʾiq al-qurʾān*. Edited by Aḥmad Farīd al-Mizyadī. 3 vols. Beirut: Dār al-Kutub al-ʿIlmiyya, 2008.

———. *Kashf al-asrār*. In *Rūzbihān al-Baḳlī ve Kitāb Kaşf al-asrār'ı ile Farsça bāzi Šiirleri*, edited by Nazif Hoca. Istanbul: Edebiyat Fakültesi Matbaası, 1971. Also in "Waqāʾiʿ al-Shaykh Rūzbihān al-Baqlī al-Shīrāzī: *Muqtaṭafāt min kitāb Kashf al-asrār wa mukāshafat al-anwār*," edited by Paul Nwyia. *Al-Mashriq* LXIV, no. 4–5 (1970): 385–406; and in *The Unveiling of Secrets* Kashf al-Asrār*: the Visionary Autobiography of Rūzbihān al-Baqlī (1128–1209 A.D.)*. Edited by Firoozeh Papan-Matin in collaboration with Michael Fishbein. Leiden: Brill, 2006. English translation: *The Unveiling of Secrets: Diary of a Sufi Master*. Translated by Carl Ernst. Chapel Hill: Parvardigar Press, 1997. French translation: *Le dévoilement des secrets et les apparitions des lumières: Journal spirituel du maître de Shîrâz*. Translated by Paul Ballanfat. Paris: Seuil, 1996.

———. *Kitāb al-ighāna aw sharḥ al-ḥujub wa-l-astār fī maqāmāt ahl al-anwār wa-l-asrār*. In *Quatre traités inédits de Rûzbehân Baqlî Shîrâzî*, edited by Paul Ballanfat, 63–136. Tehran: Institut français de recherche en Iran, 1998.

———. *Kitāb lawāmiʿ al-tawḥīd*. In *Quatre traités inédits de Rûzbehân Baqlî Shîrâzî*, edited by Paul Ballanfat, 137–66. Tehran: Institut français de recherche en Iran, 1998.

———. *Kitāb masālik al-tawḥīd*. In *Quatre traités inédits de Rûzbehân Baqlî Shîrâzî*, edited by Paul Ballanfat, 167–90. Tehran: Institut français de recherche en Iran, 1998.

———. *Kitāb maşrab al-arvāḥ va huva'l-maşhūr bi-hazār u yak maḳām (bi-alfi maḳāmin va maḳāmin)*. Edited by Naşreden Nazif M. Hoca. Istanbul: Edebiyat Fakültesi Matbaasi, 1974.

———. *Kitāb sayr al-arwāḥ aw al-Misbāḥ fī mukāshafat ba'th al-arwāḥ aw Risālat al-rūḥ*. In *Quatre traités inédits de Rûzbehân Baqlî Shîrâzî*, edited by Paul Ballanfat, 1–62. Tehran: Institut français de recherche en Iran, 1998.

———. *al-Maknūn fī ḥaqā'iq al-kalim al-nabawiyya*. Edited by 'Alī Ṣadrā'ī Khu'ī. In *Kitābkhāna-yi Madrasa-yi Fiqāhat*. 2 vols. N.p.: n.d. http://lib.eshia.ir/27484/1/255. Also available in print (with some omissions): *'Arā'is al-ḥadīth (aw al-maknūn fī ḥaqā'iq al-kalim al-nabawiyya)*. Edited by 'Alī Ṣadrā'ī Khu'ī. Tehran: Sāzmān-i Tablīghāt-i Islāmī, 1389sh/2010; also published as *al-Maknūn fī ḥaqā'īq al-kalim al-nabawiyya*. Edited by 'Alī Ṣadrā'ī Khu'ī. In *Mīrāth-i ḥadīth-i shī'a*, vol. 8, edited by Mahdī Mihrīzī and 'Alī Ṣadrā'ī Khu'ī, 255–363. Qum: Mu'assasa-yi Farhang-i Dār al-Ḥadīth, 1381sh/2002.

———. *Manṭiq al-asrār*. Edited by Mojtaba Shahsavari. Unpublished critical edition.

———. *Risālat al-quds wa Risāla-yi ghalaṭāt al-sālikīn*. Edited by Jawād Nūrbakhsh. Tehran: Yaldā Qalam, 1381sh/2002; French translation of *Risālat al-quds*: *Le traité de l'esprit saint de Rûzbehân de Shîrâz: Étude préliminaire, traduction annotée suivies d'un commentaire de son "Lexique du soufisme,"* translated by Stéphane Ruspoli. Paris: Le Cerf, 2001.

———. *Sharḥ-i shaṭḥiyyāt*. In *Commentaire sur les paradoxes des soufis (Sharh-e Shathîyât)*. Edited by Henry Corbin. Paris: Adrien-Maisonneuve, 1966.

Rūzbihān Thānī, 'Abd al-Laṭīf b. Ṣadr al-Dīn Abī Muḥammad. *Rawḥ al-jinān fī sīrat al-shaykh Rūzbihān*. In *Rūzbihān-nāma*, edited by Muḥammad Taqī Dānishpazhūh, 151–371. Tehran: Intishārāt-i Anjuman-i Āthār-i Millī, 1347sh/1969.

Rūzbihān Thānī, Sharaf al-Dīn Ibrāhīm b. Ṣadr al-Dīn Abī Muḥammad. *Tuḥfat ahl al-'irfān fī dhikr sayyid al-aqṭāb Rūzbihān*. In *Rūzbihān-nāma*, edited by Muḥammad Taqī Dānishpazhūh, 1–150. Tehran: Intishārāt-i Anjuman-i Āthār-i Millī, 1347sh/1969; also as *Tuḥfat ahl al-'irfān*. Edited by Jawād Nūrbakhsh. Tehran: Intishārāt-i Yaldā Qalam, 1382sh/2003.

al-Sam'ānī, Abū al-Muẓaffar Manṣūr b. Muḥammad. *al-Intiṣār li-aṣḥāb al-ḥadīth*. Edited by Muḥmmad b. Ḥusayn b. Ḥasan al-Jīzānī. Medina: Maktabat Aḍwā' al-Manār, 1417/1996.

Sam'ānī, Aḥmad b. Manṣūr. *Rawḥ al-arwāḥ fī sharḥ asmā' al-malik al-fattāḥ*. Edited by Najīb Māyil Harawī. Tehran: Shirkat-i Intishārāt-i 'Ilmī wa Farhangī, 1368sh/1989.

Shīrawayh, Abū Shujā' b. Shahrdār al-Daylamī al-Hamadhānī. *al-Firdaws bi-ma'thūr al-khiṭāb*. Edited by al-Sa'īd b. Basyūnī Zughlūl. 6 vols. Beirut: Dār al-Kutub al-'Ilmiyya, 1986.

Shīrāzī, Abu al-ʿAbbās Aḥmad Zarkūb. *Shirāz-nāma*. Edited by Bahman Karīmī. Tehran: Maṭbaʿa-yi Rawshanāʾī, 1310sh/1931.

Suhrawardī, Shihāb al-Dīn Yaḥyā (al-Maqtūl). *Fī ḥaqīqat al-ʿishq*. Translated by Wheeler Thackston as "On the Reality of Love." In *The Philosophical Allegories and Mystical Treatises*, 58–76. Costa Mesa, CA: Mazda Publishers, 1999; also in *The Mystical and Visionary Treatises of Suhrawardi*. London: Octagon Press, 1982.

al-Sulamī, Abū ʿAbd al-Raḥmān. *Tafsīr al-Sulamī wa-huwa Haqāʾiq al-tafsīr*. Edited by Sayyid ʿUmrān. Beirut: Dār al-Kutub al-ʿIlmiyya, 2001.

———. *The Way of Sufi Chivalry*. Translated by Tosun Bayrak al-Jerrahi. Rochester: Inner Traditions International, 1983.

al-Suyūṭī, Jalāl al-Dīn. *Jāmiʿ al-masānīd wa-l-marāsīl*. 21 vols. Beirut: Dār al-Fikr, 1994.

Ṭabarī, Abū Jaʿfar Muḥammad. *Jāmiʿ al-bayān fī taʾwīl al-qurʾān*. Edited by Aḥmad Muḥammad Shākir. 24 vols. Cairo: Dār al-Maʿārif, 1420/2000.

al-Tirmidhī. *Kitāb al-sunan*. 5 vols. Beirut: Dār al-Kutub al-ʿIlmiyya, 1994.

Part II. Secondary Sources

ʿAbd al-Raḥmān, Mamdūḥ. *al-Zīna wa-l-jamāl fī mīzān al-islām*. Cairo: Maktabat al-Zahrāʾ, 1996.

Abrahamov, Binyamin. "The *bi-lā kayfa* Doctrine and Its Foundations in Islamic Theology." *Arabica* 42 (1995): 365–79.

———. *Divine Love in Islamic Mysticism: The Teachings of al-Ghazālī and al-Dabbāgh*. London: RoutledgeCurzon, 2003.

Afrāsiyābpūr, ʿAlī Akbar. *Zībāʾī-parastī dar ʿirfān-i islāmī*. Tehran: Intishārāt-i Ṭāhūrī, 1380sh/2001.

Akkach, Samer. *Cosmology and Architecture in Premodern Islam: An Architectural Reading of Mystical Ideas*. Albany: State University of New York Press, 2005.

Alavi, Mohd. Badruddin. "Some Aspects of the Literary and Poetical Activities of Avicenna." *Avicenna Commemoration Volume*. Calcutta: Iran Society, 1956. 65–72.

Allard, Michel. *Le problem des attributs divins dans la doctrine d'al-Aš'arī et de ses premiers grands disciples*. Beirut: Imprimerie Catholique, 1965.

Anṣāriyān, Zahīr. "Falsafa-yi hunar wa zībāʾī-shināsī-yi Ṣadrāʾī [Philosophy of art and Ṣadrā's aesthetics]." In *Mullā Ṣadrā bih riwāyat-i mā: Hastī-shināsī, maʿrifat-shināsī, nafs-shināsī, dīn-shināsī, akhlāq-shināsī, falsafa-yi hunar wa zībāʾī-shināsī*, edited by Reza Akbari, 209–66. Tehran: Shirkat-i Chāp wa Nashr-i Bayn al-Milal, 1386sh / 2008.

Anwar, Etin. "Ibn Sīnā's Philosophical Theology of Love: A Study of the *Risālāh fī al-ʿIshq*." *Islamic Studies* 42, no. 2 (2003): 331–45.

Arberry, Arthur J. "Fārābī's Canons of Poetry." *Rivista degli studi orientali* 17 (1938): 266–78.

———. *Shiraz: Persian City of Saints and Poets*. Norman: University of Oklahoma Press, 1960.

Āriyā, Ghulām-ʿAlī. *Sharḥ-i aḥwāl wa āthār wa majmūʿa-yi ashʿār bi-dast āmada-yi shaykh shaṭṭāḥ Rūzbihān-i Fasāʾī (Baqlī-yi Shīrāzī)*. Tehran: Intishārāt-i Rūzbihān, 1363sh / 1984.

Avery, Kenneth S. *A Psychology of Early Sufi* Samāʿ*: Listening and Altered States*. New York: RoutledgeCurzon, 2004.

Ballanfat, Paul. "Aspects de la pensée de Rûzbehân Baqlî, soufi à Shîrâz au XIIème siècle." PhD dissertation. Sorbonne, 1994.

———. "L'échelle des mots dans les ascensions de Rûzbehân Baqlî." In *Le voyage initiatique en terre d'Islam: Ascensions célestes et itinéraires spirituels*, edited by M. A. Amir-Moezzi, 265–300. Paris: l'Ecole Pratique des Hautes Études, 1996.

———. "Légitimité de l'herméneutique dans le commentaire des traditions du Prophète de Rūzbihān Baqlī." *Annales islamologiques* 31 (1997): 17–42.

———. *Quatre traités inédits de Rûzbehân Baqlî Shîrâzî*. Tehran: Institut français de recherche en Iran, 1998.

Beardsley, Monroe C. *Aesthetics from Classical Greece to the Present*. New York: Macmillan, 1966.

Behrens-Abouseif, Doris. *Beauty in Arabic Culture*. Princeton: Markus Wiener Publishers, 1999.

Bell, Joseph Norment. "Avicenna's *Treatise on Love* and the Nonphilosophical Muslim Tradition." *Der Islam* 63, no. 1 (1986): 73–89.

Beneito, Pablo. "On the Divine Love of Beauty." *Journal of the Muḥyiddīn Ibn ʿArabī Society* 18 (1995): 1–22.

Black, Deborah L. "Aesthetics in Islamic Philosophy." In *Routledge Encyclopedia of Philosophy*, edited by Edward Craig. London: Routledge, 1998. http://www.rep.routledge.com/article/H02.

Brown, Frank Burch. *Good Taste, Bad Taste, and Christian Taste: Aesthetics in Religious Life*. New York: Oxford University Press, 2000.

Bulkhārī, Ḥasan. *Maʿnā wa mafhūm-i zībāʾī dar al-Manāẓir wa Tanqīḥ al-manāẓir*. Tehran: Intishārāt-i Farhangistān-i Hunar, 1387sh / 2008.

Cantarino, Vincente. *Arabic Poetics in the Golden Age: Selection of Texts Accompanied by a Preliminary Study*. Leiden: Brill, 1975.

Chittick, William. "The Aesthetics of Islamic Ethics." In *Sharing Poetic Expressions: Beauty, Sublime, Mysticism in Islamic and Occidental Culture*, edited by A-T. Tymieniecka, 3–14. New York: Springer, 2011.

———. "Chapter 9 The Fall of Adam." In *Sufism: A Short Introduction*, 111–36. Oxford: Oneworld, 2000.

———. *Divine Love: Islamic Literature and the Path to God*. New Haven: Yale University Press, 2013.

———. *Sufi Path of Knowledge: Ibn 'Arabi's Metaphysics of Imagination*. Albany: State University of New York Press, 1989.

Corbin, Henry. "*ʿAbhar al-ʿĀšeqīn*." In *Encyclopaedia Iranica*, edited by Ehsan Yashater, vol. 2, 214–15. London: Routledge and Kegan Paul, 1982–.

———. *Creative Imagination in the Ṣūfism of Ibn ʿArabī*. Translated by R. Manheim. Princeton: Princeton University Press, 1969.

———. *En Islam iranien: Aspects spirituels et philosophiques*. 3 vols. Paris: Gallimard, 1971–72.

———. *The Man of Light in Iranian Sufism*. Translated by Nancy Pearson. Boulder: Shambhala, 1978.

———. "Quiétude et inquiétude de l'âme dans le soufisme de Rūzbehān Baqlī de Shiraz." *Eranos-Jahrbuch 1958* (1959): 51–194.

———. "Rûzbehân Baqlî de Shîraz." In *Henry Corbin*, edited by Christian Jambet, 150–67. *Les Cahiers de l'Herne*. Paris: Éditions de l'Herne, 1983.

Dakramanjī, ʿĀʾida. *Qāmūs al-aḍdād al-kabīr*. Beirut: Maktabat Lubnān Nāshirūn, 2005.

Dānishpazhūh, Muḥammad Taqī. *Rūzbihān-nāma*. Tehran: Intishārāt-i Anjuman-i Āthār-i Millī, 1347sh / 1969.

de Bruyne, Edgar. *The Esthetics of the Middle Ages*. Translated by Eileen B. Hennessy. New York: Frederick Ungar, 1969.

de Wulf, Maurice. "Beauty." In *Encyclopaedia of Religion and Ethics*, edited by James Hastings et al., I.444–48. Edinburgh: T. and T. Clark, 1979.

El-Bizri, Nader. "God: Essence and Attributes." In *The Cambridge Companion to Classical Islamic Theology*, edited by Tim Winter, 121–40. Cambridge: Cambridge University Press, 2008.

Elias, Jamal. *Aisha's Cushion: Religious Art, Perception, and Practice in Islam*. Cambridge: Harvard University Press, 2012.

Ernst, Carl. *Rūzbihān Baqlī: Mysticism and the Rhetoric of Sainthood in Persian Sufism*. Richmond: Curzon, 1996.

———. "Rūzbihān Baqlī on Love as 'Essential Desire.'" In *Gott ist schön und Er liebt die Schönheit: Festschrift für Annemarie Schimmel zum 7. April 1992 dagebracht von Schülern, Freunden und Kollegen*, edited by Alma Giese and J. Christoph Bürgel, 181–89. Bern: Peter Lang, 1994.

———. "The Stages of Love in Early Persian Sufism from Rābiʿa to Rūzbihān." *Sufi* 14 (1992): 16–23; also in *Classical Persian Sufism from its Origins to Rumi*, edited by Leonard Lewisohn, 435–55. London: Khaniqahi Nimatullahi, 1994.

———. "The Symbolism of Birds and Flight in the Writings of Rūzbihān Baqlī." In *The Legacy of Medieval Persian Sufism*, edited by Leonard Lewisohn, 353–66. London: Khaniqahi Nimatullahi, 1992.

———. *Teachings of Sufism*. Boston: Shambhala, 1999.

———. "Vertical Pilgrimage and Interior Landscape in the Visionary Diary of Rūzbihān Baqlī (d.1209)." *Muslim World* 88, no. 2 (1998): 129–40.

———. *Words of Ecstasy in Sufism*. Albany: State University of New York Press, 1985.

Ettinghausen, Richard. "Al-Ghazzālī on Beauty." In *Art and Thought: Issued in Honour of Dr. Ananda K. Coomaraswamy on the Occasion of His 70th Birthday*, edited by K. Bharatha Iyer, 160–65. London: Luzac, 1947.

Fackenheim, Emil L. "A Treatise on Love by Ibn Sina." *Mediaeval Studies* 7 (1945): 208–28.

Faḍīlat, Maḥmūd. *Zībāʾī-shināsī-yi qurʾān*. Tehran: Sāzmān-i Muṭālaʿa wa Tadwīn-i Kutub-i ʿUlūm-i Insānī-yi Dānishgāhhā, 1387sh / 2008.

Farley, Edward. *Faith and Beauty: A Theological Aesthetic*. Aldershot: Ashgate, 2001.

Frank, Richard M. "Elements in the Development of the Teaching of Ashʿarī." *Le Muséon* 104 (1991): 141–90.

Gimaret, Daniel. *Dieu à l'image de l'homme: Les anthropomorphismes de la sunna et leurs interprétations par les théologiens*. Paris: Editions du Cerf, 1997.

———. *La doctrine d'al-Ash'arī*. Paris: Editions du Cerf, 1990.

———. *Les noms divins en Islam: Exégèse lexicographique et théologique*. Paris: Editions du Cerf, 1988.

———. *Théories de l'acte humain en théologie musulmane*. Paris: Vrin-Peeters, 1980.

Gloton, Maurice. "The Quranic Inspiration of Ibn 'Arabi's Vocabulary of Love." Translated by Cecilia Twinch. *The Journal of the Muhyiddin Ibn 'Arabi Society* 27 (2000): 37–52.

Godlas, Alan. "The *ʿArāʾis al-bayān*, the Mystical Qur'anic Exegesis of Rūzbihān al-Baqlī." PhD dissertation. University of California at Berkeley, 1991.

———. "Influences of Qushayrī's *Laṭāʾif al-ishārāt* on Sufi Qurʾanic commentaries, particularly Rūzbihān al-Baqlī's *Arāʾis al-bayān* and the Kubrawi *al-Taʾwīlāt al-najmiyya*." *Journal of Sufi Studies* 2, no. 1 (2013): 78–92.

———. "Psychology and Self-transformation in the Sufi Qurʾān Commentary of Ruzbihān al-Baqlī." *Sufi Illuminations Journal* 1, no. 1 (1996): 31–62.

Gonzalez, Valérie. *Beauty and Islam: Aesthetics in Islamic Art and Architecture*. New York: I. B. Tauris, 2001.

Gonzalo Carbó, Antoni. "El cielo teñido de rojo: La visión del color en el Diarium spirituale de Rûzbihân Baqlî (m. 606/1209)." *Convivium: Revista de Filosofia* 13 (2000): 31–59.

Grabar, Oleg, et al. "Islamic Aesthetics." In *Encyclopedia of Aesthetics*, edited by Michael Kelly, vol. 2, 535–41. Oxford: Oxford University Press, 1998.

Gutas, Dimitri. "Plato's *Symposion* in the Arabic Tradition." *Oriens* 31 (1988): 36–60.

Gwynne, Rosalind W. "Beauty." In *Encyclopaedia of the Qurʾān*, edited by J. D. McAuliffe, I, 212–13. Leiden: Brill, 2001.

Ḥamdān, Nadhīr. *al-Ẓāhira al-jamāliyya fī al-qurʾān al-karīm*. Jiddah: Dār al-Manāra, 1991.

Haque, Serajul. "The Concept of Beauty in Islam." *Pakistan Philosophical Journal* 6 (1962): 73–77.

Ḥijāzī, Muḥammad ʿAbd al-Wāḥid. *al-Iḥsās bi-l-jamāl fī ḍawʾ al-qurʾān al-karīm*. Alexandria: Dār al-Wafāʾ, 1998.

Hillenbrand, Carole. "Some Aspects of al-Ghazālī's Views on Beauty." In *Gott ist schön und Er liebt die Schönheit: Festschrift für Annemarie Schimmel zum 7. April 1992 dargebracht von Schülern, Freunden und Kollegen*, edited by Alma Giese and J. Christoph Bürgel, 249–65. Bern: Peter Lang, 1994.

Hoca, Nazīf. "Das arabische Werk *Kitāb mašrab al-arwāḥ*." In *Akten des VII. Kongresses für Arabistik und Islamwissenschaft, Göttingen, 15. bis 22. August 1974*, edited by Albert Dietrich, 208–11. Abhandlungen der Akademie der Wissenschaften in Göttingen, Philologischhistorische Klasse, Dritte Folge. No. 98. Göttingen: Vandenhoeck u. Ruprecht, 1976.

Holbrook, Victoria Rowe. Introduction to *Hüsnü Aşk*, by Seyh Galip. Edited by Victoria Rowe Holbrook. New York: Modern Language Association of America, 2005.

Hoos, Mark. "The Unknown Treasure: The Metaphysical Aesthetics of Ibn ʿArabī." *Journal of Turkish Studies* 26, no. 2 (2002): 1–14.

Hughes, Aaron. "'God Is Beautiful and Loves Beauty': The Role of Aesthetics in Medieval Islamic and Jewish Philosophy." In *The Texture of the Divine: Imagination in Medieval Islamic and Jewish Thought*, 146–84. Bloomington: Indiana University Press, 2004.

Ivanow, Vladimir Alekseevich. "A Biography of Ruzbihan al-Baqli." *Journal and Proceedings of the Asiatic Society of Bengal* N.S. 24 (1928): 353–61.

———. "More on Biography of Ruzbihan al-Baqli." *Journal of the Bombay Branch of the Royal Asiatic Society* 7 (1931): 1–7.

Izutsu, Toshihiko. *Ethico-Religious Concepts in the Qur'an*. Montreal: McGill-Queen's University Press, 2002.

Jabbur, Jubrail. *The Bedouins and the Desert: Aspects of Nomadic Life in the Arab East*. Translated by Lawrence Conrad. Albany: State University of New York Press, 1995.

Kalīb, Saʿd al-Dīn. *al-Bunya al-jamāliyya fī al-fikr al-ʿarabī al-islāmī*. Damascus: Wizārat al-Thiqāfa, 1997.

Keeler, Annabel. *Sufi Hermeneutics: The Quran Commentary of Rashīd al-Dīn Maybudī*. London: The Institute of Ismaili Studies, 2006.

Kemal, Salim. "Aesthetics." In *History of Islamic Philosophy*, edited by S. H. Nasr and O. Leaman, 969–78. London: Routledge, 1996.

———. "Ibn Sina's Intersubjective Aesthetics." *BRISMES Proceedings of the 1986 International Conference on Middle Eastern Studies* (1986): 27–36.

———. *The Philosophical Poetics of Alfarabi, Avicenna, and Averroës: The Aristotelian Reception*. New York: Curzon, 2003.

Kermani, Navid. "The Aesthetic Reception of the Qurʾān as Reflected in Early Muslim History." In *Literary Structures of Religious Meaning in the Qurʾān*, edited by Issa J. Boullata, 255–76. Richmond: Curzon, 2000.

———. *Gott ist schön: Das ästhetische Erleben des Koran*. München: Beck, 1999; English translation: *God Is Beautiful: The Aesthetic Experience of the Quran*. Translated by Tony Crawford. Cambridge: Polity Press, 2015.

Khalifa, Laila. *Ibn ʿArabi: L'initiation à la* futuwwa. Paris: La Librarie de l'Orient, 2001.

Latiri Azouz, Rajet. "L'amour mystique comme amour de la beauté chez Ibn Sina et Ruzbihan de Shiraz." *Actes du colloque: L'homme, la femme et les relations amoureuses dans l'imaginaire Arabo-Musulman, Tunis 26, 27, et 28 Octobre 1992*. Cahier du C.E.R.E.S. série Psychologie n° 8. Tunis: Secrétariat d'état à la recherche scientifique et à la technologie: Université des lettres, des arts et des sciences humaines, Tunis I, Centre d'études et de recherches économiqes et sociales, 1995.

———. "Esthétique et mystique chez Sohrawardi." *IBLA: Revue de l'Institut des belles lettres arabes* 61, no. 182 (1998): 245–62.

Leaman, Oliver. *Islamic Aesthetics: An Introduction.* Edinburgh: Edinburgh University. Press, 2004.

Lewisohn, Leonard, ed. *Hafiz and the Religion of Love in Classical Persian Poetry*. London: I. B. Tauris, 2010.

———. "Shihab ad-Din ʿUmar Suhrawardi: Treatises on Sufi Chivalry." In *Windows on the House of Islam: Muslim Sources on Spirituality and Religious Life,* edited by John Renard, 235–44. Berkeley: University of California Press, 1998.

———. "Sufism's Religion of Love, from Rābiʿa to Ibn ʿArabī." In *The Cambridge Companion to Sufism,* edited by Lloyd Ridgeon, 150–80. Cambridge: Cambridge University Press, 2015.

Lindberg, David C. "Alhazen's Theory of Vision and its Reception in the West." *Isis* 58 (1967): 321–41.

———. *Theories of Vision from al-Kindī to Kepler.* Chicago: University of Chicago Press, 1976.

Lowin, Shari L. *The Making of a Forefather: Abraham in Islamic and Jewish Exegetical Narratives*. Leiden: Brill, 2006.

Lumbard, Joseph E. B. "Aḥmad al-Ghazālī (d. 517 / 1123 or 520 / 1126) and the Metaphysics of Love." PhD dissertation. Yale University, 2003.

Madadpūr, Muḥammad. *Ḥikmat-i insī wa zībāʾī-shināsī-yi ʿirfānī-yi hunar-i islāmī.* Tehran: Shirkat-i Intishārāt-i Sūra Mehr, 1386sh / 2007.

Mahjub, Jaʿfar. "Spiritual Chivalry and Early Persian Sufism." In *Classical Persian Sufism: From Its Origin to Rumi,* edited by Leonard Lewisohn, 549–82. London: Khaniqahi Nimatullahi, 1993.

Massignon, Louis. "Le 'jour du covenant' (*yawm al-mīthāq*)." *Oriens* 15 (1962): 86–92.

———. "La notion de l'essentiel désir." *Mélanges Joseph Maréchal II.* Brussels-Paris, 1950. 263–96. Reprinted in Massignon, *Opera Minora,* vol. 2, 226–53. Beirut: Dar al-Maaref, 1963.

———. *The Passion of al-Hallāj: Mystic and Martyr of Islam.* Translated by Herbert Mason. Princeton: Princeton University Press, 1982.

———. "La Vie et les œuvres de Ruzbehan Baqli." *Studia Orientalia, Joanni Pedersen Septuagenario A.D. VII id. nov. anno MCMLIII a collegis, discipulis, amicis dictata.* Hauniae: Munksgaard, 1953.

Mayer, Toby. "Theology and Sufism." In *The Cambridge Companion to Classical Islamic Theology,* edited by Tim Winter, 258–87. Cambridge: Cambridge University Press, 2008.

Melchert, Christopher. "God Created Adam in His Image." *Journal of Qur'anic Studies* 13, no.1 (2011): 113–24.

Mīr, Muḥammad Taqī. *Sharḥ-i ḥāl wa āthār wa ashʿār-i shaykh Rūzbihān-i Baqlī*. Tehran: Dānishgāh-i Pahlawī, 1354sh / 1975.

Moulim, Elaroussi. *Esthétique et art islamique.* Casablanca: Afrique Orient, 1991.

Murata, Sachiko. *The Tao of Islam: A Sourcebook on Gender Relationships in Islamic Thought*. Albany: State University of New York Press, 1992.

———, and William C. Chittick. *The Vision of Islam*. St. Paul: Paragon House, 1994.

Nadīmī, Ghulām-Ḥusayn. *Rūzbihān yā shattāḥ-i Fārs: Shaykh Abū Muḥammad Rūzbihān-i Abī al-Naṣr Baqlī-yi Fasawī*. Shiraz: Kitābkhāna-yi Aḥmadī, 1966.

Nasr, Seyyed Hossein. "Islamic Aesthetics." In *A Companion to World Philosophies*, edited by Eliot Deutsch and Ronald Bontekoe, 448–59. Malden, MA: Blackwell, 1997.

———. "XI Islam and Music: The Views of Rūzbihān Baqlī, the Patron Saint of Shiraz." In *Islamic Art and Spirituality*, 151–62. Albany: State University of New York Press, 1987.

Nurbakhsh, Javad. *Sufi Symbolism: The Nurbakhsh Encyclopedia of Sufi Terminology*. 16 vols. London: Khanqah-i Nimatullahi Publications, 1986–2004.

Nwyia, Paul. "Waqāʾiʿ al-Shaykh Rūzbihān al-Baqlī al-Shīrāzī: Muqtaṭafāt min kitāb *Kashf al-asrār wa mukāshafat al-anwār*." *Al-Mashriq* 64, no. 4–5 (1970): 385–406.

Pourjavady, Nasrollah. *Bāda-yi ʿishq: Pazhūhishī dar maʿnā-yi bādah dar shiʿr-i ʿirfānī-yi fārsī* [The wine of passionate love: Study on the meaning of wine in Persian Sufi poetry]. Tehran: Nashr-i Kārnāma, 1387sh / 2008.

———. "The Concept of Love in ʿErāqi and Ahmad Ghazzāli." *Persica* 21 (2006–07): 51–62.

———. "*ḥusn*." *Dānishnāma-yi jahān-i islām*, edited by Ghulām Riḍā Ḥaddād ʿĀdil et al. Tehran: Bunyād-i Dāʾirat al-Maʿārif-i Islāmī, 1996–. Vol. 13, #384. http: / / rch.ac.ir / article / Details / 12004.

———. "Ḥusn wa marātib-i idrāk-i ān: Nigāhī bih naẓar-i ḥukamā wa ʿurafā [*Ḥusn* and the levels of its perception: An observation on the views of the philosophers and Sufis]." In *Ishrāq wa-ʿirfān: maqālahā wa naqdhā* [Illumination and Sufism: Articles and reviews], 178–92. Tehran: Markaz-i Nashr-i Dānishgāhī, 1380.

———. "Maʿnī-yi ḥusn wa ʿishq dar adabiyāt-i ʿirfānī [The meaning of *ḥusn* and *ʿishq* in Sufi literature]." *Sophia Perennis* 2, no. 1 (1976): 43–51.

Puerta Vílchez, José Miguel. *Historia del pensamiento estético árabe: Al-Andalus y la estética árabe clásica*. Madrid: Ediciones Akal, 1997.

Qaiser, Shahzad. "Islamic Metaphysics of Beauty." *Iqbal Review* 36, no. 3 (1995): 135–40.

Raine, Kathleen. "The Use of the Beautiful." In *Defending Ancient Springs*, 156–75. London: Oxford University Press, 1967.

Redhouse, J. W. *On "the Most Comely Names," i.e. The Laudatory Epithets, or The Titles of Praise, bestowed on God in the Qur'ān or by Muslim Writers*. London: Trübner, 1880.

Ridgeon, Lloyd. *Jawanmardi: A Sufi Code of Honour*. Edinburgh: Edinburgh University Press, 2011.

Ritter, Hellmut. *The Ocean of the Soul: Man, the World and God in the Stories of Farīd al-Dīn ʿAṭṭār*. Translated by John O'Kane. Leiden: Brill, 2003.

———. "Philologika VII: Arabische und persische Schriften über die profane und die mystische Liebe." *Der Islam* 21 (1933): 84–109.

Riyāḍī, Ḥishmat-Allāh. *Āyāt-i ḥusn wa ʿishq*. Tehran: Intishārāt-i Ḥaqīqat, 1381sh / 2002.

Robson, James. *Tracts on Listening to Music*. London: Royal Asiatic Society, 1938.

Rosenthal, Franz. "On Art and Aesthetics in Graeco-Arabic Wisdom Literature." In *Four Essays on Art and Literature in Islam*, 1–19. Leiden: Brill, 1971.

Rundgren, Frithiof. "Avicenna on Love: Studies in the 'Risāla fī māhīyat al-'išq' I." *Orientalia Suecana* 27–28 (1978–79): 42–62.

Ruspoli, Stéphane. *Le traité de l'esprit saint de Rûzbehân de Shîrâz: Étude préliminaire, traduction annotée suivies d'un commentaire de son "Lexique du soufisme."* Paris: Le Cerf, 2001.

Sabra, Abdelhamid. I. *The Optics of Ibn al-Haytham: Books I–III On Direct Vision*. London: Warburg Institute, 1989.

———. "Sensation and Inference in Alhazen's Theory of Perceptual Vision." In *Studies in Perception: Interrelations in the History of Philosophy and Science*, edited by Peter K. Machamer and Robert G. Turnbull, 160–85. Columbus: Ohio University Press, 1978.

Saʿīdī, Gul Bābā. *Farhang-i iṣṭilāḥāt-i ʿirfānī-yi Ibn-i ʿArabī*. Tehran: Shafīʿī, 1383sh / 2004.

Salamah-Qudsi, Arin. "The Will to Be Unveiled: Sufi Autobiographies in Classical Sufism." *Al-Masāq* 24, no. 2 (2012): 199–207.

Sattārī, Jalāl. *Dard-i ʿishq-i Zulaykhā: Pazhūhishī dar qissa-yi Yūsuf*. Tehran: Intishārāt-i Tūs, 1373sh / 1994.

Saunders, Corinne, Jane Macnaughton, and David Fuller, eds. *The Recovery of Beauty: Arts, Culture, and Medicine*. Basingstoke: Palgrave Macmillan, 2015.

Scarry, Elaine. *On Beauty and Being Just*. Princeton: Princeton University Press, 1999.

Schimmel, Annemarie. *Mystical Dimensions of Islam*. Chapel Hill: University of North Carolina Press, 1975.

———. "Tiny Mirrors of Divine Beauty: Classical Persian Mystical Poetry." In *As Through a Veil: Mystical Poetry in Islam*, 49–81. New York: Columbia University Press, 1982.

———. "Turk and Hindu: A Poetical Image and its Application to Historical Fact." In *Islam and Cultural Change in the Middle Ages*, edited by Speros Vryonis, 107–26. Wiesbaden: Otto Harrassowitz, 1975.

———. *A Two-Colored Brocade: The Imagery of Persian Poetry*. Chapel Hill: University of North Carolina Press, 1992.

Sells, Michael. *Approaching the Qur'ān: The Early Revelations*. Ashland: White Cloud Press, 1999.

———. *Mystical Languages of Unsaying*. Chicago: University of Chicago Press, 1994.

Shalaq, ʿAlī. *al-ʿAql fī al-turāth al-jamālī ʿind al-ʿarab*. Beirut: Dār al-Madā, 1985.

Shamīsā, Sīrūs. *Shāhidbāzī dar adabiyāt-i fārsī*. Tehran: Intishārāt-i Firdaws, 1381sh/2002.

Shehadi, Fadlou. "Islamic Aesthetics: Islamic Music." In *Encyclopedia of Aesthetics*, edited by Michael Kelly, II, 536–38. Oxford: Oxford University Press, 1998.

Sharīat Kāshānī, ʿAlī. "La préeternité et la pérennité de l'amour et de la beauté en littérature mystique persane de Rūzbehān à Ḥāfeẓ." *Luqmān* 17, no. 2 (2001): 25–54.

Sherry, Patrick. *Spirit and Beauty: An Introduction to Theological Aesthetics*. 2nd ed. London: SCM Press, 2002.

Shiloah, Amnon. *The Epistle on Music of the Ikhwan al-Safa (Baghdad, 10th century)*. Tel-Aviv: Tel-Aviv University, Faculty of Fine Arts, School of Jewish Studies, 1978.

———. *La perfection des connaissances musicales:* Kitāb kamāl adab al-ghināʾ. Paris: Geuthner, 1972.

Silvers, Laury. *A Soaring Minaret: Abu Bakr al-Wasiti and the Rise of Baghdadi Sufism*. Albany: State University of New York Press, 2010.

Sulaymānī, Parwīz. "*Jalāl wa jamāl*." In *Dānishnāma-yi jahān-i islām*. Edited by Ghulām-Alī Ḥaddād ʿĀdil, et al. Tehran: Bunyād-i Dāʾirat al-Maʿārif-i Islāmī, 1996–. Vol. 10, #442. http://rch.ac.ir/article/Details/9813.

Takeshita, Masataka. "Continuity and Change in the Tradition of Shirazi Love Mysticism." *Orient* 23 (1987): 113–31.

———. "Kami no sugata ni tsukurareta Adam: Rūzubihān Bakurī no ningenron [Adam who was created upon God's image: Rūzbihān Baqlī's theory of human beings]. *Chūsei no ningenzou* [The medieval imagery of the human being]. Tokyo: Sōbunsha, 1987.

Terry, Graham. "Ruzbihan: Psychologist of Visions." *Sufi* 37 (1998): 43–49.

Tottoli, Roberto. *Biblical Prophets in the Qur'ān and Muslim Literature.* Richmond: Curzon, 2002.

———. "Early Muslim Attitudes Towards Prostration (*sujūd*). I. Arabs and Prostration at the Beginning of Islam and in the Qur'ān." *Studia Islamica* 88 (1998): 28–33.

Türker, Habip. "Beauty and Its Projection in Christian and Islamic Tradition." In *Sharing Poetic Expressions: Beauty, Sublime, Mysticism in Islamic and Occidental Culture,* edited by A-T. Tymieniecka, 69–79. New York: Springer, 2011.

von Grunebaum, Gustave E. "The Aesthetic Foundation of Arabic Literature." *Comparative Literature* 4, no.4 (1952): 323–40.

Wafer, Jim. "Vision and Passion: The Symbolism of Male Love in Islamic Mystical Literature." In *Islamic Homosexualities: Culture, History, and Literature,* edited by Stephen O. Murray and Will Roscoe, 107–31. New York: New York University Press, 1997.

Walzer, Richard. "Aristotle, Galen, Palladius on Love." In *Greek into Arabic: Essays on Islamic Philosophy,* 48–59. Cambridge: Harvard University Press, 1962.

———. *Al-Farabi on the Perfect State: Abū Naṣr al-Fārābī's* Mabādi' ārā' ahl al-madīna al-fāḍila. Oxford: Clarendon, 1985.

Watt, William Montgomery. "Created in His image." *Glasgow University Oriental Society* 18 (1959–60): 38–49.

Wheeler, Brannon M. *Prophets in the Quran: An Introduction to the Quran and Muslim Exegesis.* London: Continuum, 2002.

Wright, Owen. "[Chapter] Eight: Music and Musicology in the *Rasā'il Ikhwān al-Ṣafā'.*" In *Epistles of the Brethren of Purity: The* Ikhwān al-Ṣafā' *and Their* Rasā'il*: An Introduction,* edited by Nader El-Bizri, 223–24. New York: Oxford University Press, 2008.

Yāsūf, Aḥmad. *Jamāliyyāt al-mufradāt al-qur'āniyya.* Damascus: Dār al-Maktabī, 1419/1999; Persian translation: *Zībā'ī-shināsī-yi wāzhagān-i qur'ān.* Translated by Ḥusayn Sayyidī. Tehran: Sukhan, 1388sh/2009.

Zargar, Cyrus Ali. *Sufi Aesthetics: Beauty, Love, and the Human Form in the Writings of Ibn 'Arabi and 'Iraqi.* Columbia: University of South Carolina Press, 2011.

GENERAL INDEX

INDEX OF QUR᾿ĀNIC VERSES

INDEX OF ḤADĪTHS AND SAYINGS